Theory as a Prayerful Act

Studies in the
Postmodern Theory of Education

Joe L. Kincheloe and Shirley R. Steinberg
General Editors

Vol. 22

PETER LANG
New York • Washington, D.C./Baltimore • San Francisco
Bern • Frankfurt am Main • Berlin • Vienna • Paris

Theory as a Prayerful Act

The Collected Essays
of James B. Macdonald

Edited by
Bradley J. Macdonald

PETER LANG
New York • Washington, D.C./Baltimore • San Francisco
Bern • Frankfurt am Main • Berlin • Vienna • Paris

Library of Congress Cataloging-in-Publication Data

Macdonald, James Bradley.
    Theory as a prayerful act: the collected essays of James B. Macdonald/
edited by Bradley J. Macdonald.
      p.   cm. — (Counterpoints; vol. 22)
    Includes bibliographical references.
    1. Education—Philosophy. I. Macdonald, Bradley J. II. Title.
III. Series: Counterpoints (New York, N.Y.); vol. 22.
LB885.M23M32   370'.1—dc20   95-8005
ISBN 0-8204-2792-6
ISSN 1058-1634

Die Deutsche Bibliothek-CIP-Einheitsaufnahme

Macdonald, James Bradley:
Theory as a prayerful act: the collected essays of James B. Macdonald/ ed.
by Bradley J. Macdonald. - New York; Washington, D.C./Baltimore; San
Francisco; Bern; Frankfurt am Main; Berlin; Vienna; Paris: Lang.
    (Counterpoints; Vol. 22)
    ISBN 0-8204-2792-6
NE: Macdonald, Bradley J. [Hrsg.]; GT

Cover design by James F. Brisson.

The paper in this book meets the guidelines for permanence and durability
of the Committee on Production Guidelines for Book Longevity of the
Council of Library Resources.

Printed in the United States of America.

Life moves in circles.
Surrounding one another,
we give of our inner beings
valuing all we possess,
by celebrating and sharing
the human condition.
Our circles expand and constrict,
like the ebb and flow
of our minds' evolution.
Moving inward to reflect
and back out again,
our outer edges,
and most sacred expressions
swell with discovery.
In the surge of our anticipation,
we are most vulnerable.
Tossing anxiously in our journey,
touching circle upon circle,
we come face to face
with the creation of self and world.
At the moment we assume
placid resolve has found us,
we again begin our movement.
A predetermined destiny,
of choosing and creating,
acting and experiencing,
loving and revelling,
in the lifelong pilgramage
of personal, social, and emotional integration.

—Jamie Macdonald-Furches

Contents

Preface

If anything, it is my hope that this collection of essays will provide a way to fully appreciate the scope, breadth and depth of my father's thinking as it evolved over a twenty year period. One of tragedies in the history of curriculum theory—and we might add, in the history of educational theory in general—is that my father never published one of his continually evolving book-length manuscripts, mainly because they *were* continually evolving. I distinctly remember him bemoaning the fact that he could not finish one of his many "book projects," not because the task was too difficult, but because it would demand that he stop his intellectual growth and conceptual dreaming. As is so often the case, one's personal trajectory has a way of working itself into the interstices of one's conceptual discourse. Thus, if my father felt that the development of creative human potential should be the goal of schooling, his own continual project of personal growth is reflected in his theoretical trajectory, indeed in its very *form* let alone content.

The task of determining which essays and/or manuscripts were to be included within this collection was a hard one. As the bibliography attests, my father published scores of essays, articles, chapters, let alone wrote much that was never published. On the whole, my guiding criteria were threefold: first, I wanted to include essays that would give the reader a sense of the overall development of his thought as well as the subtantive areas of his theoretical concern; secondly, I included essays that seemed to develop some of the central issues that would preoccupy him in his other work—that is, I attempted to include those essays that were "seminal" or "provocative" when they first appeared, either in terms of their effect on the discipline in general or their rippling effect on other aspects of his work; thirdly, I felt it would be necessary to bring forth those essays that could still be part of the "conversation" of theory today. This latter criterion was overlaid by the fact that I am a theorist, though from a different discipline and generation. While I consider myself a "political theorist" and not a "curriculum theorist," it is increasingly the case today that those who can still speak to each other within the cacophony of disciplinary voices are theorists. That is, those practicing theory today, no matter the particular disciplinary site from which they are constituted, are involved in a rather exciting interdisciplinary venture, one that is increasingly making older disciplinary and subject-matter differences obsolete. Given my own background, I searched for those essays and works that spoke to me as a theorist today, that seemed to engage some of the central problematics and issues with which theorists within the social sciences and humanities are still concerned.

Of course, I could not have done this task alone. There were many people who have offered their help, support and hard work. First and foremost, I want to thank my mother, Susan Macdonald Hyman, and my sister, Jamie Macdonald Furches, for their continual support and inspiration. This collection could not have been possible without their structural, emotional and practical help. Without exaggeration, my mother provided the "hidden," and not so hidden, curriculum for my father's development as a theorist, and still provides such an infrastructure for my own. My sister embodies the moral values and realism that so defined my father's life and work, and is a constant inspiration to those around her. I might also add that her poetic skills are evident on the dedication page of this collection.

In more practical terms, I want to thank Joe Kincheloe and Shirley Steinberg, the general editors of the Counterpoints series at Peter Lang, for their unerring excitement about the project. Need I say that without their interest and support, none of this would have been possible. Early in the planning stages, Henry Giroux was instrumental in keeping the flame of this project going, and he used whatever time he had left over from his own projects to help search for a publisher of this project. Esther Zaret has provided continual moral support for this project, and her early attempts at cataloguing my father's oeuvre were extremely important in searching for appropriate essays. I might also add that the bibliography published in this text owes much to her work in this respect. Among my father's near contemporaries, Bill Pinar has consistently supported my father's work as an editor as well as in his own theoretical work, and I deeply appreciate him taking time from his busy schedule to write the introduction to this collection. Moreover, Bill's focus upon the Heideggerian quality of my father's work inspired the actual title of this collection. I want to also thank Dwayne Huebner and Peter McLaren for offering their encouragement during the process of putting this collection together. One of the most wonderful consequences of this project has been that I have been able to interact and dialogue with these scholars in the field of education, some of whom I have known since childhood and others whom I have just gotten to know. Such interdisciplinary interaction is the fruit of intellectual life.

Last but not least, I want to thank Brian Heckard for his technical and practical help in getting this manuscript together. My father wrote his pieces during the pre-computer days, which meant that they had to be inputted onto diskette, a long and sometimes dreary task. Of course, it is not clear that even if he were alive today he wouldn't still put his essays in the strange mimeographed form he used so often. Brian persevered wonderfully in inputting and editing the manuscript, and we have him to thank for the fact this project is off the ground.

Aside from Chapter Nine, all of these essays have been published previously. In almost all cases, they have been unaltered from their original form. Every now and then, when I felt it was necessary for structure, clarity or flow, I have edited their original published form. When this was done, I made sure this did not depart from my father's intentions. This is particularly the case for Chapters Ten and Eleven. I had to go back to my father's original typed copies to correct what were some errors in their initially published versions. In all of this, I am deeply grateful to the Association for Supervision and Curriculum Development, McCutchan Publishing Corporation and the *Journal of Curriculum Theorizing* for their permission to reprint these essays.

Bradley J. Macdonald
Colorado State University
June 1995

Chapter One, "An Image of Man: The Learner Himself," originally appeared in *Individualizing Instruction*, R. C. Doll, ed. (Washington, DC: Association for Supervision and Curriculum Development, 1964), pp. 29–49.

Chapter Two, "The School as Double Agent," originally appeared in *Freedom, Bureaucracy and Schooling*, V. F. Baubrich, ed. (Washington, DC: Association for Supervision and Curriculum Development, 1971), pp. 235–246.

Chapter Three, "A Vision of a Humane School," originally appeared in *Removing Barriers to Humaneness in the High School*, J. G. Saylor and J. L. Smith, eds. (Washington, DC: Association of Supervision and Curriculum Development, 1971), pp. 2–20.

Chapter Four, "A Transcendental Developmental Ideology of Education," originally appeared in *Heightened Consciousness, Cultural Revolution, and Curriculum Theory*, W. Pinar, ed. (Berkeley, CA: McCutchan Publishing Corporation, 1974), pp. 85–116.

Chapter Five, "Curriculum and Human Interests," originally appeared in *Curriculum Theorizing: The Reconceptualists*, W. Pinar, ed. (Berkeley, CA: McCutchan Publishing Corporation, 1975), pp. 283–294.

Chapter Six, "The Quality of Everyday Life in Schools," originally appeared in *Schools in Search of Meaning*, . Zaret and J. Macdonald, eds. (Washington, DC: Association of Supervision and Curriculum Development, 1975), pp. 78–94.

Chapter Seven, "Living Democratically in Schools: Cultural Pluralism," originally appeared in *Multicultural Education: Commitments, Issues, and Applications*, C. A. Grant, ed. (Washington, DC: Association for Supervision and Curriculum Development, 1977), pp. 6–13.

Chapter Eight, "Value Bases and Issues in Curriculum," originally appeared in *Curriculum Theory*, A. Molnar and J. Zahorik, eds. (Washington, DC: Association of Supervision and Curriculum Development, 1977), pp. 10–21.

Chapter Ten, "Curriculum, Consciousness and Social Change," originally appeared in *Journal of Curriculum Theorizing*, 3, 1, 1981, pp. 143–153.

Chapter Eleven, "Theory, Practice and the Hermeneutic Circle," originally appeared in *Journal of Curriculum Theorizing*, 3, 2, 1981, pp. 130–138.

Introduction

Thirteen years ago, at the relatively young age of 58, James B. Macdonald died. Given the traditionally ahistorical character of the field, it is probable that there are younger scholars working today who do not remember Jim's work as a source for theirs. Reread these papers. You will see that they either anticipated or coincided with the appearance of thematically similar essays. Not a little of the scholarship that has followed his merely provides detail to his foundation. It is an event of great importance that James Macdonald's son—Bradley Macdonald, a professor of political science at Colorado State University—has collected his father's most memorable and influential papers. The field will be grateful to you, Brad Macdonald. And the field will thank Joe Kincheloe and Shirley Steinberg for publishing this collection in their famous Counterpoint Series.

Who was James B. Macdonald? Macdonald's ground-breaking scholarship provoked the Reconceptualization of the American curriculum field, influencing an entire generation of curriculum scholars (Searles, 1982; Holland & Garman, 1992; Pinar, Reynolds, Slattery, Taubman, 1995). Like the other major figure of the 1960s and 1970s—Dwayne E. Huebner—Macdonald received his Ph. D. from the University of Wisconsin-Madison, advised by Virgil Herrick.

Macdonald's first university position was as Assistant Professor in Curriculum and Extension at the University of Texas-Austin during the 1956–1957 academic year. From 1957–1959 he served as Assistant Professor in Elementary Education at New York University. From 1959–1963, Macdonald was Associate Professor and Director of School Experimentation and Research at the University of Wisconsin-Milwaukee. He was a Professor in the Department of Curriculum and Instruction, and Department of Educational Policy Studies at the University of Wisconsin during the period 1963–1966. From 1966–1972 Macdonald served as Professor of Curriculum and Social and Philosophical Foundations of Education at the University of Wisconsin-Milwaukee. From 1972 until his death on November 21,1983, Macdonald was Distinguished Professor of Education at the University of North Carolina at Greensboro (Brubacker & Brookbank,1986). Macdonald's contribution was acknowledged by an international conference in his honor (Apple, 1985; Grumet, 1985; Huebner, 1985; Molnar, 1985; Pinar, 1985; Spodek, 1985; Burke, 1985; Wolfson, 1985a, 1985b).

In an autobiographical reflection which prefaced his essays collected in *Curriculum Theorizing: The Reconceptualists* (1975d), Macdonald wrote:

Personally, my own work in the field in retrospect is best explained to myself as an attempt to combine my own personal growth with a meaningful social concern that has some grounding in the real world of broader human concerns. Thus, education has served as a societal pivotal point to explore myself and the broader human condition in a meaningful context (1975a, p. 3).

This integration of the personal and the social is strikingly evident throughout Macdonald's remarkable career. For instance, as early as 1964 he discussed the relationship between society and the individual, and specifically the ways in which society defined individuals. He called for a new image which could shape schools in general and the curriculum in particular. He called those schools which recognized a new image of children as self-actualizing as "reality-centered." This early essay would mark the beginning of his enormous contribution to the Reconceptualization of curriculum. Macdonald (1964) wrote:

We simply mean that the school does not exist primarily to inculcate our cultural heritage, not principally to develop role players for society nor primarily to meet the needs and interests of the learners. The school exists to bring learners in contact with reality, of which our society, ourselves, and our cultural heritage are parts (p. 47).

During the 1960s Macdonald challenged the supremacy of the structure-of-the-disciplines approach to curriculum development (although he was supportive of Schwab's later work on the practical). In addition, he challenged both socially and psychologically oriented curriculum theory, positing another concept in which these become elements. The point of this concept—reality-centeredness—is to rationalize a curriculum in which the student can be free to develop his or her own thinking and values, and to encourage creative responses to reality (Burke, 1985). It was frontier work which would be continued and extended over the remaining twenty years of his important career.

These concerns are evident in Macdonald's 1966 essay, entitled "Learning, Meaning and Motivation: An Introduction." Here he discussed the problems associated with the structure-of-the-disciplines movement and urged a concern for the person. Macdonald challenged directly the former:

There is, after all, no reason to suspect that the reformulation of content alone in the schools will suffice to counter the loss of self, the dehumanization and depersonalization of people living in a technological society such as ours.   Further, there is no reason to suspect that the structure of the disciplines can by magic of organization reduce the threat of nuclear holocaust, bring justice and equality to all people or provide a basis for freedom from poverty for all (Macdonald & Leeper, 1966, pp. 5-6).

This challenge would constitute the thematic heart of the Reconceptualization of the 1970s, resulting in the field in which we work today.

A second major statement by Macdonald on the primacy of the person was published in *Precedents and Promise in the Curriculum Field* (Robison, 1966). Dwelling on the theme of dehumanization, Macdonald advocated a person-oriented curriculum:

We will create our own image of ourselves through the ways we structure and relate to our own world. This image is in dire peril of becoming characterized by a partially ordered and conditioned set of regimented performances in the modern age. What we must strive for is to make men what they ought to be—complete human beings (Macdonald, quoted in Robison, 1966, p. 52).

School   structure   was   dehumanizing.   What   was   necessary   was   a reconceptualization of what school and curriculum could be, the cultivation of self-conscious and complete human beings. Again, early on Macdonald sounded a challenge that would be repeated over and over again in the 1970s.

At the 1967 Ohio State University Curriculum Theory Conference, chaired by Paul R. Klohr (1967), Macdonald's paper was noteworthy. On this occasion, he delineated between "framework" and "engineering" theories at work in curriculum. Framework theorists were said to interpret curriculum issues by means of "aesthetic rationality," a concept Macdonald borrowed from Herbert Marcuse (1964), the well-known critical theorist widely read during the 1960s. Macdonald argued that aesthetic rationality pointed to the human capacity to cope rationally with the world on an intuitive basis. The individual must return to the world as experienced for insights which enabled one to transcend one's present systems of thought and to move to new paradigms or fresh perspectives.

Macdonald focussed on the danger of the engineering theorists, predominant at that time. In this 1967 statement, one finds the heart of the political theory so influential in the decades to follow.   Indeed, Macdonald's concerns foreshadowed those of nearly an entire generation of curricularists: "The danger of our present 'systems approach' to human behavior is that as we gain greater control over ourselves, the systems concept will become so useful in solving our problems of efficiency and effectiveness that we shall be in grave danger of losing contact with reality through 'aesthetic rationality.'" Further: "Schooling will be reduced to objectification of this systematic process [efficiency and effectiveness]. This process is already demonstrable in other aspects of our society. It is especially obvious in the realm of our national economic security policies" (Macdonald, 1967, p. 168). The "systems approach"—a succinct characterization of the Tyler Rationale and its behavioristic offspring such as performance objectives—would not prove popular due to its success but due to its failure. The more it failed, the more its use was intensified. The objectification process, including the objectification of students into categories (gifted, etc.) of the interpersonal process would further bureaucratize educational institutions.

Calling for a very different field, Macdonald (1967) began by acknowledging that curriculum theorizing is "a challenging undertaking" (p. 166). At this stage, and quite beyond the mainstream thinking of the period, Macdonald discerned that "there appears to be framework theorists and engineering theorists. Both may be needed" (p. 166). Framework theorists are those interested in larger, non-technical issues, and he identified himself with this group: "This paper will focus upon theory as the development of frameworks from which designs can be generated rather than theory as the testing of designs," which represented a form of "technological rationality" (p. 166). In technological rationality:

> phenomena are identified as separate objects (always in transaction or flux); common qualities are abstracted, related to one another, and put into a system. The danger of using technological rationality in human behavior is that, in our desire to gain control, understand, and predict, we may (and perhaps already have) come to see ourselves as objects or the representation of these objects that we find useful for our purposes. . . . We will then become what Marcuse called one-dimensional (pp. 166–167).

Macdonald then discussed the notion of "aesthetic rationality [which] is meant here to mean man's [sic] capacity to cope rationally with the world on an intuitive basis—to return to the world for insights which will enable him to transcend his present systems of thought and move to new paradigms. . . or fresh perspectives" (p. 167–168). In contrast to technological rationality, which is "closed," aesthetic rationality "is a rationality of means applied to ends which

are always open" (p.168).   Macdonald (1967) then moved directly to the field
of curriculum:

> Obviously, if education is to escape a similar entrapment (as a
> weapons delivery system locks us into nationalism, and an arms race),
> theorizing in curriculum must remain broad enough in scope to
> include the use of aesthetic rationality—this means specifically, that
> the systems metaphor is not enough and must be used carefully. . . .
> The central question is whether theory and theorizing are neutral or
> committed. Yet, its [curriculum theory's] central utility may well be
> the creation of forms which lead to interpreting curriculum
> phenomena, not so much to solving curriculum problems by applying
> scientific generalizations. At present, the most appropriate role for
> curriculum theory is probably an interpretive role. . . . Theory in
> curriculum has an essentially heuristic role. Curriculum theory should
> be committed, not neutral. It should be committed to human fullness
> in creation, direction, and use. All of man's rational potential should
> be committed to the processes and goals in curriculum theorizing. . .
> . Curriculum theorizing is an act of disciplined thinking.   It is
> disciplined by the vertical awareness of curriculum theory as it has
> developed historically and by the horizontal awareness of man's
> contemporary status of development in various formal disciplines. . .
> . Rather than place emphasis only upon the discipline of technical
> reason, curriculum theory should be disciplined by the total rational
> potential of man [sic], both aesthetic and technological (pp. 168–169).

This was a major paper, one which went well beyond public curriculum debates
(although correctly locating them in national defense issues) to the very character
of thought employed in curriculum research. He rejected rationalistic and
technical systems of theorizing as distortive and finally inhuman, endorsing an
aesthetic rationality which holds political, historical, and technological potential.
Note that Macdonald suggested an interpretative role for curriculum theory, one
that in fact the field would take up a decade later, i.e. the project to
understand—not only develop—curriculum.

   In another seminal paper first published in 1971 entitled "Curriculum
Theory," James Macdonald foreshadowed the movement to reconceptualize the
field by laying out three categories of curriculum theorists, a scheme I employed
in my mapping of the field (Pinar, 1975; Giroux, Penna, & Pinar, 1981; Pinar
& Grumet, 1988). Extending the notion of "framework" theorist that he had

developed in 1967, Macdonald wrote that:

> One group (by far the largest) sees theory as guiding framework for applied curriculum development and research and as a tool for evaluation of curriculum development. . . . A second "camp" of oftentimes younger (and far fewer) theorizers is committed to a more conventional concept of scientific theory. This group has attempted to identify and describe the variables and their relationships in curriculum. The purpose of this theory is primarily conceptual in nature, and research would be utilized for empirical validation of curriculum variables and relationships, rather than as a test of the efficiency and effectiveness of a curriculum prescription. A third group of individuals look upon the task of theorizing as a creative intellectual task which they maintain should be neither used as a basis for prescription or as an empirically testable set of principles and relationships. The purpose of these persons is to develop and criticize conceptual schema in hope that new ways of talking about curriculum, which may in the future be far more fruitful than present orientations, will be forthcoming. At the present time, they would maintain that a much more playful, free-floating process is called for by the state of the art (Macdonald, 1975b, p. 6).

After a decade of Reconceptualization, this third group would come to dominate the field.

In yet another major paper, this one delivered at the 1973 University of Rochester Curriculum Theory Conference and entitled "A Transcendental Developmental Ideology of Education" (1974), Macdonald began by citing the limitations of developmental models in curriculum and in education generally. In the context of a reference to Freire [the Brazilian theorist whose work would influence certain strands of American political curriculum theory; see Freire, 1968; McLaren & Leonard, 1993], Macdonald pointed to the development of the autobiographic (which he termed romantic) and the political discourses (which he linked with earlier reconstructionist discourses) which would become influential in the Reconceptualization. Macdonald (1974) wrote:

> We still do not generally recognize this radical thrust in curriculum thinking, but the growing edge of writing in the past five to ten years leans toward a resurgence of romanticism and a renewal of past reconstructionist terms of the radical tradition. Neither. . . is the same

as its predecessor (Macdonald, 1974, p. 87).

Macdonald goes on to note that the political or radical criticism of the autobiographic emphasis upon the individual asserts that it is a conservative reassertion of the status quo, i.e. of conservative political theory. He (1974) wrote:

> . . . a radical ideology claims that liberal developmental ideology and romantic ideology are embedded in the present system. That is, the emphasis upon the individual and his unfolding or developing necessitates acceptance of the social structures as status quo in order to identify in any empirical manner the development of the individual. Thus, developmental theory is culture and society bound, and it is bound to the kind of a system that structures human relations in hierarchical dominance and submission patterns and alienates the person from his activity in work and from other people (p. 88).

However, like the developmental/psychological view, the radical perspective was flawed as well.

> Yet I find this [radical] view limiting in its materialistic focus, and I suspect that it is grounded fundamentally in the Industrial Revolution and reflects the same linear rationality and conceptualizing that characterizes the rise of science and technology. . . . The world today is not the same, and a different reading of history is needed to help make sense of the contemporary world. . . . The radical-political perspective as a home for curriculum thinking does not adequately allow for the tacit dimension of culture: it is a hierarchical historical science that has outlived its usefulness both in terms of the emerging structure of the environment and of the psyches of people today (Macdonald, 1974, pp. 89–90).

This critique of Marxism would become loud with the arrival of poststructuralism in the field not ten years later (Taubman, 1979, 1982; Daignault & Gauthier, 1982).

Then Macdonald the visionary surfaced. He (1974) wrote that "today's technology is yesterday's magic" (p. 91). He continued:

Technology is in effect an externalization of the hidden consciousness of human potential. Technology. . . is a necessary development for human beings in that is the means of externalizing the potential that lies within. Humanity will eventually transcend technology by turning inward, the only viable alternate that allows a human being to continue to experience oneself in the world as a creative and vital element. Out of this will come the rediscovery of human potential (Macdonald, 1974, p. 91).

Political and economic analysis cannot, to borrow Jean-Paul Sartre's concept, "totalize" culture, society, and history. Rather, political and social theory represents:

> . . . a radical social adjunct to conceptual culture. Now we are facing the opening of doors of perception in human experience, not as the minor mystical phenomena that have appeared throughout history, but as a large-scale movement of consciousness on the part of our young. A multimedia world is perceptual, not linear, in the utilization of concepts, but patterned concepts are received upon impact as perceptual experience. The psychological attitude born in this culture is a psychology of individuation, not individualism or socialism. . . Thus the conscious attitude of integration is one of acceptance, of ceasing to do violence to one's own nature by repressing or overdeveloping any part of it. This Jung termed a "religious" attitude, although not necessarily related to any recognizable creed (Macdonald, 1974, p. 92, p. 98).

Macdonald's thought represents a major contribution to the American curriculum field. First, we have here a rather comprehensive curriculum theory, one rooted in the historical world, as well as in the history of curriculum discourses. It contains within it the major theoretical elements of the field's history, and it has made them over in a view of complexity and moral power. Second, as Melva Burke (1985) has chronicled, Macdonald's career spans what some might call the four theoretical moments of the field: scientific thinking, personal humanism, sociopolitical humanism, and transcendental thought. For Macdonald curriculum theory was fundamentally a creative act. Perhaps his view is summarized in his statement that "curriculum is an exciting venture for persons whose dispositions lead them in this direction. There is an article of faith involved. . . [because it is] 'the study of how to have a world'" (Macdonald, 1975b, p. 12).

In a videotaped autobiography Macdonald identified four stages of his development. The first stage was scientism, which he eventually felt excluded too much—especially affect. From scientism Macdonald moved to what he termed person-centered humanism, and third to what he termed sociopolitical humanism. His fourth and final stage was transcendentalism, with its significant secular and religious implications and its need for cultural revolution. He believed that each stage was necessary and important to his study of what he considered the key question in curriculum: How shall we live together? (Brubacker & Brookbank, 1986; Macdonald, 1986)

The path-breaking work of James B. Macdonald not only challenged the traditional field during the 1960s and 1970s, it suggested a thematic route for Reconceptualization in the 1970s. Its thematic outlines would be political, autobiographic, and would include European traditions such as phenomenology and theology. What sounded like "faint voices" in the 1960s and like sheer speculation in the very early 1970s would turn out to be "fact" by 1980. This swift movement from the traditional to the reconceptualized field was, in part, a consequence of the scholarship of James B. Macdonald.

In the early 1980s, Macdonald sketched the outlines of the relations between gender and curriculum, collaborating with his wife Susan Colberg Macdonald. They pointed to the scale of the problem of sexism and the links among sexism, world armaments, and the environmental crisis. The Macdonalds connected politics, economics, and culture with the production of gendered personalities in the family and the school. They distinguished between the "agentic" or agency-oriented personality (typically male), and the "communal" one (typically female), concepts which generally parallel the gender distinctions drawn by object relations theorists (Grumet, 1988). These psychoanalytic theorists typify contemporary man (in countries like the U.S.) as achieving independence at the price of relationship and intimacy, and the contemporary woman as sometimes submerged in relationship at the cost of independence and autonomy. These psychological constellations of self-formation support and express political inequalities.

The Macdonalds (1988) argued that sexism permeates all aspects of the school, including its organization, status hierarchy, and curriculum. They noted that concepts such as behavioral objectives, behavior modification, competency analysis, instructional systems, and so on, support agency-oriented value orientations. The so-called hidden curriculum reproduces familial sex-role stereotyping at worst, and fails to challenge the gender status quo at best. No aspect of school life seems to escape these influences. What course of action is possible? The Macdonalds suggested that "social engineering" was inappropriate and ineffective. Rather, incremental social action, taken in individual ways according to what is possible at each institutional site, offers hope for long-term change. In addition, scholarship (especially theoretical work) is necessary to justify and explicate what must be done. The Macdonalds suggested that the school must be reconceived to support a concept of "sociability" or community, in which patterns of independence, relationship, and intimacy could be lived by both sexes within the institution. At stake, the Macdonalds insisted, is not only gender equity in the school but the survival of the planet.

James B. Macdonald's scholarly range was very remarkable. The reader of this collection will find citations not only from curriculum specialists, but from social theorists, poets, and scholars in the humanities and arts as well. For instance, Jim illustrated and amplified his ideas by drawing upon the work of Adler, Apple, Berger, Blake, Bloom, Bruner, Buber, Casteneda, Coleman, Dewey, Elkind, Freidenberg, Freire, Freud, Fromm, Goodlad, Goodman, Habermas, Heisenberg, Herrick, Huebner, Illich, Jackson, James, Jung, Klein, Kliebard, Koestler, Kohlberg, Langer, Lefebvre, Mann, Marcel, Marcuse, Marx, McLuhan, Miel, Mills, Myrdal, Nietzsche, Phenix, Polanyi, Ricoeur, Rogers, Schwab, Soleri, Steiner, Stratemeyer, Tolstoy, Tyler, Watts, Whitehead, and Yeats, among others. To give you an impressionistic sense of the conceptual range of his interests—as well as their presence in 1990s scholarship—prepare to find the following concepts in this collection: embeddedness, self, culture, identity, meaning, listening, empathy, unspoken assumptions (i.e. hidden curriculum), technology, gender, bureaucracy, depersonalization, morality, human development, transcendence, romance, powerlessness, inwardness, individuation, being, Zen, Christianity, ecology, mathematics, aesthetics, imagination, mind, body, love, ideology, dialogue, relationship, understanding, psychoanalysis, science, hermeneutics, objectivism, scientism, emancipation, life-world, consumption, power, politics, economics, language, democracy, multiculturalism, bisexuality, decadence, community, God, goodness, values, anarchy, passion, and always the school. Jim's modest self-presentational style could not hide the scope, rigor, and integrity of his scholarly accomplishment.

Throughout his career, James Macdonald argued against the traditional structures of curriculum research that excluded the ethical dimension of education. From several perspectives, Jim explored curriculum from a "utopian impulse for justice, equity, and fairness." He wrote:

> Education [is] a moral enterprise rather than simply a set of technical problems to be solved within a satisfying conceptual scheme. . . .
> Thus, the struggle for personal integration, educational integrity, and

social justice go on, necessitating a constant reevaluation of oneself, one's work and one's world—with the hope that with whatever creative talent one possess will lead toward something better that we may all share (1975a, p. 4).

He concluded that "the act of theorizing is an act of faith, a religious act. . . . Curriculum theory is a prayerful act" (Macdonald, 1981 p. 136).

A prayerful act, an act of faith. Perhaps before any of us, Jim knew how profoundly we were moving away from the taken-for-granted and the everyday. His work and presence were openings to worlds not here, worlds many have turned against as impractical. But James B. Macdonald knew that to give up praying to that world, dreaming of that world, is to collapse defeated into this one, is to abandon hope of our redemption, and the redemption of our children. In a world and a field sometimes contracted by stinginess, blinded by loss of vision, and embittered by loss of heart, James B. Macdonald's life and career offers us a powerful and clear vision of a new world. Let us celebrate his monumental achievement by reading and rereading his essays, and proceeding, with his help, toward that new world.

William F. Pinar
Louisiana State University
1995

References

Apple, M. (1985). There is a River: James B. Macdonald and Curricular Tradition. *JCT*, 6 (3), pp. 9-18.

Brubaker, D. & Brookbank, G. (1986). James B. Macdonald: A Bibliography. *Journal of Curriculum and Supervision*, 1 (3), pp. 215-220.

Burke, M. (1985). The Personal and Professional Journey of James B. Macdonald. *JCT*, 6 (3), pp. 84-119.

Freire, P. (1968). *Pedagogy of the Oppressed.* New York: Seabury.

Daignault, J. & Gauthier, C. (1982). The Indecent Curriculum Machine. *JCT*, 4 (1), pp. 177-196.

Giroux, H., Penna, A., & Pinar, W. (Eds.). (1981). *Curriculum and Instruction: Alternatives in Education.* Berkeley, CA: McCutchan.

Grumet, M. (1985). The Work of James B. Macdonald: Theory Fierce with Reality. *JCT*, 6 (3), pp. 19-27.

_____ (1988). *Bitter Milk: Women and Teaching.* Amherst, MA: University of Massachusetts Press.

Huebner, D. (1985). The Redemption of Schooling: The Work of James B. Macdonald. *JCT*, 6 (3), pp. 28-34.

Holland, P. & Garman, N. (1992). Macdonald and the Mythopoetic. *JCT*, 9 (4), pp. 45-72.

Klohr, P. (1967). This Issue. *Theory into Practice*, 6 (4), p. 165.

Macdonald, J. (1964). An Image of Man: The Learner Himself. In R. Doll (Ed.), *Individualizing Instruction* (29-49). Washington, DC: ASCD.

_____ (1967). An Example of Disciplined Curriculum Thinking. *Theory into Practice*, 6 (4), pp. 166-171.

_____ (1974). A Transcendental Developmental Ideology of Education. In W. Pinar (Ed.), *Heightened Consciousness, Cultural Revolution, and Curriculum Theory: The Proceedings of the Rochester Conference* (85-116). Berkeley, CA: McCutchan.

_____ (1975a). Autobiographical Statement. In W. Pinar (Ed.), *Curriculum Theorizing: The Reconceptualists* (3-4). Berkeley, CA: McCutchan.

_____ (1975b). Curriculum Theory. In W. Pinar (Ed.), *Curriculum Theorizing: The Reconceptualists* (5-13). Berkeley, CA: McCutchan.

_____ (1975c). Curriculum and Human Interests. In W. Pinar (Ed.), *Curriculum Theorizing: The Reconceptualists* (283-294).

Berkeley, CA: McCutchan.

_____ (1981).   Theory, Practice and the Hermeneutic Circle. *JCT*, 3 (2), pp. 130-138.

_____ (1986).   The Domain of Curriculum.   [Foreword by D. Huencke.] *Journal of Curriculum & Supervision*. (1)3, pp. 205-214.

_____ (1988).   Curriculum, Consciousness, and Social Change. In W. Pinar (Ed.), *Contemporary Curriculum Discourses* (156-174). Scottsdale, AZ: Gorsuch Scarisbrick.

Macdonald, J., Anderson, D. & May, F.   (Eds.).   (1965). *Strategies for Curriculum Development: The Works of Virgil Herrick*. Columbus, OH: Charles E. Merrill.

Macdonald, J. & Leeper, R.   (Eds.).   (1966). *Language and Meaning*. Washington, DC: ASCD.

_____ (1968).   *Theories of Instruction*.   Columbus, OH: Charles Merrill.

Macdonald, J. & Macdonald, S.   (1988).   Gender, Values, and Curriculum.   In W. Pinar (Ed.), *Contemporary Curriculum Discourses* (476-485). Scottsdale, AZ: Gorsuch Scarisbrick. [First published in *JCT*, 1981.]

Macdonald, J. &   Purpel, D. (1987).   Curriculum and Planning: Visions and Metaphors. *Journal of Curriculum and Supervision*, 2 (2), pp. 178-192.

Macdonald, J. & Zaret, E.   (Eds.).   (1975). *Schools in Search of Meaning*. [1975 yearbook.] Washington, DC: ASCD.

Marcuse, H. (1964).   *One-Dimensional Man: Studies in the Ideology of Advanced Industrial Societies*. Boston, MA: Beacon Press.

McLaren, P. & Leonard, P.   (Eds.).   (1993). *Paulo Freire: A Critical*

Encounter. New York: Routledge.

Molnar, A. (1985). Tomorrow the Shadow on the Wall will be that of Another. *JCT*, 6 (3), pp. 35-42.

Pinar, W. (Ed.) (1975). *Curriculum Theorizing: The Reconceptualists.* Berkeley, CA: McCutchan.

Pinar, W. (1985). A Prayerful Act: The Work of James B. Macdonald. *JCT*, 6 (3), pp. 43-53.

Pinar, W. & Grumet, M. (1988). Socratic *Caesura* and the Theory-Practice Relationship. In W. Pinar (Ed.), *Contemporary Curriculum Discourses* (92-100). Scottsdale, AZ: Gorsuch Scarisbrick.

Pinar, W., Reynolds, W., Slattery, P. & Taubman, P. (1995). *Understanding Curriculum*. New York: Peter Lang.

Robison, H. (Ed.). (1966). *Precedents and Promise in the Curriculum Field*. Washington, DC: ASCD.

Searles, W. (1982). A Substantiation of Macdonald's Models in Science Curriculum Development. *JCT*, 4 (1), pp. 127-155.

Spodek, B. (1985). Reflections in Early Childhood Education. *JCT*, 6 (3), pp. 54-64.

Taubman, P. (1979). *Gender and Curriculum: Discourse and the Politics of Sexuality*. Rochester, NY: University of Rochester, Graduate School of Education and Human Development, unpublished doctoral dissertation.

Wolfson, B. (1985a). Preface: Special Issue in Commemoration of James B. Macdonald, 1925-1983. *JCT*, 6 (3), pp. 5-7.

_____ (1985b). Closing Remarks. *JCT*, 6 (3), p. 65.

Chapter One

An Image of Man: The Learner Himself

Knowledge about teaching is directly related to, and at times is a direct corollary of, man's knowledge of human nature. It is hardly possible to conceive of a teaching situation that does not involve, at some level of operation, beliefs concerning human learning, development and relationships. These beliefs are present and embodied in the actions of teachers as they plan, organize, interact and evaluate in classrooms.

The sources of beliefs about man are varied. Some beliefs are learned through our own developmental experiences as primarily incidental matters, perhaps through the attitudes of others. Other beliefs arise from our common sense analysis of life. Religious beliefs are further common sources of our beliefs about man. And, of course, scientific knowledge can be the cornerstone of our beliefs.

During the past fifty years many attempts have been made to shape the beliefs of teachers about the nature of man. Child study movements, courses in the nature of learning and human development, and the use of psychologists, social workers and psychiatrists in school settings come readily to mind. Whatever form these attempts have taken, they reflect a common belief of a most fundamental nature: that the functions of teachers which promote learning are inseparable from the nature of the human beings who are functioning and learning in the school situation. It is the purpose of this essay to reaffirm this belief and to rephrase it in the form of a specific image of man which reflects our empirical knowledge of human nature.

Knowledge of man that is open to empirical validation requires more than empirical methodology. It requires a schema for selecting and organizing empirical data. These organizing schemata have been called many things—from metatheory to images of man.

The sources of our images of man are not at all clear. These images are not entirely empirical in derivation; rather they are emergent through the totality of man's experiences. We believe, however, that an image of man is necessary for the selection, organization and interpretation of empirical data. Further, it is our image of man, rather than so called "facts," which guides us in our conscious cognitive interaction with others. It is this understanding that may help to explain why many research data lie untouched, for without a coherent image of man we cannot expect useful research or intelligent understanding of the results.

Images of man are, however, not free of their empirical groundings. They are heuristic devices to be accepted solely on their successful ordering of the data of human experience within the framework of empirical methodology. Thus, images change as man develops more knowledge about himself and in turn fertilizes the development of further knowledge.

The social scientist as a man is never free from the basic social and cultural value orientations and forces in the milieu of his existence. There are of necessity deep and lasting psychological relationships between the social scientist's scientific images of man and the fundamental values of his total existence. Yet within that limitation there is a range of images within which to order the data of his experiences. Nevertheless, one would be remiss in failing to point out the corollary of the proposed scientific image of man and such fundamental social values as freedom, individuality and human dignity.

As we have implied, the purpose of this essay is to present the outlines of an image of man which at present seems most harmonious with scientific knowledge. This image also corresponds with the personal values of the writer in relation to the task of ordering and selecting experiences with human behavior in the classroom. The outlines of this image of man will be given substance by addressing ourselves to four questions: What process of development? What conditions for growth? What kind of self image? And, especially, what kind of education?

The Process of Human Development

The process of human development is considered here to be a process of becoming.[1] As such, the process cannot be described by analogy as an unfolding of an organism along predetermined paths. It is, rather, a process whereby the person is always in a transactional relationship with his environment. This relationship includes individually unique choices and the vagaries of unpredictable circumstances as well as the mechanisms of biological growth and the predominant socialization processes of a society. Development is, in other words, a creative, self-actualizing[2] phenomenon, as well as a predictable pattern of growth and socialization.

The essence of development eludes the viewer unless the realm of personal responsiveness is considered as foremost in the appraisal of development processes. Or, to put it another way, growth, maturation and socialization are much more useful for understanding similarities than they are for the consideration of differences. Thus, when viewing the socialization process, we may readily see how language becomes a part of the child's development; how self-concepts emerge; and so on. What is missing is the dimension of personal responsiveness to the socialization process. Likewise, in the biological realm, the forces of maturation explain much about walking, sexual maturation, etc., but little about personal responsiveness to these developments.

What this means is illustrated when we view man historically and individually. Rather than ask the question, "How could man have come so far in developing such technology and social life?," we are more prone to ask, "Why has man failed so miserably in ridding the world of war, disease, famine and starvation?" Or rather than marveling at individual men and asking, "How could an Einstein be?" we may ask, "Why are there so few great men?" It is because the answer must lie in the realm of what man and society do to the element of personal responsiveness that the questions are phrased differently. In other words, we are not concerned here with how man can condition, and has conditioned, himself to the present state, but how this very conditioning process has affected the creative, self-actualizing, personal aspect of his development.

The basic propositions underlying the approach are, then, that man has a personal, self-actualizing and creative capability not limited solely by biology or conditioning; that personal response is the avenue through which individuals stretch and may reach their potentialities; and that a view of human development which wishes to focus upon human potentialities must center upon the developmental aspects of personal responsiveness. Gordon Allport catches this feeling well when he says:

> We maintain, therefore, that personality is governed not only by impact of stimuli upon a slender endowment of drives common to the species. The process of becoming is governed, as well, by a disposition to realize its possibilities, i.e., to become characteristically human at all stages of development. And one of the capacities most urgent is individual style of life that is self-aware, self-critical, and self-enhancing.[3]

In another context, Allport says:

> Hence the individuality of man extends infinitely beyond the puny individuality of plants and animals, who are primarily or exclusively creatures of tropism or instinct. Immense horizons for individuality open when billions of cortical cells are added to the neutral equipment of lower species. Man talks, laughs, feels bored, develops a culture,

prays, has a foreknowledge of death, studies theology, and strives for the improvement of his own personality. The infinitude of resulting patterns is plainly not found in creatures of instinct. For this reason we should exercise great caution when we extrapolate the assumptions, methods and concepts of natural and biological science to our subject matter. In particular, we should refuse to carry over the indifference of other sciences to the problem of individuality.[4]

The individual life cycle is a process of becoming characterized by the individuality and uniqueness of the human being: not each becoming a man in a generic sense, but each becoming a human individual with myriad potentialities not known or predictable in any absolute sense.

Just as an historical view of man may be seen as facing a "triad of limitations"[5] with the goal of overcoming them, the life cycle view of man has its purposefulness. This purpose may be seen as Buber[6] views it in relatedness, or as Tillich[7] sees it in freedom from anxieties. Fromm[8] calls this goal productivity; and Lindner,[9] productive rebellion. Whatever view of purposefulness we choose, throughout each view runs the thread of freedom and individuality, whether for individual maturities' sake or as the basis for higher relatedness. Whatever its terminal status, it is as Maslow says, "a self-actualizing process," and it is unique to the circumstances and heredity of the given individual.

The development of an individual is an extremely complex and perplexing matter. Theories abound and organizing schemata vary from Freudian phases[10] to development tasks,[11] or normative behaviors.[12] What is most often omitted is consideration of personal response and/or responsibility in the developmental process, and upon this aspect the image presented here is focused.

What Conditions for Growth?

The optimum development of human potential is related to three sets of conditions which have been called "the *a priori* conditions," "the social conditions," and "the maximal conditions."[13] Full opportunity for potential to develop is dependent upon the existence of all three sets of conditions, each in its own way.

The *A Priori* Conditions

A priori conditions are genetic and physical in character. An individual must possess an adequate genetic structure to develop humanness, must experience normal (for him) physical growth, and must have proper nutritional care throughout. The lack of any or all of these conditions will result in the thwarting of the development of human potential. These conditions are important to all animal life but are necessary before human potential may develop. They are "givens" which are basic but not specifically human in nature.

An understanding of physical growth, nutrition, and genetic lack or physiological damage is essential for providing the background of the development of human potential. It is considered here to be the necessary condition for developing potential and will be assumed as background in further discussion.

The Social Conditions

Human beings develop and are distinctly recognizable as such in the context of social relationships which involve the use of signs and symbols. Societies and cultures provide frameworks for the development of human beings. They teach the individual how to act, how to symbolize and conceptualize, and how to perceive himself and his environment.

In order to become minimally human, an individual must learn how to interact with others and must operate through the prevalent symbolic system; and in the process, he must learn to "see" himself and his world as others see him. His basic quest is toward mastery of common understandings about status and roles, objects and ideas, himself and others.

The manner by which the individual is "socialized" is also of great importance. The degree of understanding, love, acceptance, recognition, hostility and aggression, for example, will have deep consequences upon his personality formation. So, the content of his world and the process which he encounters will be set by his particular social conditions.

Social conditions are minimal conditions. They provide a framework by which the individual becomes human. They are, however, essentially *closed* in nature. No matter what the structure of a specific culture may be, the individual is closed in its symbolic universe and world view, its customs and mores, its functions and objects.

Thus, the basic problem of developing human potential appears. In order to be human, one must experience the closure of the socialization process. One is taught what it is appropriate to be curious about; what things exist and what they are called; how one manipulates these objects of attention symbolically and physically; how one may maintain one's personal integration in this culture (often via defense mechanisms); and how one should perceive and interact with others. Yet, to develop his potential, a person must be open, and it is openness that provides the maximal conditions for human development.

The Maximal Condition

To be open to life is the maximal condition for developing human potential. To be open in thought—fluent, flexible and original; and open in affect—experiencing the potential feelings in an activity; and open in perception—meeting the potential stimuli in the world: these are the ways to maximum development of human potential. To be open to life, however, is a risky business demanding a "courage to be" and a sound ego integration.

Fingarette[14] has presented an insightful viewpoint for conceptualizing the maximal conditions for reaching potentialities. In essence, this framework proposes that anxiety and ego integration are "two sides of a coin." The state of anxiety (which is more than the common feeling labeled anxiety) is essentially a state of ego disintegration. Ego integration or disintegration is seen in terms of meaning schemes. Thus when life is vital, meaningful, and purposeful, the ego is relatively integrated. When life is experienced as meaningless, dull, or purposeless, a state of anxiety or ego disintegration is predominant.

Meaning schemes are the ways in which one personally relates oneself to one's past experiences, present situations and aspirations in his existent world; and to his understanding of himself, others and phenomena in his object world. Thus, the individual and/or the culture creates meaning schemes to orient himself and/or itself to life as a personal and unique existence, and to life as part of a general structure or system of objects.

When experience is meaningless, living is a state of general anxiety in the sense that present meaning schemes do not promote ego integration at higher levels, but reflect a process of disintegration which most often causes the ego to restrict its functioning in controllable areas. Thus, the process of closure is evident, and the use of defense mechanisms to ward off the movement of the ego into potentially open areas short-circuits the potential enlargement of ego-relevant new experience.

Schachtel[15] speaks of a similar phenomena in terms of the affective development of the individual. Although for our purposes here his terminology is not as useful, it embodies one concept that is especially descriptive of the viewpoint being expressed. This is the idea of *embeddedness*. Briefly, when the avenues to personal growth and potentiality are closed, they are embedded in an affective state of equilibrium. Thus, the person, under the threat of new experience and activity, is aroused emotionally to seek equilibrium, to return to a lack of arousal. Rather than turning outward and exploring the new, he turns his activity towards restoring the old.

The old may be an embeddedness in primary (personal) meanings, or an embeddedness in secondary (cultural) meanings. In either case, the circuit is closed to the development of potential, and one may say the person is *embedded*.

The individual's ego structure may be viewed according to these two basic postures described in similar terms by Fingarette and Schachtel. Meaningful situations produce either general anxiety or open activity. Anxiety, it shall be argued here, short-circuits the becoming of the individual, whereas open activity fosters becoming; and the process of becoming is creative realization and development of human potential. Thus, as one looks at development behaviors as these are received by the world and fed back to the child, one looks for the existence either of anxiety or of open activity. When anxiety exists, one may assume that potential is encapsulated; and when open activity exists, one may look for the enrichment and unfolding of capability.

Anxiety may be the feeling of boredom which is akin to knowledge of the meaninglessness of one's activity for self-becoming. Anxiety may arise from threatened or genuine separation from a state of embeddedness. Also, it may undergird pleasure when pleasure is essentially a need satisfaction which incorporates the object "pleasured" into the safe ground of embeddedness of the subject. It may be productive of hope when hope is mere wishful expectation that somehow everything will change for the better, or it may motivate joy, when joy has the quality of magical fulfillment which suddenly changes the whole character of life and of the world. Or, anxiety may be seen as psychosomatic symptoms which remove a person from an ego-threatening encounter with the world. Whatever its form, anxiety provides the vehicle by which the organism maintains a state of quiescent equilibrium in relation to the environment. This equilibrium is in effect the removal of the self from any new threat in the face of already-felt ego disorganization.

Open activity produces feelings which arise from direct encounter with the world. It is openness and responsiveness to the impact of the world not sheltered by an embeddedness in some other context, but rather a direct transaction. Open activity is stimulation and activity, involvement, and the pleasure of contact with objects "out there." Encounter with reality is the significant aspect of open activity, not the distortion and subsequent incorporation of reality for the sake of equilibrium. It is joy not linked to any expectation but is a felt experience of acts of relatedness. Open activity is realistic hope, founded in satisfactions based in the encounter with reality along the way toward goals.

On the level of thought and perception, these basic ego structures guide the behavior of the individual. When integration is dominant one "sees" what is in reality to be perceived. The individual's thoughts are bound to the structuring of cognitions to enhance the basic ego structure and affective orientation. When anxiety pervades, one thinks what one needs to think to preserve equilibrium (e.g., "rationalization"), or one thinks what one can grasp as he faces reality.

Human development, then, may be viewed as a biological given with its environmental and social conditioning, and its personal responsiveness in the form of ego orientation and its attendant affective states in the world. It is this last which seals the biological and social forces and processes in embeddedness, or which utilizes the biosocial avenues for greater realization of human potential. Human development forms the contrast between an end product and a never-ending product; the contrast between a closed system which "sees" and "thinks" what it has learned to see and think in its attempt to maintain an adjusted equilibrium, and an open system which reaches outward and inward in active search, discovery and creativeness in its encounter with reality. Furthermore, it creates the contrast between (a) an individual for whom reality *is* the defined and internalized feelings, symbols and thoughts learned in culturally or biologically embedded anxiety, and (b) an individual who experiences reality as *becoming* in the creative transaction between a person and his interactions in the world "out there" and "in here."

Self-Image: The Focus of Action

When ego processes are weak, the behavior of the individual is essentially defensive. Behavior is protective of equilibrium, and the individual adjusts to the world by means of defense mechanisms which accompany distorted perceptions that allow his equilibrium to remain rather than to encourage him to take in new information. Weak ego processes are reflected in a negative perception of self as inadequate, undeserving and unworthy; in a perception of others as threatening, hostile and controlling; and in a perception of the world as foreign and forbidding. Thus, the individual so affected experiences the environment passively, with little curiosity and manipulation. Ego strength, on the other hand, is both resultant from and reflected in openness to new experience. In contrast to ego weakness, ego strength is characterized by a positive concept of self, others and the world; and by an active participation in the world. Bower's remarks are most pertinent to the subject. He says:

Of major concern to behavioral scientists and educators are those factors which encourage a defensive reaction of a person to an event and those which encourage a coping pattern. . . [in] terms of the thinking of such writers as Klein and Ross[16] and Murphy[17] coping is an approach to the handling of stress or a problem of living in such a manner that the result is a stronger and healthier organism—an organism in a more fluid and effective homeostasis, or balance. On the other hand, a defensive pattern constitutes an approach by the organism to the stress or problem that results in a less resilient state—that is, a more fixed and rigid homeostasis. Consequently an organism that employs defensive ego processes will, in time, lose the ability to function freely with new problems.[18]

Perhaps the most useful approach to thinking about the nature of man, with reference to the classroom, is the idea of self-perception. At least it appears that the person's concept of himself is an available phenomena for inference from observation on the part of the teacher. A student's behavior can be interpreted with reasonable accuracy to reflect certain positive or negative self-perceptions, other perceptions, and modes of behaving in the world.

When the student enters the classroom, he brings with him a self, or reflection of his ego processes, which has been built through his own unique heredity and experience. If the child's self-perceptions reflect adequate ego strength, he will see himself as adequate to the performance of curricular tasks as well as liking what he sees. He will be open to new experiences, ready to grow, willing to experiment and discover. However, when self-perceptions are negative, they have a debilitating effect. Curricular tasks will be seen as too hard and as imposed unreasonably.

The sense of self is present in all children. In the child's early infancy, one sees a general acquisition of self-consciousness, a separation of "me" from the rest of the world. By the time a child is ready to walk, it is highly probable that the awareness of "I" is present.

The bodily self seems to develop first. It grows from the stream of recurrent organic sensations from within and the barriers imposed from "out there." The bodily self remains a basic cornerstone of our existence:

Recent work on sensory deprivation has shown how much we depend on our sensory stream for our sense of self-hood. Subjects who lie inactive on a bed for a day or so, receiving absolutely no outside stimulation, and a very minimum of internal stimulation, complain that they lose virtually all sense of self.[19]

As locomotion develops, the child begins his journey toward autonomy. So strong is the desire to become autonomous that this is often spoken of as a need for autonomy. Whether it is a "need" or not, the beginnings of self-esteem arise in the functioning of the child. He begins to see himself as adequate or inadequate in relation to his experiences and attempts toward autonomous behavior.

The social self-image commences to develop during or shortly after the beginning of autonomous behavior. The child gradually becomes aware that his parents want him to be a "good" boy, and that at times he is "bad." Although his conscience is not yet developed, the foundation for goals, purposes, responsibility and self-knowledge is being formed.

Upon entrance to school, the child undergoes an enlargement of his sense of identity and self-image. The presence of significant adults and his peer group provides many new and broad possibilities for the enhancement of self. Recognition of different standards and expectations from those of his parents adds immeasurably to his potential for self-growth. Shortly, the child recognizes his developing ability to cope with the world as a rational being. Objective knowledge becomes for him a fascinating quest, whether it is in the form of academic activity, baseball averages, or some other kind of socially available "know how."

As the child grows into adolescence, he in a sense withdraws from the objective world and turns inward in renewed search for identity. The brash reality-testing self becomes a more careful prober of possibilities. On a more mature level, the adolescent tries on many roles much as the preschooler wears different hats. He is searching for his self-identity, his adult personality.

A certain aspect of the total development of self is a striving, purposing function. It is though the self were continually trying to actualize itself. In some ways, one might say there is a restless, searching quality to the growth of self. Whatever this may be, the self may be said to aspire toward goals and ends which are the individual's own.

The self as a reflection of ego-processes strives toward meanings. These meanings are of two general varieties; they are perhaps best described by the prescriptions "know thyself" and "know thy world." The self is not "actualized" in a vacuum but in a world. The world is, however, primarily as it is perceived by the self. For the world to become only what one feels it is is to retreat into psychosis; but for the world to be accepted only as it is defined, in terms of rational, cultural knowledge, is certainly a form of neurosis. In neither case is the ego integrated into a functional, open and reality-oriented structure.

It should be apparent to all that the growing self must have personal meanings and cultural meanings for adequate realization. Further, it follows from this that the two meaning systems are not separate compartments within the individual. They are (in the healthy state) functionally integrated into the purposive striving of the person.

Success in the attainment of goals becomes of crucial significance to the self. When failures are recurrent in self-relevant, or ego involved areas, lasting feelings of inferiority arise, and defense mechanisms are developed in order to avert encounters which arose these feelings. When this occurs, the youngster closes his contact with reality and becomes embedded in some structured feelings which will thwart the development of his potential by warding off the learning of new meaning schemes.

Thus the pupil as self provides the teacher with a way of entering the life of the individual in meaningful ways: through helping the pupil see himself clearly, and by fostering his sense of identity and success in his striving toward selfhood. All the learner's experiences are relevant in the development of selfhood. Success or failure, joy or shame, pleasure or guilt and/or anxiety in solving an arithmetic problem feed as directly into the development of self as do peer group reactions or parental attitudes.

Furthermore, the actualizing quality of self places the destiny of the individual within his own hands. To some extent, at least, one may become what one hopes or wishes to be; and a teacher can provide the guidance of this development of realistic hope and desire which may give far more lasting meaning to the life of a child than the multiplication tables per se.

More significantly, the child's concept of self provides him with his most manageable and productive means of self-actualization. This concept is, actually, the only rational way by which the child can enter into his own development to influence growth through the setting of ideals, purposes and commitments which strengthen the ego processes as self-perceptions change. Here is a crucial point at which the teacher may hold open the world for a child.

What Kind of Education?

The implications of this image of man are numerous. The teacher as the socializing agent in the classroom must provide opportunities for children to reveal themselves, must promote relationships which bring out a positive affective climate, and must open vistas of relevant cultural knowledge. These three tasks are intricately related to each other, since the classroom environment which is relatively free of anxiety-producing elements will by necessity offer opportunities for pupils to reveal themselves to self and others and to experience the cultural and physical environment in self-meaningful ways.

Of special significance to anxiety production in the school, as in socializing agencies generally, is the imposition of authority in the context of *right* or *wrong* and *good* or *bad*, rather in the context of *appropriate* or *inappropriate*. The essential difference between the perception of an act, idea, or feeling as right or wrong, good or bad, rather than appropriate or inappropriate rests in the closing of alternatives in the developmental process, in the stultifying of individual judgement. The feeling of inappropriateness provides a qualification which allows the door to remain open for other circumstances. It poses the question, "What is appropriate in this situation?" without the finality or absoluteness of what is "good" or "right."

There is another way of viewing the concept of appropriateness. Behavior is appropriate when it is personal and a part of the individual's own becoming. We may be sure that a person "becomes" within the context of cultural values. No person is beyond these values unless he is alienated to an extreme degree, for example, as in psychosis. Appropriate behavior should also not be confused with behavior associated with amoral or psychopathetic individuals. Although the hardened criminal, for example, may behave in a completely ego-centered manner "appropriate" to his own gratification, his behavior lacks a feeling relationship to others capable of contributing to his own self-realization.

On the contrary, appropriate behavior is value-directed and moral behavior. It is value-oriented because it is purposeful, and it is moral because it includes self-relevant behavior in the context of productive human relations within which the individual assumes responsibility for his behavior. It is not, however, behavior which serves the purpose of other persons alone.

The question of the motivation of the socializing agent is central to this distinction. When the child is led to feel his behavior to be "right" or "wrong," "good" or "bad," then the motives of the socializing person are drawn from outside the immediate relationship transaction or specific growth context of a given pupil. In a sense, the socializer is attempting to prohibit or avert the emergence of critical or crucial situations by teaching the child not to respond in certain ways. In so doing, the child is deprived of any experience of his own from which he may derive his own feelings of appropriateness. Socially conditioned fears, anxiety, shame, guilt, satisfaction, gratification and pleasure thus encircle the child and cue off externally imposed response patterns, which block the child's own ego integration. The basic question is, then, not one of specific response or behavior, but of the meaning of the behavior (i.e., its function) in the existence of the child.

Bruner's comment about reward and punishment is relevant at this point:

> It is often the case that emphasis upon reward and punishment, under the control of an outside agent such as the teacher or parent, diverts attention away from success and failure. In effect, this may take the learning initiative away from the child and give it to the person dispensing the rewards and punishments. This will be more likely if the learner is not able to determine the basis of success and failure. One of the great problems in teaching, which usually starts with the teacher being very supportive, is to give the rewarding function back to the learner and the task.[20]

Thus, necessary reality testing (assessment of success and failure) can not take place when good-bad or right-wrong embeds the child in a reward and punishment system beyond his control.

Obviously, the crucial aspect of this distinction does not rest in the surface reaction of stopping a given inappropriate behavior, or of exercising authority as an adult responsible for children. The crucial dimension lies in the reflection upon the self created through the overt activity.

We may, in other words, "teach" our youngsters to be "good" and "right" so that they learn to see themselves in these terms and to have feelings of shame, guilt and anxiety when "bad" and "wrong." The "badness" and "wrongness" encapsulate the developing individual in an affect-embeddedness which becomes a powerful drive for equilibrium, for returning to the security of what is "good" and "right." What we must "teach" our youngsters is to act, feel and think "appropriately" in those situations which call for such reactions, by focusing them upon the search for self-relevant behavior in a wide variety of circumstances.

We must stress the essential difference between "right-wrong," "good-bad," and "appropriate-inappropriate," for in our cultural thinking it is easy to shift the black and white quality of one to the intended meaning of the other. Appropriate behavior, regardless of its action context, is behavior which is one's own self-relevant possession. It has the element of self-acceptance of discovered appropriateness rather than the stamp of human authority beyond the boundaries of one's self. Appropriate behavior, then, is in essence self-disciplined behavior, and more: it is behavior at the service of the individual, not behavior which serves merely something or someone beyond the individual.

The act of recognizing the word "cat" may be any of these things. At a purely cognitive, judgmental level, it is "right," "good" and "appropriate." But in terms of the affective dimension, it cannot be all things. At this level, the affective, such recognition becomes "I am a *good* person because I recognize 'cat'"; or, "I am *right* in the eyes of authority when I see 'cat'"; or "When I see 'cat', it helps me to adjust to my world *appropriately.*"

The affective impact of "good-bad" and "right-wrong" built throughout the curriculum reinforces previous embeddedness-affect in youngsters. Learning becomes an affect-embedded necessity to maintain balance by escaping shame, guilt and anxiety, and seeking socially approved satisfaction and gratification. For those incapable of academic success in the school program, embeddedness at a nonschool level is reinforced and is seen by such behavior as withdrawal, aggression, illness, and fantasy. The school, in other words, facilitates the social or autistic embeddedness of the developmental process that alienates the pupil from social norms.

The teacher stands, in many ways, at the crossroads of meaning in the life of the pupil. On the one hand, he is attempting to stimulate the accumulation of, and provide the opportunity for, growth in the understanding of human knowledge. On the other hand and at the same time, the teacher must provide or stimulate an immediate, expressive commitment to the meaning of now. The immediate meaning must be generated out of creation of a new vision which serves as the context for new commitment, or motivation. The more general and longer-range meaning is part of the development of a rational, cognitive, systematically usable world view or meaning scheme. Thus, the pupil must have a meaningful relationship to himself and his immediate commitment, and to his world and his cognitive structure of it.

The concept of motivation in learning is the closest common referent for the idea of immediate commitment to a meaningful experience. The great misunderstanding of this concept in education has led to a failure of teachers to stand between the two meaningful contexts, between the personal existence meaning scheme of the pupil and his cognitive, culture-oriented meaning scheme. Rather, the usual concept of motivation has been a manipulative procedure whereby teachers attempt to "motivate" learners from the vantage point of one meaning system.

To stand between the two meaning systems means to stand with the pupil. It does not mean to stand in the *personal meaning system* of a given individual, nor to stand in the *common meaning system* of a society. Rather, it is centered in the reality of the person whose self-realization is dependent upon the growth of ego integration through the discovery and internalizing of more and more productive meaning schemes in both spheres.

Within recent years, Louis Raths has spoken much about the process of value clarification in the schools. This would seem to be one fruitful way of stimulating a student to examine his self-image and by so doing to lead him to identification of purposes and goals and rejection of defense mechanisms. The value clarification process thus would seem to be a teacher strategy for developing self-relevant aspirations, increased ego strength and involvement in life's activities, or, in other words, a strategy for standing with the pupil between his two meaning systems. As Raths says:

> If we want these children to have a deeper understanding of themselves, and a better comprehension of their own epoch, it will be necessary to introduce curriculum materials which are consistent with these ends. And, in addition, the curriculum materials must provide the opportunity for children to express attitudes, feelings, beliefs, interests, purposes, aspirations, and to discuss their activities, in and out of school.[21]

The behavior of the teacher is central in the clarification process. It is a questioning behavior which is essentially nonjudgmental and which does not reject pupils' answers. Sometimes a teacher may repeat what a pupil has said and ask if that is what he meant. At other times, he may ask a pupil to define his terms. Always the teacher *listens*, and listens with the belief that learners try to make things clear to the teacher, but that first they must be clear to themselves. There may be times when the teacher simply asks the pupil to elaborate, or to tell what he thinks is good about a particular idea, belief, purpose or activity. Should everyone think and feel this way? Is this an important and significant idea? Perhaps the teacher may sense an inconsistency and ask the pupil to think about it. Regardless of the question asked, the interaction in the clarification process is clear. It is an attempt to help a youngster see himself more clearly and to provide him with a useful vehicle incorporated in a teaching strategy to think about and clarify his own aspirations and desires and his relation to the environment in which he lives.

The development of thinking goes hand in hand with value clarification. Clarification of values always involves thinking, and a curriculum oriented toward value clarification will have a problematic character. Both value-clarification and thinking share the unique characteristic of humanistic rationality. It is this ability to achieve rationality which the Educational Policies Commission has called "the central purpose of American education."[22] Rationality is not to be confused with cognition or knowing, for to be rational is to think with values. The process of mere knowing can lead one astray, as is illustrated by the old cliché of "knowing the price of everything and the value of nothing." This is not the process used by the rational being, for whom thinking and valuing are always interlocked.

In relation to thinking, Raths again has relevant suggestions for teachers.[23] Curriculum tasks can be oriented toward the maximizing of possibilities to develop thinking at any level and can be woven into the patterns of methodology to the enhancement of self and society. The process of making *comparisons*, of seeking similarities and differences between poems, characters, life forms, mathematical proofs, or language translations involves the exercise of thinking and judgement. *Summarizing* experiences, or stories, or text material, or discussion will foster rational behavior and expose values to be clarified. To pose *problems* for solution, to make systematic *observations*, to *classify* and *criticize* provoke thought and decision-making.

Imagine you are at the North Pole, or that you could solve the problems of our time. What would you need, and/or what would you do? What is the meaning of what Jones has written? *Interpret* these data and tell what reasonable conclusions can be drawn. Look at these advertisements and *analyze* them. Tell what you feel the methods and motives of the advertiser are. Construct *categories* to group these motives and methods. Or perhaps, follow the most mundane but fruitful procedure of all: planning—planning for activities, for projects, for gathering appropriate resources, for doing research on a topic, or for the use of personal or group time in or out of school.

Central to all these processes is their rationality, their use of reason, value and choice. Each process demands individual commitment or use of judgement as the mind is put to use by the individual. Each outcome is unique to the individual, is tied to his own ego and his perception of self, and contributes potentially to the development of a more adequate self-concept.

Implied within these processes are nuances of relatedness, relationships to human beings and to one's cultural and physical world. As Huebner observes:

> Relating to others cannot be a goal of life or education, for it is the *sine qua non* of human existence. To relate or not to relate to others is not a choice offered to the child, nor even to the adult. The problem is not to relate to others, but to find a mode of relationship, and a way of talking about that relationship, which offers the greatest meaning today.[24]

The teaching-learning situation is a relationship whose intention, on the part of the teacher, is to foster and provide other relationships or transactions. Thus we may say that the personal characteristics of individuals are important, but values, thinking and needs find their expression in relatedness. The quality of this relatedness may well determine the direction of personal development in both immediate commitment and more pervasive cognitive structures.

Ashley Montagu's *Education and Human Relations*[25] develops in detail the theme of human relations as the primary meaning in education: to be educated is to be humanized, not to be instructed. It is well to remember, however, that human relationships are not ends but the sufficient conditions for becoming a social being. What kind of relationship will provide the conditions for a maximum amount of open activity for pupils?

Bills,[26] Rogers,[27] Murphy,[28] and others most certainly offer cues concerning teacher attributes and behavior in relatedness which will facilitate the development of human potential as conceptualized in the context of this image of man. Perhaps an even more direct way of discussing this image is through the existential concept of authenticity.[29] Regardless of which approach is taken, the view of becoming which we accept will include in some form or other, what Rogers[30] discusses.

To facilitate pupil growth, teacher behavior must be *congruent*, i.e., consistent with the teacher's real self. The teacher must be what he is without false pretenses. The teacher must, in other words, meet his pupils person-to-person, not status-to-person. When teachers hide behind status, pupils do not reveal themselves, and consequently their potentiality for growth is limited, for they are closed to avenues of development. The teacher who is genuine provides the pupil with the possibility of an authentic or direct, unmediated contact with reality through a relationship. The teacher who is otherwise raises defenses within the learner.

Empathy is a second cue to teacher-pupil relatedness. A teacher must be able to sense pupils' personal meanings as if they were his own. This ability is essentially different from understanding as an evaluative judgement. This ability is, in contrast, a total feeling, one of knowing rather than making a cognitive statement about another person. The teacher enters the reality of the world of the pupil rather than arousing the perceived reality in terms of outside reality norms.

Positive regard is intricately related to congruence and empathy. It refers to having a positive attitude toward the pupil, to prizing him as a thinking, valuing person beyond his immediate actions. When a pupil is positively regarded, he is freed in his feeling to be what he is at the moment, thus opening up his reality to himself. This is not permissiveness in its paternal or sentimental aspects, but a directed respect for the individuality of the person.

Thus, in the process of clarifying values, developing thinking, and relating to pupils, the teacher may find cues to opening of experience and growth of potential in pupils. Through these processes and possibly others, the teacher can gain access to the two areas of meaning-schemes so necessary for the growth of human potential.

The child may grow large (biologically) in school, may learn well (perform academically), and may act sociably (get along with others) without the school's contributing a great deal to the development of human potential in the developmental process. The school can lay claim to the effects upon performance which would not have come without the school of experience. But developmentally, any procedure which reinforces embeddedness is a "penny wise-pound foolish" procedure which thwarts the development of self-identity and ego involvement in life. The schools may be generating adequate role players at the cost of human development. For, as Fromm says:

> It is the fact that man does not experience himself as the active bearer
> of his own powers and richness, but as an impoverished "thing,"
> dependent upon powers outside of himself unto whom he has projected
> his living substance.[31]

The school which recognizes the image of man we have been discussing, and which incorporates the image in its curriculum is not child-centered, or society-centered, or subject-matter centered. It is *reality*-centered. By this, we simply mean that the school does not exist primarily to inculcate our cultural heritage, not principally to develop role players for society, nor primarily to meet the needs and interests of learners. The school exists to bring learners in contact with reality, of which our society, ourselves, and our cultural heritage are parts.

The basic goals of the reality-centered school are to meet the unmet needs of learners, i.e., to free them: to develop thinking and values in relation to our cultural heritage; and to encourage creative response to reality. Embodied in these goals is an awareness that learners must be free to explore; must have symbolic tools for exploration; and must focus upon culturally- and socially-defined concepts or foci as points of orientation for exploration.

In the reality-centered school, a thing exists not only to be mastered and imitated, but also to be discovered and invented. Reality and man's symbolic glasses for viewing it stretch to infinity. Symbolic forms are utilized to meet all of reality. To catch a bird in the net of a child's view is to perceive something to be classified, examined, counted, described, observed, rhythmically felt, poetically known, and otherwise related to one's own personal meanings. For there is certainly as much melody in a bird as there are feathers to count, as much rhythm in the reality of a bird as there are behaviors to observe.

The basic methodology of the reality-oriented school is simple. It is founded upon the principle that all children are self-actualizing, and that curiosity is basic to this process. Children's activity is centered in seeking, searching, discovering, inventing, trying, exploring, researching and experimenting. Teacher behavior is characterized by stimulating, guiding, clarifying, helping and supporting.

The reality-centered school is an "open" school. Here, learning is seen as the outcome of personal responsiveness to wide varieties of stimulation and wide usages of symbolic media. Children are seen as unities, self-actualizers and creators. The function of the school is to challenge and stimulate the child's creative encounter with reality. Social relationships are also seen as objects for stimulation and creativeness, not simply as closed normative procedures for facilitating other kinds of learning. The communication process in this milieu is characterized by more emphasis upon object stimuli themselves without the necessity of continued mediation by the teacher and other secondary sources.

Contrast this with the "closed" school. Here learning outcomes are synonymous with evaluated performance. Learning is described as conditioning and/or reinforcement, problem solving (with predetermined answers), remembering, and recognizing. The children are organisms, or role players, or types. They are objects to be manipulated and consumers of school goods. The function of the school is simply life adjustment, or occupational preparation, or cultural indoctrination, literacy or citizenship. Social relationships are primarily bases of confirmation, sanction and motivation; and communication is a process of attending to predetermined stimuli with the production of predictable responses. Everything is, in a sense, inside the reality of prestructured relationships.

In a reality-centered school, tests and grades per se function only to facilitate a broader evaluation of two types. Individual progress is seen through the feelings of individual worth and productiveness, satisfaction and gratification experienced by the learners under the guidance of the staff. Program evaluation is in terms of the degree of involvement, vitality, enthusiasm and productive work (thinking and valuing) which exist. The key to evaluation is quality of *living* as previously described in the school environment, for the reality-centered school recognizes that *living is learning and the quality of living is the quality of learning.*

Notes

1. Gordon Allport, *Becoming* (New Haven: Yale University Press, Inc., 1955).

2. A.H. Maslow, "Creativity and Culture," in *Creativity and Its Cultivation,* H.H. Anderson, ed. (New York: Harper & Row, Publishers, Inc., 1959).

3. Allport, *Becoming*, p. 20.

4. *Ibid.*, p. 22.

5. Robert Lindner, *Prescription for Rebellion* (New York: Holt, Rinehart and Winston, Inc., 1952).

6. Martin Buber, *Between Man and Man* (Boston: Beacon Press, 1955).

7. Paul Tillich, *The Courage To Be* (New Haven: Yale University Press, 1952).

8. Erich Fromm, *Man for Himself* (New York: Holt, Reinhold and Winston, Inc., 1947).

9. Lindner, *Prescription for Rebellion.*

10. Eric H. Erickson, *Childhood and Society* (New York: W.W. Norton & Co., Inc., 1950).

11. Robert Havighurst, *Developmental Tasks and Education* (New York: David McKay Co., Inc., 1953).

12. Arnold Gesell and Frances Ilg, *The Child from Five to Ten* (New York: Harper & Row, Publishers, Inc., 1946).

13. This idea was suggested by the work of Harley Shands, *Thinking and Psychotherapy* (Cambridge: Harvard University Press, 1961).

14. Herbert Fingarette, *The Self in Transformation* (New York: Basic Books, 1963).

15. Ernest Schachtel, *Metamorphosis* (New York: Basic Books, Inc., 1959).

16. D.C. Klein and A. Ross, *Kindergarten Entry—A Study of Role Transition in Orthopsychiatry and the School* (New York: American Orthopsychiatery Association, 1958), pp. 60–69.

17. Lois Barclay Murphy, "Preventive Duplications of Development in the Pre-School Years," in *Prevention of Mental Disorders in Children*, Gerald Coplan, ed. (New York: Basic Books, 1961), pp. 218–48. See also, *The Widening World of Childhood* (New York: Basic Books, 1962), by the same author.

18. Eli M. Bower, "Mental Health and Education," *Review of Educational Research*, 32, 1962, p. 447.

19. W.A. Bexton, W. Flerar and T.H. Scott, "Effects of Decreased Variation in the Sensory Environment," *Canadian Journal of Psychology*, 8, 1954, pp. 70–76.

20. Jerome S. Bruner, "Needed: A Theory of Instruction," *Educational Leadership*, 20, 1963, pp. 31–32.

21. Louis Raths, "Sociological Knowledge and Curriculum Research," *Research Frontiers in the Study of Children's Learning*, James B. Macdonald, ed. (Milwaukee: University of Wisconsin - Milwaukee, 1961), p. 27.

22. Educational Policies Commission, *The Central Purpose of American Education* (Washington, D.C.: National Education Association, 1961).

23. Raths, "Sociological Knowledge and Curriculum Research," pp. 28–30.

24. Dwayne Huebner, "New Modes of Man's Relationship to Man," in *New Insights and the Curriculum* (Washington, D.C.: Association of Supervision and Curriculum Development, 1963), p. 144.

25. Ashley Montagu, *Education and Human Relations* (New York: Grove Press, Inc., 1958).

26. Robert E. Bills, "Education Is Human Relations," in *New Insights and the Curriculum* (Washington D.C.: Association of Supervision and Curriculum Development, 1963).

27. Carl R. Rogers, *On Becoming a Person* (Boston: Houghton-Mifflin Co., 1961).

28. Gardner Murphy, *Freeing Intelligence Through Teaching* (New York: Harper & Row, Publishers, Inc., 1961).

29. For example, Donald Vandenberg, "Experimentalism in the American Society: Existential Education," *Harvard Educational Review*, 32, 1962, pp. 155–87.

30. Carl R. Rogers, "The Interpersonal Relationship: Core of Guidance," *Harvard Educational Review*, 32, 1962, pp. 416–29.

31. Erich Fromm, *The Sane Society* (New York: Holt, Reinhart and Winston, Inc., 1955), p. 124.

Chapter Two

The School as a Double Agent

The reality of American education reminds old-timers of a radio program staring "The Shadow," who, listeners were reminded each week, was "in reality Lamont Cranston." Or, less charitably and from a more radical point of view, perhaps "Mata Hari" would do. In either case, American schools tend to be two-faced and ridden with unspoken assumptions, more often than not determining operational procedures, which are in conflict with the rhetoric and idealism of American school values.

The conflict will be no surprise to any interested observer of American culture. It has counterparts in other areas. Anthropologists have noted for many years that we display a fairly extensive set of important cultural conflicts. For example, we treat adolescents as adults for consumer purposes, but delay their entrance into the productive system. What may seem to be a shock for some is the pervasive and paralyzing extent of cultural conflict in the schools.

It is also a charitable gesture to call the school a "double" agent, for it is clear by now that "quadruple agent" would be more accurate. We shall return later to this assertion.

The American school system has been predicated upon the development of the democratic ideal. Realization of this ideal entailed an education dedicated to rational processes of problem solving with the concomitant ethical principles. It also entails honoring attitudes and values which facilitate the fulfillment of justice, equality, and liberty for all. Central to this doctrine is faith in the dignity and integrity of each human being and the resultant prizing of the necessary actions which facilitate the development of individual uniqueness and potential. The schools should serve the youth of our society by helping them to become better democratic citizens and better individuals. According to this doctrine there is no separation of the individual and society, for society's wants demand the development of individuals committed to and capable of functioning as members of a society which in turn creates the very conditions which best allow individuals to flourish. Thus, the acts of facilitating the development of individual human potential and the functional participation of persons in democratic social processes are mutually supportive.

One would be hard pressed to find evidence that the above description is in fact an accurate portrayal of goals which determine the realities of schooling. But if this seems a bit harsh let us say that *no one* who looks at schooling with a critical eye would allege that the democratic ideal and individual development are the primary determiners of programs and practices in any but a very small minority of cases.

Evidence for this conclusion is relatively easy to come by. A recent study of primary school classrooms across the land published by Goodlad, Klein, and associates, for example, reports very little evidence of individualization of instruction in classrooms;[1] this in spite of 70 years of child development research, the progressive education movement, the content and orientation of most teacher education programs, and the greatly increased activity and materials production over the past 15 years to develop increasing individualization in programs at the primary school level.

Jules Henry's case study of high schools[2] are further documentation of the failure of schools to live up to the above general ideal, as is Edgar Friedenberg's work.[3] The more limited but equally disconcerting study of Jackson and Getzels[4] on the response of the school to creative children is another case in point.

And the list goes on, to a point where one begins to wonder even where our ideals came from or if they have any influence on American social behavior at all.

The fact of the matter is that schools have not produced an informed citizenry, and there is very little evidence that rational processes of problem solving are ever learned and/or practiced by students in schools, or that they are utilized in society. Concomitantly the aura of justice, equality, and liberty which hangs over the schools (and society) is reflective of the lack of value placed in these ideals. Certainly, for example, liberty and lack of choice or freedom, justice and lack of equal opportunity, and equality and the myriad categorizing procedures in schools are not resolvable in terms of ideals.

The vast majority of schools, teachers, and other concerned persons do not trust students. The basic assumption of the schools' orientation to students is that students will do the wrong thing (what you do not want them to do) unless you make them do the right thing. If this were not so, most school policies and classroom disciplinary procedures would not be justified. Surely, faith in the worth, dignity, and integrity of individuals is not in evidence.

Institutional facilitation of the individual's uniqueness and potential is easily refuted when we examine curricula and teaching practices. By and large, curricula are standard, vary little from locale to locale, and are monitored by virtually identical quality control test devices. Further, teaching methods are predominantly group procedures, characterized by discussion procedures or assignments which discourage individuality and expect the same "right" answers of all students.

The interpersonal conditions of living in schools are perhaps the final blow to our ideal of schooling. Though there is some evidence that most teachers are well-meaning and generally have positive predispositions toward the young, an authoritarian administrative structure is infused throughout. Opportunities to learn about democracy and to build the necessary understanding of the democratic process through the living of a democratic life are almost totally absent.

To paraphrase Friedenberg, there is no difficulty in understanding why, under these conditions, a federal judge who, when he was in school, had needed a hall pass to go to the toilet until he was 17 would not hesitate to refuse the issuance of a passport to an American citizen who was a member of the Communist Party.[5]

There are at least two directions in which one might go to explain the gap between ideals and realities. One might assert, as many social reforms have, that American society is characterized by the same general conflict between ideals and administrative "necessities" and that the school merely reflects the general culture. This is a strong and difficult argument to refute. Still, the school is a rather special sort of institution, and there is much that could be done within the schools themselves to bridge the gap if we would attend to contradictions built into the structure of schooling. In this spirit of optimism let us turn to the contradictions which may be conceptualized and, hopefully, improved.

Major Contradictions: The Four Faces of Schooling

The "quadruple agent" referred to earlier may be described as four faces or orientations which only sometimes act in concert when program or practice decisions are made. We may describe them as conflicting ideas of the role of the school, although in many instances the "role" must be inferred from observation.

The first role has already been described under the guise of the "democratic ideal." The double agent aspect of schooling comes in a schizophrenic sort of activity which might be called the "four faces of schooling." The "other" aspect or agency has three personalities which we may call: (a) school as the preparation of new teachers (or discipline specialists); (b) school as preparation for the occupational structure; and (c) school as a place of work with its attention focused on status, role, and maintaining the system.

School as Preparation for School

It is one of the well-recognized truths about schooling that success in school is most closely related as a predictor variable to further success in school. No other prediction may be made with anywhere near the certainty of this. Thus, Taylor was able to show that even creative research scientists, a breed of highly trained academics, do not attribute much of their success on the job (out of school) to those variables (intellectual attributes) that are high predictors of school achievement.[6] It seems highly reasonable that we may explain many practical decisions most easily if we assume that one face of schooling represents it as an agent for the parent disciplines that provide the major substance of the traditional curriculum.

How else, for example, do we explain instruction in the division of fractions found in many sixth grade mathematics books? How else can one explain the placement of much material at grade levels in terms of a logical sequence of difficulty? How else does one readily explain the almost fanatic urge on the part of most teachers to cover the curriculum in order that students will be "ready" for the next step? Surely, these and many other behaviors and activities that can be observed are remotely connected to development of human potential, preparation for occupation (other than academician), and even bureaucratic needs of the school system. It is foolish to suggest that these practices cannot be rationalized in these terms, but the simple idea that often school practices and programs are justified in and of themselves as good because they lead to further success in schooling is a much more reasonable explanation.

We live in an era when one might argue that a highly technological society is developing a form of tyranny best called the tyranny of knowledge. It may be true that no knowledge is disastrous and that "a little knowledge is a dangerous thing," but for a culture to be dominated by knowledge is a form of tyranny. We live in such a dictatorship today. We are not speaking of knowledge in its broad anthropological meaning, as culture. Surely, all cultures through their customs and mores restrict individual choices and provide constraints upon behavior. But when a culture enshrines specialized knowledge as its fundamental "good," then tyranny as it is meant here sets in. Knowledge of this sort may free "man" from physical limitations, but it enslaves "men" in the process. We, in other words, are being subjugated by the very process which is intended to free us.

This tyranny may be seen in a number of ways in schools; priorities of the standard curriculum are hard to explain without it. Areas such as the arts and humanities are slighted because they do not represent "hard knowledge," the real stuff of the curriculum. Concepts of prerequisites and other forms of sequencing are imposed and shape experiences for the sake of knowledge. The school curriculum over the years looks like a series of separately strung beads with no attempt to relate them to each other, and the consequent experience of students is of several varied and disconnected experiences which are often forgotten shortly after they are encountered.

The educational technician is partner to this tyranny, as illustrated by the behavioral objectives movement. We often justify the procedures of schooling in terms of the knowledge (or skill) ends in the process. No one is quite clear where all this knowledge will lead to in the end; but if we sequence the whole curriculum on this basis we can be sure that it will lead to the next step, and this appears to be a satisfactory outcome for many. Thus, the technician often simply accepts the knowledge goals of experts and proceeds to develop a set of procedures and conditions which will lead to the efficient achievement of these goals. The greater the realization of their intentions, the more securely tightened is the screw which holds the life of the young to the tyranny of knowledge.

School as Preparation for Occupation

In some ways the heading of this section is somewhat misleading, for only a small part of this face of schooling is truly related to what is known as a vocational education in its curricular sense. On the other hand, many school practices and programs reflect the essential commitment to the idea that a school is a degree factory, a credential provider, or a certifier that it is necessary for people to experience before they enter into the real occupational world.

It does not seem to matter whether or not there is any direct connection between credentials and later functioning, inasmuch as the social uses of schooling are apparently convenient ways of making occupational hiring decisions which provide an access to social mobility and affluence for members of our society. Paul Goodman, for example, has quoted work by Ivar Berg of Columbia which Goodman contends shows that dropouts do as well as high school graduates in less pretentious jobs in our society.[7]

Some critics have also noted that war is one of our major occupations. Thus, the schools are directly serving the military-industrial complex in our social system. A careful examination of this allegation suggests that it is overly simple, yet how can many of our reporting, grading, and testing practices, our authoritarian relationships, and our prizing of docility, punctuality, and attendance be more readily explained?

Our evaluation procedures *in toto* tell us a great deal about this. It is not so much the processes themselves, though many objections may be made to these, but the usage of results which provides the important clues. The social consequences of testing are rarely given a careful examination. Tests have become so useful that the question of whether or not they should be administered at all has been replaced by "what would you use instead?"

Teachers may often claim that test results help provide them with evidence which helps them to redesign their methodology and goals to facilitate learning. Educational psychologists will be quick to note that "feedback" is essential to reinforcement. Yet neither position justifies the social uses of testing, for the use society makes of grades and test scores transcends the learning situation. No student's slate is ever wiped clean, there is no forgiveness in schooling. Instead students are taught their abilities by continuous evaluation and allotted social slots on the basis of their cumulative performance. This provides a useful way for society to deal with the young as they emerge into the work force, for we can be assured that their predictive success (in terms of tests) has been set (psychologically and socially) as early as fourth or fifth grade.[8]

It is interesting to note further that the education industry is now one of the largest in the country. Under these circumstances, it is of considerable importance to keep as many people in school for as long as possible. This may be an accidental development, but the nature of our economic arrangements would certainly lead to a societal reinforcement of the need for schooling as the collection of more and more advanced credentials. Thus, the social use of schooling becomes an integral part of the structure of our society. The school as a consumer of goods is an important part of this economic complex, and the demands of the economy are increasingly becoming part of the role of the school as a double agent.

School as a Place of Work: The Face of Self-Serving Bureaucracy

Every school, school system, or, for that matter, every classroom is a place of work. People spend significant portions of their lives as members of a work force which by necessity has some form of structural relatedness. An organizational structure becomes necessary to coordinate the different functions and roles that inevitably arise. When the concerns for maintaining the organization become more important than the stated goals of student learning and development, a form of self-serving bureaucracy results.[9] More often than not, the policies and practices of schools are more reasonably explained by this phenomenon than as rational decisions and arrangements for facilitating their stated goals.

Maintaining a complex organization is surely not an easy task, although decentralizing large school systems might improve the situation. Yet one would be hard pressed to argue that many school policies, schedules, organizational formats, communication networks, and status-role relationships are the only way a school (or system) can be maintained. There is instead such a large degree of blatant hypocracy involved in the justification of dress codes, hall passes, schedules, and teacher and student freedom of choice and movement that we must look elsewhere for explanations. Perhaps the simple idea of inertia is a better explanation. Whatever the primary causes are, they are not justifiable in terms of the democratic ideal and individual development.

An enlightening and frightening view of the epitome of this process in American society has been provided by Goffman in regard to total institutions such as prisons and mental institutions.[10] His description of the privilege system, for example, found in total institutions has a familiar ring to observers of schools.

According to Goffman, there are three basic elements in the privilege system: (a) "House rules" or a formal set of prescriptions and proscriptions that sets the requirements of inmate conduct; (b) a small number of clearly defined rewards or privileges held out in exchange for obedience; and (c) punishments designed for occurrences of rule violations. Schools, in other words, operate in many ways like total institutions, and certainly to greater degrees than other social institutions in our society.

Perhaps the most crushing blow has been a more recent realization, as dramatically highlighted by the New York City teachers strike in the Brownsville case,[11] that teachers are not only potential classroom bureaucrats, but that teachers organizations are in a major struggle for control of the total bureaucracy. The attempts to control on the part of teachers are not what is at issue here. The dawning realization that does hurt is that we are seeing the rise of another essentially self-serving force whose major concerns and efforts have up to this date had little to do with bringing about the realization of the American ideals for education. We appear to be witnessing a struggle between those who would run the system for their own benefit. It is, in other words, the conditions of work that motivate most of the activity and concern.

Again we must hasten to add that the need to be concerned about conditions of work is not being criticized, but that the phenomena of how all this is taking place appear to show that teachers are tuned into the heart of the question—the control of the bureaucracy. It is the fact that this is the jugular vein that is cause for alarm. The classroom as a place of work comes in for its own share of bureaucratic self-serving. The nature of the composition of teaching staffs and the behavior of teachers in classrooms cannot easily be explained without granting their duplicity and perhaps open-armed welcoming of the self-serving ethic.

According to Charters, the career patterns of female teachers can be described rather accurately as "in and out," whereas the male patterns are more nearly "up or out."[12] In either case the classroom teacher today appears to have primary personal allegiances to something which his occupation gives him/her that is not inherent in the activity of teaching itself. As a career, elementary or secondary teaching is not highly prized by the education profession when compared to the role of supervisor, administrator, or college professor. Further, the persons who choose teaching as a career are primarily individuals who are upwardly mobile in the class structure (upper-lower to middle), or persons opting for teaching in order to preserve a middle class status while unable or unsure enough to pursue this through other avenues.

As a consequence, teachers tend to be security oriented and essentially conservative in many of their social attitudes. They represent, as someone remarked, a sort of "clerk" mentality in our culture, and as such fit beautifully into a bureaucratic setting.

The schools are full of a "they won't let me" syndrome on the part of teachers, and the risks that are taken for the sake of ideals are at a premium. It is difficult to see how teachers who acquiesce to the authoritarian and self-serving milieu of the system could provide conditions other than those same ones in their own classrooms. In fact, this is what one often finds.

Teachers teach from textbooks, manuals, and, if possible, commercial lesson plans. Teachers teach groups of children because it is easier to do so, and have often acquiesced to "homogenous" grouping in schools primarily because they feel it is easier to teach this way. Teachers often avoid controversial issues, deny the erotic aspects of the nature of human beings, and avoid the discussion of anything which is not planned ahead of time. Many teachers are consumed by the fear that they will lose control, that some situation will present itself in which they must operate as a responsive human being rather then a status symbol of authority. Under these sorts of circumstances, it pays to get things "organized" and to develop managerial techniques whose primary goal is the maintenance of control.

The Double Agent Revisited

In the end, the various faces of schooling lead to the fundamental schism in our society—the widening gulf between our democratic ideals and the individual human fulfillment possible through our social structure as influenced by the pressures and strictures of an industrial nation.[13] In oversimplified but rather direct terms, we must ask whether school activity essentially reflects service to democratic ideals and individuals, or service to a monolithic technological social system with all its attendant specialization, depersonalization, and self-serving forces.

McLuhan has a section in one of his latest communications entitled "Education as War."[14] To him the answer to the above question is clear. The educators (including schools) are aggressors who "simply impose upon them [youngsters] the patterns that we find convenient to ourselves and consistent with the available technologies." As a result, we are creating, maintaining, and communicating an environment in schools which is past-oriented and not a meaningful part of the new media environment as the young come to experience it.

In order to impose this we cannot afford to let rational democratic processes operate in schools or allow the unique growth and capacities of individuals to develop. The "generation gap" is more than an age gap, it is essentially a cultural gap.

Roszak characterizes this situation as a compulsion proceeding from the assumption that the young must be made to learn, "as if in truth education were *contra naturam* and required clever strategies."[15] But why this compulsion? Because, he says, the society we live in fears that its culture is not interesting or important to the young. Thus, we must compel the young to learn what we wish them to learn in order to perpetuate the status quo.

That this compulsion goes far beyond the imposition of certain courses and areas of content is clearly revealed by a recent Association for Supervision and Curriculum Development (ASCD) publication on *The Unstudied Curriculum*.[16] The nexus of the effect of teacher expectations on pupil learning, the impact of social philosophy and practice on human development, the secondary consequences of schooling, the socializing function for the middle class, and what is learned about authority and authority relationship is cogently described. It is not difficult to conclude that these are powerful social reinforcers of the compulsion noted earlier.

What we may have to do eventually is to take seriously the position frequently presented by Goodman.[17] Goodman not only agrees that the school is a double agent, but it is Goodman's contention that the schools have no real alternative to being repressive and acting out the compulsion to make students learn. The very nature of compulsory education dooms the system. Goodman feels that the total social environment is far more educative than the schools. He is convinced that with the exception of perhaps 15 percent of the young who would choose to attend, the others are being definitely harmed by attending high school and college.

Further, he feels that the attendance of all (or large numbers in college) actually destroys the legitimate functions of schooling, which are the development of a community of scholars and the commitment to the pursuit of academic activities.

The social task of education, he feels, is to make the total environment more educative and responsive to the young rather than to incarcerate the total adolescent population in one location or institution and attempt to "educate" them with an essentially single track curriculum.

Thus, the contention that the school is a double agent and that this duplicity is negative and destructive to the young is agreed upon by many critics and concerned observers of the educational scene. Accepting this perception, the question remains whether the reformation of schooling can best proceed from within the institution itself or by enlarging the domain to the broader society. McLuhan and Goodman, for example, would surely take the latter course; whereas many persons involved with the educational establishment can see myriad possibilities of radical improvement from within. One of the interesting aspects of it all is that in the opinion of almost all of these concerned persons the issue is no longer whether or not the traditional school can be adequate, but whether or not schools as we have known them can exist at all as places for productive fulfillment of human potential.

Notes

1. John Goodlad, Francis M. Klein, *et. al.*, *Behind the Classroom Door* (Worthington, OH: Charles A. Jones Publishing Co., 1970).

2. Jules Henry, *Culture Against Man* (New York: Random House, Inc., 1963).

3. Edgar Friedenberg, *Coming of Age in America* (New York: Random House, Inc., 1963).

4. Philip Jackson and Jacob Getzels, *Creativity and Intelligence* (New York: John Wiley & Sons, Inc., 1962).

5. Edgar Friedenberg, *The Dignity of Youth and Other Atavisms* (Boston: Beacon Press, 1965).

6. Calvin W. Taylor, "A Tentative Description of the Creative Individual," in *Human Variability and Learning*, Walter Waetjen, ed. (Washington, DC: Association for Supervision and Curriculum Development, 1961), pp. 62–79.

7. Paul Goodman, "High School Is Too Much," *Psychology Today*, 4 (5), October 1970, p. 25.

8. Benjamin S. Bloom, *Stability and Change in Human Characteristics* (New York: John Wiley & Sons, Inc., 1964).

9. See, for example, Amitai Etzioni, *Modern Organizations* (Englewood Cliffs, New Jersey: Prentice-Hall, Inc., 1964). This volume gives a generalized statement as to how bureaucracies become more concerned about their own incumbents than about the clients they serve.

10. Erving Goffman, *Asylums* (New York: Anchor Books, Doubleday & Company, Inc., 1961).

11. See, for example, Martin Mayer, *Teacher's Strike: New York* (New York: Harper & Row, Publishers, Inc., 1968).

12. W.W. Charters, Jr., "The Social Background of Teaching," *in Handbook of Research on Teaching* (Chicago: Rand McNally & Company, 1963), pp. 715–813.

13. See, for example, Hendrick M. Ruitenbeck, *The Individual and the Crowd: A Study of Identity in America* (New York: A Mentor Book, The New American Library, 1964).

14. Marshall McLuhan and Quentin Fiore, *War and Peace in the Global Village* (New York: Bantam Books, 1968).

15. Theodore Roszak, "Educating *Contra Naturam*," in *A Man for Tomorrow's World*, Robert R. Leeper, ed. (Washington, DC: Association for Supervision and Curriculum Development, 1970), pp. 12–27.

16. Norman V. Overly, ed., *The Unstudied Curriculum: Its Impact on Children* (Washington, DC: Association for Supervision and Curriculum Development, 1971).

17. Paul Goodman, *Compulsory Miseducation and the Community of Scholars* (New York: Vintage Books, Random House, Inc., 1966).

Chapter Three

A Vision of a Humane School

William Blake was a visionary and prophetic poet. He raged against the constraints of church and society upon the creative emergence of humanness.

Blake said: "Do what you will, this life is a fiction and is made up of contradiction."[1]

A contemporary sociologist like Peter Berger[2] might say, instead, that all social arrangements are purely contrivances of man; or a social critic like Michael Harrington[3] might prefer to call our society a historical accident or an unintended consequence.

Yet Blake was not being simply descriptive in his reminder, for he believed that the only hope for men was to be continually free to return to their humanness so that their creative vision might continually resolve contradictions.

We are presently, I believe, engaged in a serious contradiction. Blake clearly saw the meaning of it, and since his time this unresolved condition has worsened. The contradiction lies within the tension of humanness and technology. The question is whether men will dehumanize themselves through the creation of a technological environment and its consequent social arrangements.

What will awaken men from the idiocy of their technological compulsions? Will we be saved by superior intelligence from the unknown universe? Will there be a second coming of Christ? Perhaps, but then, perhaps not. Will California quake and crumble into the Pacific as a warning to men? Or shall we simply risk the possibility of beginning again after we have purged ourselves in the fire of nuclear redemption?

Perhaps the poet Yeats was prophetic when he said:

Things fall apart; the center cannot hold
Mere anarchy is loosed upon the world,
The blood-dimmed tide is loosed, and everywhere
The ceremony of innocence is drowned;
The best lack of all conviction, while the worst
Are full of passionate intensity.[4]

Perhaps it is all a little too much for any of us. However, if we believe in education we are counted among the hopeful. And, if we are hopeful, then we will hold to Erich Fromm's definition: "To hope means to be ready at every moment for that which is not yet born, and yet not to become desperate if there is no birth in our lifetime."[5] Then we would do well to attend to our work with hope.

If we are to be ready for what is yet unborn we must know where we are, what the contradictions we face mean in our own terms, and what direction we feel we are fumbling toward. It is these concerns that will pervade the ideas that follow.

Relevance

Having co-authored a book called *Education for Relevance*,[6] it is with considerable chagrin that I suggest the term "relevance" is misleading and "irrelevant" to school programs that face up to the contradiction between humanness and the press of our technological society.

To make our industrial, technological society work we must have a "one-dimensionality" in our efforts. We must produce the scientists and technologists and their supportive personnel above all else. Further, we must be highly organized into complex bureaucratic structures with little tolerance for individual deviation. "Law and order" must be maintained because the breakdown of any aspect of the system could be catastrophic for the totality.

It is not necessarily the technology, per se, that provides the basis for constraint, but the need to maintain the total system created around technology, and the generalization of technological rationality from a way of relating to things to a way of relating to people. The schools, of course, have become an integral cog in our technocratic system. Thus we see the general evidence of the alienation, boredom, law and order, regimentation, and depersonalization in the school environment also. The basic contradiction in schools as well as society resides in the paradox of the immense promise for individual happiness and well-being inherent in a technological society which is being paid for by the dehumanization of the individuals for whom the promise exists. Thus, we speak the rhetoric of progress at the sacrifice of our humanity.

The problem with our schools is that they are too relevant to our society. There is no doubt that they could be made even more efficient and effective, but when we look at the result (for example, about 50 percent go beyond high school) we have to be impressed with the schools. The schools are in fact so relevant that most persons who say they are not relevant are able to do so because the gap between perfect fit and present status is relatively narrow and calls for little imagination to see the possibilities of closure.

It is only in terms of universal human values that the idea of irrelevance takes on meaning. And it is not irrelevance, per se, even here. It is simply that living in school is an essentially inferior, vulgar, imitative, second-rate *human* experience because this is the kind of ecological press that surrounds us both in and out of school. Thus, as I have stated elsewhere, the "problem with schools is not that they are irrelevant in the sense that they are odd cultural museum pieces, but that they are a living embodiment of the very shoddiness that pervades our general social experience. . . a rather faithful replica of the whole."[7]

The Ideology of Achievement

The schools are not created and organized in terms of philosophical commitments or data about the nature of humanness, or even concern for the human condition, but on the basis of ideology; and the central ideology of the schools is the ideology of achievement.

As an ideology this serves as a justification for practices which integrate the school into the fabric of our social and academic concerns. For the sake of increased achievement we are able to justify such things as grouping practices, testing programs, grading, reporting, and scheduling, as well as most school policies.

The ideology of achievement is a quantitative ideology, for even to attempt to assess quality must be quantified under this ideology, and the educational process is perceived as a technically monitored quality control process.

It is tempting to tie the ideology of achievement to the Puritan work ethic. This, I believe, is a fundamental error, for few people would argue that achievement is "good for the soul." We would, one suspects, rather say that it is good for the "pocket."

The ideology of achievement is built upon a myth, a myth which says that the degree of achievement is fundamentally due to the kind of schooling a person receives. This myth is easily exposed, for we are unable to explain much of anything by it, even though we labor faithfully under its dictation. It is a myth which tells us a little about the individual trees, but nothing about the forest itself.

The Coleman report, for all its faults, would seem to support clearly the idea that achievement of groups of youngsters cannot be accounted for easily by schooling practices. Why are there wide gaps in achievement between social classes? Why do youngsters with high IQ's achieve better than youngsters with more modest scores? Why do children with emotional problems often experience more difficulty than so-called normal children?

If we have learned anything in education in the past 50 years we most certainly must now know that the school is not the center of a child's learning, but merely one of his environmental situations which he experiences in the context of his own unique historical, biological, and total environmental fabric.

Admission of this truth may be found in such things as Head Start, infant modification projects, kibbutz-like residential proposals, behavior modification techniques, and autotelic environment experiments. The problem with most of these kinds of approaches is that they admit the myth is not accurate, but they display a "faith" in the ability of education to make the myth a reality. They make me feel like William Blake must have felt when he wrote of Hayley:

Thy Friendship oft has made my heart ake;
Do be my enemy for Friendship's sake.[8]

The rhetoric of the ideology of achievement is an important aspect of it. It is the rhetoric of behaviorism, scientism, and psychologism. People are "learners," who have to be "motivated" and "measured," and who possess certain "traits," "capacities," and "needs" which we "diagnose." Goals are talked about in "behavioral" terms. This rhetoric has the effect of lifting the burden of our moral responsibility to children (and other people). It creates a mystique about schooling into which one must be initiated through a teacher education program and the rite of certification, and it creates a jargon which obscures our fundamental moral concern.

The Individual and the Collective

Thus, it becomes easy to keep our focus upon the achievement of learning goals and to forget the fundamental goal of freeing persons for self-responsible and self-directed fulfillment of their own emerging potential. It is easy to talk about norms, percentiles, concepts, skills, methods, and so forth; and it is equally as easy to forget about the persons involved.

Schooling must be for the benefit of individuals, not the collective society within which it takes place. Many people talk as though there were no conflict between the two. There isn't, if the school absolves itself from any moral responsibility. When schooling simply reflects the desires of the collective and serves to train the young for that purpose, there is no conflict between the individual and society.

Yet this is a fundamentally amoral position for educators to take. It is a position that dehumanizes both the teacher and child and absolves the teacher and school from any personal moral responsibility, asking only for collective accountability. Thus, without moral responsibility we become merely socially accountable to others.

There *is* a major conflict between the individual and the collective. If we, as educators, are morally responsible for our actions in school, then we are centrally responsible to the children we educate and only technically accountable to the collective within which we live.

This is not a matter of opinion, of debate about the role of the school in society. It is a fundamental commitment to the fullness of human potential versus an acceptance of a technical role. One will perform technical acts in either case, but one can escape the moral responsibility for his acts if one is mainly accountable to the collective. However, if one assumes moral responsibility, then the individual must come before the collective.

The Humane Goal—Freedom

Education in formal schools is essentially a moral enterprise. This is simply and fundamentally true inasmuch as adults decide that the young should grow up in certain prescribed ways and learn certain kinds of things rather than others. There are judgements which directly influence the development of each human being and provide both possibilities for freedom and sets of constraints upon individuals.

Contrary to Rousseau's[9] famous opening sentence, "Man is born free and everywhere he is in chains," man is born into chains and everywhere he tends to remain so. Man is chained at birth to his own internal needs and external conditions. He is neither free to survive in external environments, nor is he free to survive through the exercise of his internal structures.

A man's freedom is his personal self-developing project in life. It is through his own efforts and experiences that he comes to be free to choose, to gain freedom from the constraints of others, of the environment, and of his own internal structures.

Freedom, then, is the only tenable moral goal of individual development, and freedom is at the same time the only process by which freedom can realize itself as a goal.

If this is not so we may dispense with all further talk about education. Without freedom and choice it is only necessary to acquiesce to conditions, to live out our passions, and to be shaped by our circumstances. We need not argue about what is good, or right, or beautiful, or true. We can simply accept. Schooling then becomes what it is. It is, and that's the way it is.

There are many educators who appear to operate upon that assumption. It is an assumption that eliminates any need for moral justification of what we do. It all becomes a simple matter of power, of who can organize the power in the environment to bring about whatever influences upon others are desired. It is a form of "might makes right," a "realistic" posture.

Yet freedom is hardier than this. Men feel they choose and have potential for freedom; societies have struggled to manage their own destinies. Men everywhere have codes of conduct, and hold each other responsible for them, and feel regret when these codes are violated.

Freedom is harder to know today. Yet even if our advancing sophistication tells us more and more about the impact of the environment upon us, about the "contingencies" that shape us, about the instincts and needs which drives us, it does not negate the potentiality of freedom. It simply highlights the cruciality of keeping freedom central in our minds, of keeping a moral stance in our actions.

It is a mistake, for example, to say that our youth counter culture is an escape from technology per se; it is mainly a search for freedom and humanness, a positive quest with often questionable means. And the tragedy of it all is that the positive medium for transcendence lies at the heart and substance of the humanities.

The ideology of achievement and the technical acquiescence to the accountability of the collective have had deleterious effects on schooling and the curriculum. The curriculum has become more and more what we can be held accountable for in the eyes of the collective, and more and more what is currently needed for collective goals. This has meant an increasing press for curricula that can be measured and specified in detail, and for curricula which emphasize the academic knowledge and skill necessary for collective needs—primarily reading, mathematics, and science.

The potentialities of men are much broader than these areas. As important as these prized areas are for the technological society we live in, they are not by themselves sufficient for human beings. What is missing is what are called the humanities.

The humanities, the arts, literature, philosophy, and some aspects of social studies have either been downgraded because they cannot easily be included in the rhetoric of the ideology of achievement, or they have dehumanized themselves in order to specify bits and pieces of measurable substance and in the process have lost their unique potential for man.

It is to the humanities, however, that we must look for broadened freedom through self-development of individual potentiality. The humanities promise freedom to man's aesthetic or qualitative relation to the world as well as his quantitative scientific bent.

The Humanities—A Counter Culture in the Schools

What is needed is akin to what Theodore Roszak[10] calls a counter culture, but in this instance within the schools themselves. The humanities are the vehicle for this counter culture.

In early December of 1968, the Association for Supervision and Curriculum Development (ASCD) sponsored a small invitational conference on the Humanities Curriculum. A group of some 20 persons spent a number of days interacting and exchanging ideas on the subject. As the days passed it became clear that what began as a concern for specific disciplines called humanities became a generalized concern for humane schooling.

An examination of the definition and goals of the humanities led this group of persons to fundamental concerns for individuals in schools and the development of individual freedom. The humanities would not stay put in neat categories without being dehumanized.

Instead of a new package for old ideas, the longer we talked the more it became apparent that we were talking about a counter culture; perhaps an "up with people" culture, as the Utah ASCD group might call it.

Fifteen months and a considerable number of books and articles later, I am even more convinced that this realization is the one hopeful way of helping resolve our basic cultural contradiction through the curriculum of the schools.

It is, in fact, clear to me now that the need of our young for new experiences through consciousness-expanding drugs, communal life, mysticism, and other cultural regenerations must surely lie with the failure of the humanities, broadly conceived, in the modern age.

To "take a trip" is essentially to yield to the flight of imagination, perception, and sensation. There is little for us to identify and relate with in our culture which will provide our "trips." Yet the very substance of the humanities is nothing if not the essence of human expression in creative form.

Susanne Langer discusses art (the humanities here) in much the same way. She says: "The only way we can envisage vital movement, the stirring and growth and passage of emotion, and ultimately the whole direct sense of human life, is in artistic terms," and "self knowledge, insight into all phases of life and mind, springs from artistic imagination. That is the cognitive value of the arts."[11]

The "trips" of the hippie are in search of this essence of aesthetic experience. They amount to being "turned on" by outside influences because many of us have lost our sense of human identity and the cultural roots from which we can "turn ourselves on."

The modern dilemma, says John MacMurray, is that we have set the intellect free and kept emotion in chains. "Knowledge is power, but emotion is the master of our values and of the uses, therefore, to which we put power. . . unless the emotions and intellect are in harmony, rational action will be paralysed."[12]

The development of rationality is generally credited to be the fundamental purpose of education. Yet rationality, as MacMurray indicates, means more than intellectual activity; it means thinking with values and commitments. Rationality is an integrated human activity.

The dilemma, though, does not rest between "head and heart," but *in* our "heart," for we are essentially facing a situation where we cannot decide what is best to do, because we do not know what is of most value. The intellectual power to achieve our goals is useless without the direction of our feelings.

We must be careful, however, that the concept of feeling is not counterposed to the rational and interpreted as irrationality. There is great difficulty with such words as feelings, emotions, and passions. Yet most thoughtful persons would accept, at least as a heuristic device, the idea of thought, feeling, and action as meaningful categories of human experience. Further, there would be a fair consensus that action is both cognitively and affectively oriented; and that it is the feeling dimension which powers the cognitive in action.

Our feelings are personal and human, our thoughts (in the sense of cultural data) are impersonal and common. It is the thinker who is human, not the thought; and the humanness flows into the thought through the formatting of emotion, as value, commitment, involvement, and action.

As Langer says:

Art, in the sense intended here—that is, the generic term subsuming painting, sculpture, architecture, music, dance, literature, drama, and film—may be defined as the practice of creating perceptible forms expressive of human feeling.

Perceptive rather than sensuous because some works of art are given to imagination rather than to the outward senses (e.g., literature); feeling as it applies to everything that can be felt; creating in the sense of making and constructing; a form in the sense of an apparition given to a perception, a perceptible, self identical whole which has unity and individual reality; and, expressive in the sense that it is both self expressive and yet the presentation of an idea in symbolic form.[13]

The humanities as a counter culture in the schools are focused squarely upon the development of individual persons as human beings, upon the welding of feeling with thought and action, and upon the awareness, experiencing, and analysis of cultural forms as expressive symbols. The validation of the truth of the humanities lies within the process of creating personal meaning in experiences, not in experimental abstractions and manipulations.

This is such a simple truth that as educators we know and act on this intuitively. The best possible example lies in our use of educational research findings. When one considers the rather large data bank of research findings available to educators, and then assesses the actual use of this knowledge in practice, one is at first perplexed by the lack of correlation in most cases between the two. One major reason for this is simply that there is no personal meaning in the lives of teachers and other staff members in reference to experimental results. The trouble as MacMurray said, lies in the heart, not the head; in the phenomena of teaching as a human ethical enterprise. We do not value research findings because our intuition or perhaps common sense tells us they are essentially abstractions and we live in a world of concrete phenomena.

The gulf between theory and/or philosophy and practice is another form of evidence of the same fundamental problem. But here, I believe, the case is poorly stated. Theoretical prescription or philosophical principles in education are essentially humanistic expressive symbols. They are not intended to be (or should not be) taken as literal statements and directly translated into action in the same way an experimental finding is intended to be used. They are essentially art forms which may bring some perspective and may create personal meaning within the persons who practice. It is only further witness to the contemporary power of the culture of science and technology that we should expect the same kind of results from them. As William James once said, "better chaos forever than an order based upon any closet-philosopher's rule;"[14] and we might add any laboratory experimenter's findings.

This suggests that the human activity involved in curriculum development and teaching is of the very same essence within which the studies called humanities are grounded. Joseph Wood Krutch defined the realm of art as "whatever is not found in nature and yet is treated as real."[15] Certainly the curriculum and most of what passes for formal schooling fall into that realm. Thus, the enterprise of schooling is a moral and personal process. If education can be called a discipline, then it is a member of the humanities, not the sciences. Curriculum and teaching are not based upon abstract universals as the sciences are; they are based upon concrete expressive forms. The curriculum can never be a map of the way things are. It is a creative characteristic form involving selection and organization of symbols from many diverse areas, during which process all data that are relevant to concrete phenomena are welcomed. But the total pattern, the balance and integration, are essentially assessed by aesthetic criteria.

The same holds true for teaching, else why do we have our perennial argument about what is a good teacher? We continually return to the impasse of realizing that no scientifically isolated practices, traits, abilities, actions, or relationships reveal a commonly accepted "goodness" in teaching. Why can we not agree on criterion variables for assessment? It would appear most likely that it is because the activity of teaching is known intuitively to be an expressive form with the integrity of a wholeness which comes from the integration and synthesis of an extremely complex set of personal and environmental factors. As such, it is patterned more nearly after an art form than a set of scientific principles or practical prescriptions.

Thus, a vision of a humane school is a vision which is predicated upon the idea that the educational process is a humanistic process which flows out of the integration of substance with values and becomes operative through the feelings and personal meanings of the participants.

The Humane Attitude

The most fundamental part of a humanities perspective is a basic attitudinal orientation toward school. William James came close to what is intended here when he distinguished between "the easygoing way" and the "strenuous mood" of life.[16]

The "easygoing way," James felt, was the way of science. It is the objective way whereby man is basically a recorder not a maker of truth. It is the attitude of waiting for further evidence before making decisions. As Wild says of James, ". . . once we are involved in enterprises of this sort, the decisions are not primarily in our hands. We are really not active agents in this way."[17]

In contrast, the "strenuous mood" embodies the intrinsic values of freedom, seriousness, responsibility, energy, courage, meaning, and devotion. James felt that the man who believes choice really matters will take life seriously, and the first necessity for living the strenuous life is "choosing to really choose." Thus, the strenuous mood is a mood of freedom and involvement.

In school settings the strenuous mood means taking things seriously, making free choices, and assuming the responsibility for these choices. It means trying to find the greatest meaning out of our living in schools, to be a vital and energetic person in our activity.

It is the strenuous mood that is needed for a humanistic orientation to schooling. The easygoing way is primarily the way of intellectual abstraction and results in objectifying, analyzing, and categorizing everything, in letting the results come in and sitting back. It is not really taking responsibility for one's choices and actions in the living context of the schools. If school really matters we would thus engage ourselves fully in all aspects of schooling as persons combining passion with intellect, with what James referred to as "the heart."

Implicit in what this position means for curriculum is that no specific theory, ideology, or research result can provide an absolute structure that is best, for this is the way of science and technological rationality and is not amenable to the phenomena of curriculum.

Joseph Schwab points this out beautifully in his book *The Practical: A Language for Curriculum*.[18] Schwab maintains that theory by itself has three major weaknesses: (a) it is incapable of dealing with the scope of the phenomena of curriculum; (b) theories are based upon abstraction, not concrete phenomena; and (c) for every theory there is an opposite and equally defensible theory—what Schwab calls radical pluralism.

Thus, if we base our curriculum development on abstract theory alone, we have adequate evidence that all theories fail to cope adequately with the realities of schooling. Further, we will by the necessity of the present state of theory commit ourselves to partial theories which exclude more than they include (for example, learning: reinforcement versus gestalt), all of which are essentially abstractions and seem equally remote from the day-to-day business of schooling.

Schwab's answer is *the practical*. But it is not a naive "experience is the best teacher" approach. It is a call for building curriculum upon a practical inquiry basis, for collecting a wealth of understanding of what actually goes on in schools and working piecemeal out of the concrete situation toward the improvement of schooling.

This is an important statement and one which will touch a feeling of reality in all who have struggled with curriculum development. Yet it appears to lack one basic element. It fails to cope adequately with the problem of ethical commitment in human activity.

If Aristotle and others since were right, then there are three basic approaches to human activity—the intellectual, the aesthetic, and the practical. The intellectual is, as James pointed out, the easy way. Schwab simply says it does not work. Schwab commits himself to the practical; and my position here is that the aesthetic is preferable.

It could well be that in the end the aesthetic and the practical may not conflict. At the moment this is difficult to see, for in my mind the aesthetic approach deals not only with practical phenomena, but with a form of situation ethics as well. It is a commitment, like the practical, to see activity through the concrete uses of actual phenomena but in light of the criteria of aesthetic patterns.

C. Wright Mills[19] criticized sociology with similar intent. He lampooned what he called "the grand theorists" for their abstraction, jargon, and unreal qualities; but he was equally hard on the overly empirical fact gatherers. Mills opted for the "sociological imagination" which grew out of creative insights guided by ethical commitment and grounded in the phenomena of society. This is similar to what is intended here as an aesthetic approach—a *curriculum imagination.*

The aspects of a humane school must be engaged imaginatively. They must be engaged with seriousness, and a "strenuous mood;" they must be looked at in terms of the concrete activity of day-to-day experiences, and always from an aesthetic point of view.

The ethic of freedom, as a process of engagement and an end of development, must be taken into each situation and seen in the light of aesthetic criteria. Since freedom must be won by each individual, we must guide ourselves by encouraging choice and generating alternatives; and we must make our decisions in concrete situations in terms of the aesthetic values of living.

There is no master plan; no secret of structuring subject matter; no secret formula for relating to others; no special methods of teaching the sciences or the humanities that are not inherent in the activity and substance themselves provided the breath of ethical commitment and the pulsation of the aesthetic heart are present.

Each situation is entered anew with the serious attitude of freedom and choice, with the goal of providing maximum opportunity for all to engage freely in meaningful doing through self-expressive activity in each new context.

The Shape of Activity in a Humane School

Alfred North Whitehead[20] made two important statements which may help us when we think about the nature of activity in a humane school. One was "The Rhythm of Education" and the other "The Rhythmic Claims of Freedom and Discipline."

The rhythm of education, Whitehead said, was a cyclic pattern moving from a stage of what he called "romance" to a stage he called "precision" and then to "generalization." This rhythmic cycle he felt went on in all areas and at all ages, though it also progressed generally in that pattern from infancy to adulthood. He said that "lack of attention to the rhythm and character of mental growth is a main source of wooden futility in education."

The stage of romance is a stage of novelty. It is not dominated by systematic procedure. It is an immersion in new experiences, with half-glimpsed connections growing out of our encounters with new phenomena. It arouses romantic emotion as bare facts begin to take some form. Whitehead warned that we tend to confine ourselves to the second state—precision—but that the cycle is fruitless without romantic ferment, precision, and generalization.

The state of precision is an ordering stage. It is the development of knowledge and technique, the stage of grammar, either in science or language. It is barren without the previous stage because you cannot educate the mind *in vacuo*.

The final stage of generalization is a stage of synthesis. It is a return to romanticism with the added advantage of classified ideas and relevant technique.

Whitehead's insights fit well with Piaget's later findings. David Elkind,[21] in a recent speech, summarized the three aspects of the development of mental capacity inherent in Piaget's work, as follows: (a) stimulus exploration; (b) stimulus gaiting and storage; and (c) stimulus generalization. The parallel is striking, and we again see that our educational system under the ideology of achievement is focused upon precision or stimulus gaiting and storage.

Whitehead went on to talk about the rhythmic claims of freedom and discipline:

The drop from the divine wisdom, which was the goal of the ancients, to the textbook knowledge of subjects, which is achieved by the moderns, marks an educational failure, sustained through the ages. . . . The only avenue towards wisdom is by freedom in the presence of knowledge. But the only avenue for knowledge is by discipline in the acquirement of ordered fact. Freedom and discipline are two essentials of education. . . . Accordingly it should be the aim of an ideally constructed education that the discipline should be the voluntary issue of free choice, and that freedom should gain an enrichment of possibility as the issue of discipline.[22]

The activity in schooling, talked about as the selection and organization of learning experiences in technical curriculum language, is more nearly a pulsating, spiraling process of freedom and discipline in the form of exploration, precision, and generalization. No two individuals are necessarily at the same stage in any area at any specific time or age.

This suggests the creative evolution of what Virgil Herrick called organizing centers,[23] which have within them the potentiality for romance and exploration, precision, and generalization at different levels of sensation, perception, and ideation. This is much more akin to the selection of "globs" of activity than it is to the highly organized selection of "means" hung between objectives and an evaluation, and manipulated between these abstractions.

Yet the selection process is equally important as the selection. Given teachers and areas of cultural substance with youngsters as unique persons, the selection process must continually evolve out of the ever renewed realities of schooling. Thus, guided by the rhythmic cycle of intellectual growth and the dynamic interacting of the persons present, the patterns of activity will emerge. And as unsatisfactory as this statement may be to the orientation of some persons, there is simply no other alternative which does not violate the character of the total vision of a humane school offered here. Nothing short of an article of faith in the creative potential of feeling and thinking human beings, in contrast to objective assessment by itself, will do.

Curriculum Criticism

The improvement of schooling will continue to be a major concern, given our culture, no matter what orientation we take. *Evaluation* is a perfectly good word for describing what one does when one attempts to improve matters. Yet it is unfortunately true that the connotation of the evaluation process in schooling has become technically loaded toward scientism; and we would be better served, as John S. Mann[24] has pointed out, by using the term *criticism*.

According to Mann, curriculum is like a story in the sense that what we choose to include, via the choice of some teacher, state legislature, film maker, or textbook writer, is a representation of life. The end product is not altogether different from a novel or a short story, since the writer too must choose what he wishes to represent, how he wishes to represent it, and in what context it will occur.

A curriculum, too, may be said to have a design and a style. It prescribes rhythms of activity through such mechanisms as scheduling; it has patterns of emphasis and significance found, for example, in required and elected experiences and the placement of activity during the day; it has a list of characters playing various roles; and it has a plot which may rise and fall with grades and come to a climax at graduation. It even has a moral to the story which goes something like, "all is well that ends well."

The effort to criticize curriculum would be no less strenuous or less important than it would be to evaluate. What would differ, however, is the fact that criticism would not begin with a unidimensional absolute, in this case the achievement of youngsters. Criticism differs from this because it is essentially after the fact. It is reflection about what is done which presupposes that we find out about what we are doing about it, rather than by thinking about it. Once we have done it we may then criticize what we have done, in the hope that the next time we do something we will be more satisfied with it when we finish.

It is essential to note here the weakening of the concept of objectives as major determinants of action. Now objectives are all well and good, but as Schwab[25] noted in his work on the practical, it is better to contemplate what we have accomplished rather than what was intended. Good intentions have a history of getting men into deep trouble, for we seem unable to let go of them when the reality of the ongoing situation makes them inapplicable or no longer good, as when in the desire to achieve our goals we begin to justify any concomitant result as worth it.

Dwayne Huebner[26] has developed the idea which may be paraphrased to mean that we tend to be as illiterate in ways of talking about schooling as we are in ways of talking to people who do not speak English. There are many ways to talk about such a complex phenomenon, and the fact that we use the technical language of our time does not preclude the usefulness and, in fact, the necessity of being multilingual.

Criticism should be a conversation in the sense that Michael Oakeshott[27] used the term. We may speak scientifically from our data, and we may speak practically from our experiences of what is desirable; or we may speak historically in terms of our understanding of contributing influences, but we must also speak aesthetically (poetically in Oakeshott's terminology) through our imagination.

These are four different ways of talking. One does not take precedence over another. "Their meeting place is not an inquiry or argument, but a conversation."[28] All ways are appropriate, but their appropriateness is determined by the course of the conversation itself, not by external standards.

The distinction here is not between utterances of fact and non-fact. All ways of talking are forms of images. IQ scores or standardized test scores, for example, are images, not facts. Practices derived from experience are also images rather than concrete facts, just as the discussion of historical antecedents is a process of selecting images of facts for explanation. The voice of art (aesthetics) is the voice of images created for their own sake.

At the risk of negating my purpose through taking what some call an irrational position, it is suggested that the aesthetic approach to curriculum and schooling is similar to a "change for change's sake" premise. But this does not mean blind or random change. It is change which is predicated upon creative making, remaking, observing, turning about, playing with, delighting in, and composing in larger patterns. This is in contrast to the innovation which evokes approval or disapproval principally upon cause-effect or means-ends basis.

The positive thrust of this idea is the image of schooling as the continuous creating and recreating of meaningful experiences among the participants involved, and patterns and experiences evolving in terms of individual self-development and the ever changing differences in life circumstances and persons—through freedom guided by imaginative contemplation.

Yet there are negative reasons that might cause us to consider this approach, for when we look carefully at talk about schooling and innovation in scientific, practical, and historical terms there are many puzzling occurrences.

Historically we seem to be caught in some sort of irrational cyclical phenomena explainable perhaps in broad social terms but not from within schooling. We often appear to be swept up in fads, even those as respectable as "structure," which seem continually to repeat a theme or a promise, which then fails to produce, and which soon tends to return to its opposite or some other alternative. There is a high failure rate in the cause-effect, means-ends, promise of change.

Scientifically and practically we are also puzzled. Our problems appear to be little changed with the increase in data from these sources. Statistically significant differences seem hollow in practical terms, and practical differences seem arbitrary and nongeneralizable. Tolstoy,[29] for example, said over 100 years ago that a teacher should use the reading method (from among the basic approaches) that he is most comfortable with, and we have not made much progress scientifically or practically since then.

It is at least suggestive, then, that our contradictions in schooling may be due to our refusal to accept the position of curriculum criticism rather than curriculum evaluation. Curriculum criticism may be a more natural way for people to enter into the reality of schooling. If so, then we must admit this and deliberately encourage and support the aesthetic and creative potential in this approach.

John Dewey remarked in 1929 that "quantification, mechanization, and standardization are the marks of Americanization." He felt these factors had their good side in the improvement of external conditions; but he warned that their effects were not limited to these matters: "they have invaded mind and character, and subdued the soul to their own dye."[30]

Forty years later this is essentially the growing impassioned cry of our youthful counter culture. If we are to take hopeful, positive action in schooling to face this contradiction, we must return to the source of creative humanism, the humanities; and we must infuse this spirit throughout our substance and processes. And we would do well to keep in mind Dewey's comment that ". . .it is impossible to develop integrated individuality by any all-embracing system or program. . . . No individual can make the determination for anyone else; nor can he make it for himself all at once and forever."[31]

Notes

1. William Blake, "The Everlasting Gospel," in *William Blake: A Selection of Poems and Letters*, J, Bronowski, ed. (Middlesex, England: Penguin Books, 1950), p. 78.

2. Peter L. Berger, *Invitation to Sociology* (Garden City, NY: Doubleday & Company, Inc., 1963).

3. Michael Harrington, *The Accidental Century* (New York: Macmillan Company, 1965).

4. W.B. Yeats, in *Poetry: A Modern Guide to Its Understanding and Enjoyment*, Elizabeth Drew, ed. (New York: Dell Publishing Co., Inc., 1959), pp.149–150.

5. Erich Fromm, *The Revolution of Hope* (New York: Harper & Row, 1968).

6. Carlton Beck, *et. al.*, *Education for Relevance* (Boston: Houghton Mifflin Company, 1968).

7. James B. Macdonald, "The School Environment as Learner Reality," *Curriculum Theory Network*, Toronto, Institute of Education, Winter 1969–1970, pp. 45–54.

8. Blake, in *William Blake*, p. 236.

9. Jean-Jacques Rousseau, *The Social Contract*, Charles Frankell, ed. (New York: Hafner Publishing Company, 1954).

10. Theodore Roszak, *The Making of a Counter Culture* (Garden City, NY: Doubleday & Company, Inc., 1969).

11. Susanne K. Langer, *Philosophical Sketches* (New York: Mentor Books, 1964), p. 82.

12. John MacMurray, *Freedom in the Modern World* (London: Faber and Faber Ltd., 1958), p. 47.

13. Langer, *Philosophical Sketches*, p. 76.

14. William James, quoted in John D. Wild, *The Radical Empiricism of William James* (Garden City, NY: Doubleday & Company, Inc., 1970), p. 268.

15. Joseph Wood Krutch, *Experience and Art: Some Aspects of the Esthetics of Literature* (New York: Collier Books, 1962).

16. William James, "The Moral Philosopher and the Moral Life," in *Pragmatism and Other Essays*, J.L. Blau, ed. (New York: Washington Square Press, 1963), pp. 214–235.

17. Wild, *The Radical Empiricism of William James*, p. 280.

18. Joseph J. Schwab, *The Practical: A Language for Curriculum* (Washington, DC: Center for the Study of Instruction, National Education Association, 1970).

19. C. Wright Mills, *The Sociological Imagination* (New York: Oxford University Press, 1953).

20. Alfred North Whitehead, *Aims of Education* (New York: The Macmillan Company, 1929).

21. Speech presented by David Elkind at conference on "Open Schooling" sponsored by the National Association for the Education of Young Children (NAEYC), Denver, Colorado, March 5, 1970.

22. Whitehead, *Aims of Education*, pp. 45–46.

23. Virgil E. Herrick, in *Strategies of Curriculum Development*, Dan W. Anderson, James B. Macdonald, and Frank B. May, eds. (Columbus, OH: Charles E. Merrill Publishing Company, 1965).

24. John S. Mann, "Curriculum Criticism," in *Curriculum Theory Network*, Toronto, Institute of Education, Winter 1968–1969, pp. 2–14.

25. Schwab, *The Practical*.

26. Dwayne Huebner, "Curricular Language and Classroom Meanings," in *Language and Meaning*, James B. Macdonald and Robert R. Leeper, ed. (Washington, DC: Association for Supervision and Curriculum Development, 1966), pp. 8–26.

27. Michael Oakeshott, *The Voice of Poetry in the Conversation of Mankind* (London: Bowes and Bowes, 1969).

28. *Ibid.*, p. 10

29. Leo Tolstoy, *Tolstoy on Education*, Leo Wiener, trans. (Chicago: University of Chicago Press, 1967).

30. John Dewey, *Individualism: Old and New* (New York: G.P. Putnam's Sons, 1962).

31. Ibid., p. 157.

Chapter Four

A Transcendental Developmental Ideology
of Education

The title of this essay was prompted by the recent Kohlberg and Mayer article entitled "Development as an Aim of Education."[1] They talk about three ideologies: *romantic, developmental,* and *cultural transmission.* It is clear to me that there are at least two other potential ideologies that I would call *radical* and *transcendental developmental.* I shall attempt to step off from Kohlberg and Mayer's framework to discuss briefly the radical ideology and to develop what I believe to be a transcendental developmental ideology. It is my contention that the radical and transcendental ideologies are the most potentially useful in the modern world.

The elements or components of ideologies as described by Kohlberg and Mayer are psychological theories, epistemological components, and ethical value positions. These correspond roughly with the philosopher's concern for ontological, epistemological, and axiological considerations. Essentially this amounts to a statement of the nature of man, the nature of knowledge, and the nature of values.

The romantic ideology Kohlberg and Mayer perceive is fundamentally concerned with human nature and the unfolding or maturation of the individual. Knowledge in this ideology is said to be existential or phenomenological, and it refers directly to the inner experience of the self. Truth is self-knowledge and extends to others by sympathetic understanding of other selves. The ethical theory of the romantic is based upon the freedom of the individual to be himself, assuming that individuals, when free, are essentially good unless society makes them otherwise.

The cultural transmission ideology is grounded in behaviorist psychology. Essentially the individual is shaped by his environmental experiences in terms of the associations and stimulus-response sets he encounters and acquires. Knowledge is the outer reality, the "objective" world, that can be found in sense experience and culturally shared. Value theory is either an ethically neutral stance or a social relativism that accepts the present cultural values for which there would appear to be consensus.

Between these two, in the sense that it is neither a model of inner experience or outer experience but a dialectic between inner and outer, lies developmental ideology. The transaction itself creates reality which is neither an inner nor an outer phenomena, but something else. Dewey's method of intelligence and the cognitive-developmental work of Piaget with its concern for inner structures and outer structures encountered in interaction are the psychological models for this ideology. Knowledge is equated with a resolved relationship between inner experience and outer reality. Truth is pragmatic in that it depends upon its relationship to the situation in which we find ourselves. Values are based upon ethical universals derived philosophically, and they serve as developmental means and ends. Thus, rational ethical principles, not the actual values of the child or the culture, serve as arbiters for defining aims.

Analysis of these ideologies suggests that the following elements are the critical aspects of ideology. Figure 1, a – c illustrate these different ideologies.

Figure 1 is of course highly simplistic, but it illustrates the inner and outer aspects of ideology and the dominant directions of the critical flow of the human encounter. Thus, the romantic conception is mainly from inner to outer, the cultural transmission from outer to inner, and the developmental is dialectical.

Kohlberg and Mayer assume that the radical position is equivalent to the romantic, or at least they use these terms interchangeably at times. This I believe to be an error. It is in error, that is, if radical is meant to imply a political radicalism of a Marxian persuasion.

The political radical is committed to a dialectical model, as is the developmental. However, as the work of Paulo Freire[2] shows, it has a fundamentally different interpretation of the dialectic. (See Figure 1, d).

The developmental and radical models look identical only on the surface, for the radical model is weighted on the side of social realities. The developmental model is weighted on the side of inner cognitive structures. The progressive position assumed that democracy was the ideal social reality and continued its analysis of the interaction process with that assumption in mind. The radical model, on the other hand, is essentially based upon an analysis of why democratic ideas are not realized, thus emphasizing environmental structures.

We still do not generally recognize this radical thrust in curriculum thinking, but the growing edge of writing in the past five or ten years leans toward a resurgence of romanticism and a renewal of past reconstructionist terms of the radical tradition. Neither is, I believe, the same as its predecessor, and I shall try to use historical perspectives to validate both assertions.

The political view of curriculum that appears to provide the most satisfying analysis is Marxian in orientation. There are classical and Neo-Marxian differences of opinion that are of great interest and impact. However, I shall try

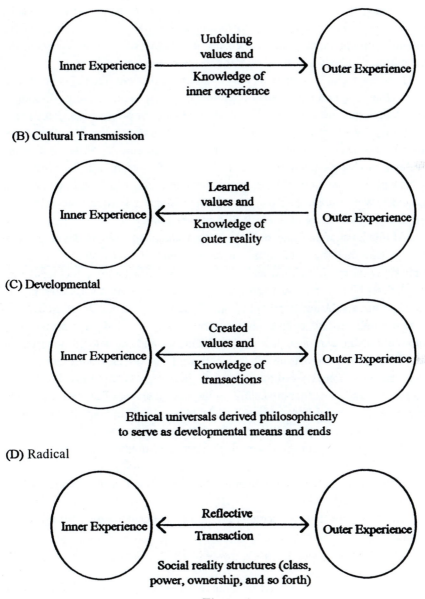

Figure 1

to generalize the radical position as an ideology in terms of what Kohlberg and Mayer left out.

The radical point of view takes off from the essential proposition that the critical element in human life is the way people live together. It further posits that the way people live together is determined essentially by the structure of our economic arrangements, the ownership of means of production, and the distribution of goods and services through the possession of power.

It is the social structures of the environment that provide the radical with his developmental impetus, rather than the biological structures of development in the individual that are so important for the liberal or progressive. This is not to say that either group ignores the other, but it is to say that the democratic ideal of the liberal (as the social condition best able to foster individual development) leaves much to be desired in terms of its usefulness for a historical analysis of why democracy appears to operate in a rather different manner than its rhetoric would suggest. Thus, the radical ideology raises questions that could lead us to another level of analysis of the curriculum.

At this level of analysis, radical ideology claims that liberal developmental ideology and romantic ideology are embedded in the present system. That is, the emphasis upon the individual and his unfolding or developing necessitates an acceptance of the social structures as status quo in order to identify in any empirical manner the development of the individual. Thus, developmental theory is culture and society bound, and it is bound to the kind of a system that structures human relationships in hierarchical dominance and submission patterns and alienates the person from his own activity in work and from other people. Given the level of analysis of the radical, the individual cannot fully develop out of the very conditions that are central to the improvement of human life. Only when new social conditions arise will we be able to begin to empirically identify and talk about human development in the new social context.

At this level of questions a radical curriculum thinker might ask:

1. How are the patterns of human relationships found in the broader society revealed in schools?
2. What function does the school have in the system, and how does this affect practice?
3. Why is there unequal opportunity to learn in schools, at least in terms of race and social class?
4. Why are textbooks biased in terms of race and sex, and why is history nonauthentic or biased?

5.   Do schools provide for unequal access to knowledge by the way they operate?

6.   How should we structure human relationships in school?

There are, of course, radical answers to such questions. However, questions tend to frame the answers we get, and the critical point here is that educational problems become quite different when one looks at them from a radical perspective.

My problem with the radical or political view of curriculum is not its level of analysis or the questions it asks, per se; instead, it is the feeling I have that it is also one step behind the world. Thus, I feel that, as McLuhan once said, we are traveling down a superhighway at faster and faster speeds looking out the rear-view mirror. Kohlberg and Mayer's three ideologies are "over the hill," so to speak, but the political view is in the mirror. It does provide us with some idea of how straight the road is ahead provided our speed does not exceed our reaction time. What we need is some way to look beyond, if only a few feet.

The radical view of education in its political manifestations does provide us with a historical analysis—as well as with concepts for analyzing contemporary phenomena. Yet I find this historical view limiting in its materialistic focus, and I suspect that it is grounded fundamentally in the Industrial Revolution and reflects the same linear rationality and conceptualizing that characterizes the rise of science and technology. It is a "social science" of human relations and a "science" of history. Like all history, this is a special reading of the past that helped make sense out of the nineteenth-century present. The world today is not the same, and a different reading of history is needed to help make sense of our contemporary world.

The radical-political perspective as a base for curriculum thinking does not adequately allow for the tacit dimension of culture: it is a hierarchical historical view that has outlived its usefulness both in terms of the emerging structure of the environment and of the psyches of people today. I propose that the structure of the world environment today must be approached through the existence of a nuclear, electronic-computerized, multimedia technology rather than the more linear, single-media machine world. Further, I would propose that concomitant psychological structures in individuals must be viewed in a different perspective. I would like to reflect briefly upon these two ideas and then project some new questions for curriculum thinking.

Our present technology and our present world population have restricted our political options in ways we could not have readily foreseen. We are faced with such problems as energy crises that threaten the very survival of members of our population. Short of detechnologizing society, we are faced with the fact that political action that in any way threatens our fundamental technological cultural base is no longer a viable alternative unless we are willing, in the name of ideals, to inflict untold suffering and the threat of extinction on millions of human beings. Freedom to stop the workings of "the system" via revolution of some sort is no longer simply a threat to the power factions in our society; it is indeed a threat to all human beings.

I believe we have entered a new hierarchical level with our electronic world. The passage may have seemed gradual, but its impact has essentially been to produce a difference in kind (instead of in degree) in the condition of human existence. The institutionalization of nuclear and electronic technology, though dependent upon what its industrial predecessor has contributed, is an operating pattern, a cultural milieu that has never existed before.

The sense of powerlessness and impotence we feel is not a sign of alienation in the traditional Marxian sense. It is a true reflection of the state of the human beings to the extent that we transfer psychological states grounded in a premodern society. With an industrial psychological outlook we are indeed powerless when we consider our destructive nuclear capacity and our dependence upon computers and power sources to simply maintain our existence. No longer are we dominated by the owners of the tools of work; they are also dominated by the need for survival and power sources.

We have in effect created our first man-made gods in material form. We have created a human condition that, should it collapse by disaster or human direction, would destroy rich and poor alike. Now all people must serve the technical "gods" in some nonthreatening way in order to insure social and perhaps personal survival. Political action and political analysis of the human condition is now too limited a perspective with which to view our conditions of existence. They can threaten our very survival if used by people having an outmoded attitudinal structure. Precisely because radicals have been so busy pushing and tugging at the means of production and distribution, they do not see that they share the same technological world view—what liberals love, radicals hate, and both are equally possessed by technology.

A key phenomena in understanding this transition is television. It is incomprehensible to me how people raised as children in a nontelevision world can miss the fact that the youth of today have been and are being dramatically affected by this overriding multimedia impact on our lives. To grow up with television is to grow up in an obviously mediated world.

Curriculum thinking should be grounded in cultural realities. One may see cultural realities in terms of a relativistic perspective or in long-range developmental terms. In my own developmental speculation I see the present and future technological domination of man as a step on the road toward human evolution. It is my personal myth that today's technology is yesterday's magic. Further, it is my intuitive feeling that technology is in effect an externalization of the hidden consciousness of human potential. Technology, in other words, is a necessary development for human beings in that it is the means of externalizing the potential that lies within. Humanity will eventually transcend technology by turning inward, the only viable alternative that allows a human being to continue to experience oneself in a world as a creative and vital element. Out of this will come the rediscovery of human potential.

Social Signals of Transcendence

We are not completely without sociological validation of a transcendent ideology. Peter Berger,[3] for example, has presented a sociological analysis of human behavior that is relevant. Berger suggests that the one major implication of modern relativistic sociology is that it relativizes the relativizers as well. That is, taking a relativistic position also puts the relativists in the historical position of having their doctrine relativized.

He suggests that we examine the behavior of people and look empirically, using sociological methods, for what he calls signals of transcendence. In so doing, Berger finds as a beginning hypothesis that there are at least four such signals, that is, prototypical human gestures: the propensity for order and the automatic assurance of the adult to the child that everything is all right (that is, you can trust the world); the existence of play; the existence of hope; and the existence of damnation. Berger finds these gestures difficult to explain without some sense of transcendence. The propensity to order and have faith and trust in the meaning of things, playing, hoping, and the sense of indignation that some human action lies beyond the acceptable are all unnecessary and inexplicable if everything is simply relative and realistic. Humor is also difficult to explain in such a context.

Thus, humans have both the propensity to play and laugh as if we need not be serious and the propensity to trust, order, and damn with a seriousness that transcends everyday political and economic concern. The case for nothing but social reality and psychological development, he feels, must be proved by the proponents of those views, not by those who see signals of transcendence.

The doors of human conception opened and ushered in the technological revolution. Political thinking is a rational social adjunct to a conceptual culture.

Now we are facing the opening of the doors of perception in human experience, not as the minor mystical phenomena that have appeared throughout history, but as a large-scale movement of consciousness on the part of our young. A multimedia world is perceptual, not linear, in the utilization of concepts, but patterned concepts are received upon impact as perceptual experience. The psychological attitude born in this culture is a psychology of individuation, not individualism or socialism.

The human race is beginning to take another major step into the unknown source of its imagination, that same source that has created technology and all of the cultural trappings we possess. The signs are apparent in today's world and in the history of human *being*. In a very real sense it is as if we are coming to know that what we have imagined and conceptualized resides within us as potential, rather than having to be made into conceptual and material form.

Think for a moment about the mysteries of human experiences rather than our achievements. How can people walk on coals as hot as 2500 degrees without visible signs of burning on either their feet or clothing? What explains the various forms of extrasensory perception? How can people dream the future? What are teleportation, telekinesis, and similar experiences? What is a mystical experience?

You may write them off as empirically unfounded, just as Julius Caesar would have written off the technological world of today as an utter impossibility. But the testimony of human history in terms of witnessing and personal experience cannot be ignored, for it is out of this very source of the unknown that whatever we have achieved has emerged. There is no reason to suspect that we have realized our human potential, and there is reasonable evidence that we may be rapidly approaching a new level of psychological and cultural growth from which dramatically new understandings of human potential will emerge.

It is my best guess that the next step, already begun, is an inward journey that will manifest itself by discovery, through perception and imagery, of human potential only slightly realized until now, and an outer journey for new communal life stages that are pluralistic and limited to small groups (tribes?) of people. The new communities will, of necessity, not threaten the technological superstructure that supports life, but they will seek pluralistic life styles within the superstructure.

A Transcendental Developmental Ideology

A transcendental ideology seems to be necessary because I find the source of value positions to be inadequate in the other four. It is never clear on what basis or by what source the values of objective neutrality, social relativism, or ethical principle are derived. In other words, I find all four ideologies unclear in their ontological and phenomenological grounding.

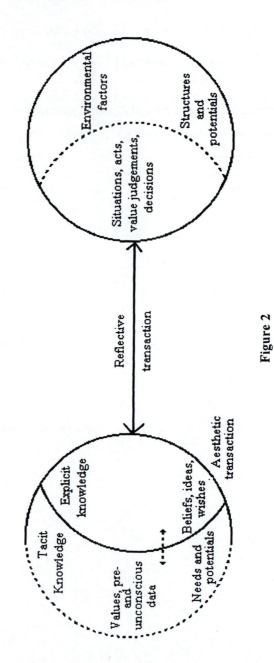

Figure 2

There are two directions I could take at this point: the transcendental or the hermeneutic. I am not now equipped to pursue the later course. From what I do know of this line of analysis, it seems to result in a cultural relativism that I find unacceptable at present. I will leave this door ajar for further study, however. What follows is fundamentally addressed to critical problems I see in the four ideologies described earlier.

My position is best approached through the concept of a dual dialectical process. A dialectic exists not only between the individual and his environment but also within the individual himself. Figure 2 will help to illustrate what I mean.

The relatively closed portions of Figure 2 represent the explicit knowledge systems of the individual and the situational context within which he acts. This represents a position similar to that held by radical ideologists, as far as it goes. Thus, I would agree that human activity is in part created by the reflective transaction of human consciousness in situational contexts.

It is clear, however, that, within the limits of the closed part, there can be no access to values or ethical principles that do not arise out of a utilitarian reflection upon the objective historical or personal consequences of human activity. Without positing a method of reflective intelligence based upon an analysis of the consequences of human activity, there could be no assessment of "good" other than a bare survival adjustment to reality, much in the manner of most other animals.

Utilitarianism as a source of values is, however, a relatively unsatisfactory position. It does not allow for, or account for, phenomena in human experience that have been readily apparent to persons throughout history and in contemporary society. Central to this discontent is the cognitive orientation of reflection as a method of intelligence and the only source of analysis for human activity. Thus, an a priori valuing of rationality is necessary in utilitarianism. Where does it come from?

That this gives only a partial account of human being is indicated by the dialectic, between the explicit awareness of the individual and the nonexplicit nature of the individual. The self, in other words, is composed of both conscious awareness and unconscious data at any given time.

Values, I believe, are articulated in the lives of people by the dual dialectic of reflecting upon the consequences of an action and sounding the depths of our inner selves. Only a process something like this can explain why "what works is not always good." Some dual dialectic is also needed to explain the existence of reason, or aesthetic rationality, to counterbalance purely technological rationality.

The self as a concept has suffered at the hands of everyone from behaviorists to analytic philosophers. I find this interesting but neither the empirical reductionism of behaviorists nor the analysis of common usage convince me that there could not be an agency where phenomenological experience would permit the analyst to analyze and the behaviorist to behaviorize. Neither come to grips with what allows them to perform at all. I find the concept of self as an experiencing agency to be useful for this purpose, and I would suggest that a self is no less mystical than a culture or a society since all three can only be structured as hypothetical constructs by some languaging agency.

The inner dialectic of the self is a critical element if we are to advance the position that culture is in a way created by human beings. The possibility of value may well be limited in alternatives by the individual-biological-social dialectic, but the validation of values would seem to demand some source other than explicit and rational knowledge.

Herbert Marcuse[4] seemed to recognize a need for something similar—a new sensibility as well as a raised level of critical consciousness—in the idea of aesthetic rationality. Aesthetic rationality, Marcuse suggested, can serve as a sort of gauge for a free society. He found a source for the form that a new society could take in the area of sensibility. Marcuse would argue, however, that sensibility is formed from conditions of the social structure as well as from the explicit and rational data of the world. He would further argue that sensibility and rationality can only be transformed by engaging in praxis, the collective practice of creating an environment.

It is not clear where this leaves Marcuse. On the one hand, he appears to assume some biological base for sensibility; and, on the other hand, he appears to see new sensibility as emerging from new social conditions. I strongly suspect that Marcuse has, at least as a sensibility of his own, a basic idea of the "good man" grounded in his biology. If freed, it could redirect the formation of a rational world.

The importance here of Marcuse's position is the recognition of an area of sensibility or aesthetic rationality. The dual dialectic of inner aesthetic and technical rationality and outer individual and social condition is implicit in his statements. The difference between our views would apparently be the poverty of sources of aesthetic rationality that he appears to accept and the necessity of treating sensibility only in the context of the construction of new social environments. I propose that there are phenomenologically identifiable sources of aesthetic rationality not accounted for by Marcuse, and phenomenologically identifiable methods of creating individual perceptual environments and enlarging human sensibility that do not depend upon praxis as he defines it.

The problem of the source and validation of values is thus not adequately resolved in the ideologies described by Kohlberg and Mayer or by the radical position. We are left essentially with values that are either picked up culturally by association or conditioned in us behavioristically, emergent from our biological nature, or derived from cognitive reflection upon experience (individually or historically).

None of these approaches can account for the emergence, validation, and source of all values without ignoring a sizable segment of our own cultural history and personal experience. Values, I would submit, as with knowledge, are personal, developed from a dual dialectical process that represents development in a hierarchical structure that surpasses one's biology, culture, or society.

Psychological theory, if there must be such an adjunct to educational ideology, must also be seen as a focus upon the question of human being. That is, narrow empirical or developmental views lead us away from our ontological ground of being rather than causing us to come to grips with human nature. They must also be grounded in something beyond their own conceptions. Thus, psychological theory must be grounded in existence and utilize the methods of phenomenology if it hopes to cope with being.

I have found much of value in the works of C.G. Jung[5] and William James.[6] The sense of their works for me lies in their apparent willingness to cope with all forms of psychological manifestation in human activity and to discipline their inquiries through observation and phenomenological methodology. I am less concerned with their conceptualizations than their orientation and methodology, although their concepts have been useful in many instances.

Jung was concerned with metaphysics throughout both his practical work and his theoretical writing. His biography is a rare experience in reading; it tells us that he was a fascinating, introspective, and idiosyncratic individual, but, more important, it shows how he used his personality in his work. He is perhaps a modern paradigm of man's unified struggle for meaning, using his own personality and culture and methodologically disciplining that inner struggle and cultural potential to probe the nature of human being.

As an analytical psychologist, he never developed a theory of child development. He felt that the ideas of Freud and Adler were perfectly usable with the young. Instead, he focused on the process of individuation, and it is the implications of this concept that contribute to the transcendental ideology of education.

Jung worked most often with people who were successful in life, but who, upon reaching middle age, found that life lacked meaning. He felt that the tasks of the first half of life were best symbolized by the myth of the hero. What concerned him was, as Anthony Storr says, what happened when the hero emancipated himself from the past, proved his (Adlerian) power, and gained his (Freudian) mate?

This led Jung and his patients to a search for values, and for Jung the supreme value was that of integration, of "wholeness." Thus, the conscious attitude of integration is one of acceptance, of ceasing to do violence to one's own nature by repressing or overdeveloping any part of it. This Jung calls a "religious" attitude, although not necessarily related to any recognizable creed.

Then, the second half of life became a spiritual quest. He believed, contrary to Freud, that the concept of God was a "psyche aptitude" of human nature appearing everywhere in culture and history. He further believed that only by recognizing some higher authority than the ego could people detach themselves sufficiently from sexuality, the will to power, and other compulsions. If man had no spiritual inner experience, he would make a God of something else, whether sex, power, or even rationality. The God Jung discovered through his work was the sense of "wholeness," the undiscovered self.

The problem of alienation for Jung was an alienation from the ground of his being. Thereby it created loneliness, and his life lacked meaning and significance. Loneliness did not, he felt, come from having no people around; it came from being out of touch with oneself and thus being unable to communicate things that seem important or from holding views that others deem inadvisable.

Concepts that Jung used to express his views such as "archetypes," the "collective unconscious," his psychological typology of "introversion-extroversion," are more or less useful as the case may be. They are not central to my thinking except to point toward an inner potential that the person must come to experience.

Of perhaps greater use is Jung's concept of the psyche being self-regulating. That, for Jung, was a psychology of "individuation" based upon the idea that the person is self-regulating when he has attained a balance and integration in his potentialities. Self-regulation strives toward unity, toward the integration of inner and outer realities in a meaningful wholeness.

James, on the other hand, was a self-proclaimed supernaturalist, in contrast to a naturalistic perspective of what he called a "crass" or pluralistic nature. He was, I suspect, as American as "apple pie" in his generally optimistic, searching, pluralistic, pragmatic, and radical empirical bent. Yet he was an unusual person for a psychologist because he had an insatiable curiosity about all the phenomena of human personal experience, and an aversion to closed or absolute meaning.

James felt as at home examining extrasensory perception or religious experiences as the more mundane aspects of attention, perception, cognition, and so forth. Jung refers to James's earlier work in a number of instances, but James probably died before he was well acquainted with Jung's work.

The lesson James leaves us is similar to Jung's in that his openness and methodology reflect an attitude toward psychology that is especially useful for our purposes. What James brings to our thought is a more critical use of the dialectic between inner implicit and outer explicit reality. By acceptance of the inner realm as a source of meaning, James only intends that we test it in our lives, that we accept it as phenomenological fact but verify it for ourselves by its meaning for us in our human activity. It is, in other words, a dialectic of self-reflection of the commerce between our inner and explicit consciousness, and its verification for us (as in the case of psychoanalysis) does not necessarily invalidate or validate concretely the experiences of others or limit the potential of human beings.

Thus, for James, Jung's concepts might well be what James called "overbeliefs." What he would agree to is the critical acceptance of human experiences seemingly arising from within but central to the understanding of humanness. Thus, he would say, "Disregarding overbeliefs, and confining ourselves to what is common and generic, we have found in the *fact that the conscious* person is continuous with a wider self through which. . . *experiences* come, a positive content of experience which, it seems to me, is *literally and objectively true as far as it goes*."[7]

He concluded his work in religious experiences with his expression of his own overbelief, sounding somewhat like Carlos Casteneda and his adventures with Don Juan. "The whole drift of my education goes to persuade me that the worlds of consciousness that exist, and that those other worlds must contain experiences which have a meaning for life also; and that although in the main their experiences and those of this world keep discrete, yet the two become continuous as certain points, and higher energies filter in."[8]

Components of Epistemology

The epistemological components of a transcendental ideology are grounded in the concept of personal knowledge. Thus, knowledge is not simply things and relationships that are real in the outer world and waiting to be discovered, but it is also a process of personalizing the outer world through the inner potential of the human being as it interacts with outer reality.

At this level I am speaking not of idiosyncratic individual worlds, although these are important, but I am referring to the idea that the created culture of human life is a common set of personal constructs. Personal in the sense that all cognitive constructs are grounded in individual personal meaning and that our shared culture, as well as language usages, serves as a pragmatic survival device. This outer necessity does not change the fundamental nature of knowledge.

The work of Michael Polanyi[9] is instructive at this point. He develops the idea of the tacit dimension of knowledge. By this I take him to mean that any explicit knowing is grounded in a tacit knowing that makes sense out of explicit statements. Thus, Polanyi begins with what he calls the fact "that we can know more than we can tell."

It is necessary to understand what one knows in order to make sense of it. Polanyi refers to this as a process of "indwelling." Understanding, however, is tacit in that understanding may only be inferred from the explicit knowledge we possess. This process of tacit knowing exists in both practical and formal knowledge structures, and in aesthetic and scientific realms.

As Polanyi remarks, "The skill of a driver cannot be replaced by a thorough schooling in the theory of motorcar: The knowledge I have of my own body differs altogether from the knowledge of its physiology; and the rules of rhyming and prosody do not tell me what a poem told me, without any knowledge of its rules."[10] And, a mathematical theory can be constructed only by relying on prior tacit knowing and can function as a theory within an act of knowing, which consists in our attending from it to the previously established experience on which it bears.

Many of our present educational problems seem more understandable if we accept the tacit dimension of knowing. It is useful, for example, to consider the problem of school achievement among culturally different populations as fundamentally a problem of tacit knowing.

In Polanyi's terms, explicit knowledge use requires an act of commitment that cannot be formalized since "you cannot express a commitment noncommittally." The lack of commitment among culturally different students has been referred to as motivation and attention or value problems. Essentially it can be thought of as an absence of tacit knowing which makes sense of (helps the student understand) the meaning of the explicit knowledge he is encountering. In mundane terms he lacks the experiences that make sense of his school tasks. Thus, he is unable to *understand* and *commit* himself to the enterprise.

On a more general level, the problems of testing take on a more understandable quality when seen in the light of tacit knowledge. The sense of injustice and unfairness encountered frequently among students in reference to tests is helpfully explained when one accepts the idea that "we can know more than we can tell" and that it is possible not to understand the meaning or direction of tests and err because the tacit awareness we bring to a test situation may well not match the tacit assumptions of the test maker.

A positive side to this problem may be seen in the use of humor. Much of our humor in the form of stories is grounded in the development of a story line that arouses a tacit understanding in the listener and is revealed to be in error when the punch line is delivered. The punch line is frequently "funny" because the listener quickly realizes that the tacit base in the story has been juxtaposed to his own tacit knowledge. A good humorist is a past master of utilizing the tacit dimensions.

An epistemology must further come to grips with the so-called hard knowledge of our culture. It seems doubtful if any knowledge is "harder" than modern physics, and it is instructive to note epistemological implications found in the knowledge of modern physical science.

According to Arthur Koestler[11] modern physics has entered a phase of epistemology whereby modern physicists are ever more receptive to the possibility of the seemingly impossible. In a way one might say, at least in relation to the subatomic or supergalactic dimension, that physicists have literally gone out of their senses.

According to Koestler, Werner Heisenberg, in the field of quantum physics, has remarked that "atoms are not things. . . when we get down to the atomic level, the objective world of space and time do not exist, and the mathematical symbols of theoretical physics refer merely to possibilities, not to facts." The Principle of Uncertainty or Indeterminacy, credited to Heisenberg, demonstrates that the more accurately a physicist is able to determine the velocity of an electron, the less able he is to determine its location (and the reverse).

Further, matter as entity behaves as waves or particles, but on mutually exclusive terms. This concept of complementarity means that two mutually exclusive frames of reference are complementary. Both are needed to provide an exhaustive view of phenomena.

As Sir James Jeans said, "Today there is a wide measure of agreement, which on the physical side of science approaches almost to unanimity, the stream of knowledge is heading toward a mechanical reality; the universe begins to look more like a great thought than like a great machine."[12]

The story of neutrinos is perhaps the most bewildering. Neutrinos, it appears, have virtually no physical properties and apparently pass through solid bodies as if they were empty space. Koestler further tells how V. A. Firsoff described neutrinos as existing in a different kind of space, governed by different laws.

There is, of course, much more to modern physical theory, but it is a journey that I am ill prepared to take. I can only relate what reporters in this field seem to feel the knowledge implications are. In essence, the materialistic cause-effect world has collapsed as explanation of newly perceived phenomena. These phenomena appear to operate in a different dimension of reality and are referred to by many in mentalistic rather than materialistic terms.

Koestler, in his work, sees a convergence between physical theory and the data of extrasensory perception. At least the findings and theories of modern physicists are no less "unusual" and tend to be partially integratable with such things as precognition and psychokinesis. Fundamentally, he feels they reveal a basic polarity in matter which he describes as a causal self-assertive tendency and an acausal integration tendency to function as a part of a larger whole. He ends his essay by saying, "the limitation of our biological equipment may condemn us to the role of Peeping Toms at the keyhole of eternity. But at least let us take the stuffing out of the keyhole, which blocks even our limited view."[13]

An article by Bilanvik and Sundarshan[14] further illustrates the incredible potential of emerging physical theory. They remark that there is an unwritten precept in modern physics that "anything which is not prohibited is compulsory." They then go on to attempt to demonstrate that in terms of relativity theory there is no contradictory reason why "negative energy particles" traveling "backward in time" cannot exist. In the process they posit the existence of what they name "transcendent" tachyons.

An epistemology that does not recognize tacit knowledge components, or the fantastic possibilities and implications of our most advanced fields of inquiry, is simply weighted down with the baggage of philosophical and materialistic biases. How, what, and why are far more open questions than we are often led to believe, and the possibilities of accessibility to knowledge from "hidden" inner sources operating on acausal, or integrative, or serial and synchronistic bases point directly toward the awareness of another ground of knowledge in human being.

Centering as the Aim of Education

The aim of education should be a centering of the person in the world. Mary Caroline Richards[15] has expressed this idea beautifully. Much of what I have to say is at least consonant with her views, if not directly adapted from them.

Centering does not mean mental health. Though I have no quarrel with the intentions of people who want everyone to be mentally healthy, the term is too ridden with a psychologism that limits our perspective about human beings. It appears as a statistical concept, and those who are mentally healthy may in fact be "other-directed" persons, having little sense of a core or center.

Further, centering does not mean self-actualization, for that process, at least as I interpret it, is filled with assumptions about personal development that seem arbitrary and somewhat closed to me. One's personality, I would feel, is better thought of as something to be used to find a centering rather than something to be developed. Our efforts are better spent helping personalities as we find them ground their selves in a center of their being.

The idea of centering may be found in a wide variety of sources throughout history and the contemporary world. It is essentially what William James called a religious experience, although here it seems more appropriate to refer to the *spiritual*.

It is important that centering be recognized as a process that may occur in a religious context, but it is not dependent upon any sect or creed, whether Eastern Zen or Western Christianity, for its validation. It is a human experience facilitated in many ways by a religious attitude when this attitude encompasses the search to find our inner being or to complete one's awareness of wholeness and meaning as a person.

The work of some psychologists is important in helping us recognize the existence of inner potential, but the science of psychology, with its methodological and assumptive base, can only point toward the existence of the experience of centering. It cannot deal directly with it.

The "back door" or "front door" of human being, whichever suits your purpose, must be unlocked and left ajar if centering is to occur. The process draws its power and energy from sources that are not completely explicable. The naming of these sources of energy is not terribly helpful, even though one word that occurs frequently in relation to this experience is God. But God is not known; He is not understood; He is used. Thus, centering occurs through the use of spiritual resources, whatever one wishes to call them.

Spiritual energy does not shape the explicit knowledge of the person in absolute or noncultural ways. Centering takes place within the culture of the individual, and the process of centering utilizes the data of an individual's culture, what he explicitly knows through social praxis. The variety of religions, mystics, spiritualists, and other manifestations found throughout history fundamentally tells us that inner resources and strength can be made available and used but not what verbal form or perceptual reality this potential takes.

Centering as the aim of education calls for the completion of the person or the creation of meaning that utilizes all the potential given to each person. It in no way conflicts with the accumulated knowledge of a culture; it merely places knowledge in the base or ground from which it grows. As such, centering is the fundamental process of human *being* that makes sense out of our perceptions and cognitions of reality.

It is important we do not turn away from examining the ideas of centering simply because it is connected with spirituality. This term simply is the best one available in the attempt to refocus our fundamental educational concerns, even though it is fraught with heavy cultural biases in our society.

The data of spiritual literature when related to the axiological, psychological, social, and epistemological components I have alluded to make it quite difficult for us to reject the possibilities of centering. It appears to me that we are witnessing a period of discovery and transition leading toward convergence of phenomena very much like centering. I, personally, am satisfied with the particular term.

What kinds of questions can we now ask about curriculum in view of the developmental aim of centering?

1. What kinds of activities are encouraged that provide for opening up perceptual experiences?
2. What kinds of activity facilitate the process of sensitizing people to others, to inner vibrations?
3. What kinds of activity provide experiences for developing close-knit community relationships?
4. What kinds of activity encourage and facilitate religious experiences?
5. What kinds of activity facilitate the development of patterned meaning structures?
6. What ways can we organize knowledge to enlarge human potential through meaning?
7. How can we facilitate the development of inner strength and power in human beings?

Curriculum Content

Let me take a mundane example of the implications of this perspective of centering on the so-called discipline by focusing upon mathematics. Then we can reflect on more speculative but less mundane matters.

It is apparent that the substance of the culture we call "disciplines" may be used to create new knowledge to be passed on, to provide substantive content within social roles to attack social problems, and to enlarge human potential.

If we were fundamentally concerned about enlarging human potential, we would view mathematics, for example, as a way of conceptualizing or thinking and creating a special kind of meaning system. Being able to think mathematically would result in the development of a human potential that could not be gained through any other avenue. Mathematics, in other words, could be seen as a special world perspective, not as a single view, but one of a number of potential cultural views for opening up individuals to their potential.

This is counterposed to, though not mutually exclusive from, either the language use of mathematics for creating science, or pure mathematics, or the functional uses of computation. Teaching mathematics "for its own sake" means for the sake of enlarging the human potential of individuals in a way that is unique.

The importance of this perspective may be referred back to the developmental point of view provided by Kohlberg and Mayer. If we accept Dewey's concept of providing experiences that both interest people and contribute to their long-range development, it is clearly essential that the kind of long-range development be identifiable. Is the long-range development to be seen in terms of the discipline of mathematics? Or is it to be viewed in terms of its social usefulness to the individual in society? Or is it to be oriented toward the development of potential patterns of meaning for individuals?

Though, as I said, these ends are not mutually exclusive, they are functionally different in the sense that, when we make educative value judgements about the kinds and patterns of experience people encounter, we create a situation which in practice reflects one of these orientations as a primary view of the goal of development.

What is problematical about mathematics? If we assume, for lack of a better term, that a desirable mathematical problem for an individual is one which he sees as problematic and which promises to contribute to his long-range development, does it make any difference how we help him to create experiences that will meet both criteria in terms of one or another of the possible long-range perspectives? I think that it clearly does make a fundamental difference in the way we create curriculum environments and the manner in which we enter into instructional practices.

It is very difficult for me to see exactly what kinds of experiences would facilitate the long-range development of meaning perspective through mathematics. I can only alert mathematicians or mathematical thinkers to this task. But I think that I can clearly see some things we presently do that do not contribute directly to this end.

It makes no sense to me from this view, for example, to have a highly sequenced, logically programmed mathematics curriculum. The kind of mathematics, and when it is encountered, must be based upon a far more sensitive awareness of the meaning systems of individuals. Further, it makes little sense to structure the great majority of learning tasks in a convergent manner. It would appear to me that "playing" with numbers in a much freer kind of problem situation would be far more valuable.

Nor does it make much sense to "package" mathematics textbooks and other materials around narrow tasks, skills, or computations. It would be far better to set out to create mathematics as a set of problem situations that can be entered at different levels by different persons who can then branch out, if they wish, into geometry, algebra, calculus, or what have you. Thus, the emphasis upon individuated entrance in mathematical meaning systems, open and playful encounters, and highly diverse materials built around a problem situation that can go in a variety of directions sound much more satisfying to me.

Ecology is an emerging social concern that has a corollary in the centering process. It takes a unitary view of the world. Thus, the inner unity of the centering process has an outer reality in the concern for a unitary world built upon an understanding of ecology. It appears that any sane attempt to educate the young must deal substantively with the impact of man and technology on his own living environment, and there appears to be little hope that we can simply solve our ecological problems with the next generation of technological developments. Ecological problem solutions call for the same value search and commitment growing from the inner knowledge of what we are and what we can be. There is a need to transcend the linear and technical problem-solving approaches of the past if we are to survive our ecological crises. Thus, a global view of the interrelationships of human structures and activities must be a central aspect of any curriculum which purports to have a transcendent developmental view.

This section on content can be concluded with one last reflection that I owe to Charity James, with whom I worked for a year at Goldsmith College at the University of London. If we were intent upon developing human potential, we would realize that we live in a highly verbal, conceptual culture. We would further realize, as Lawrence Kubie[16] has pointed out, that we tend to pay a high price in potential for this human achievement. The price is fundamentally related to the dialectic of our explicit and inner selves, and it is focused upon the withering away of portions of our creative potential. This is not new, but what is rarely noted is that the emphasis upon nonverbal or body language, hidden culture, or the arts, is not crucial in this matter.

What we seem to lose is our ability to gain access to ourselves and our creative potential through the process of visualization. We have in fact created a negative concept called hallucinations to guard against the very use of some of the visualizing potential. We seem not to trust ourselves.

Dreams are, I suppose, a human example of the process of visualization, yet dreams are rarely in our control. What I speak of is the power to control and create visualization, to bring to our vision things not present to our senses. To have visions is not the same as to create them.

A somewhat dramatic illustration of the human potential for visualization is provided by Colin Wilson[17] in his biography of Abraham Maslow. Wilson was lecturing in one of Maslow's classes when he remarked that in the human act of masturbation it is possible by imagination to carry on a sexual activity where the mental act needs no object.

Maslow objected and pointed out that monkeys also masturbate. Wilson responded with the question of whether Maslow (whose early work was in the primate laboratory at Wisconsin) had ever seen a male monkey masturbate in total isolation, without the stimulus of a female monkey somewhere in the vicinity. Maslow remarked that he had not. Thus Wilson illustrated the capacity of the human being to make a physical response via visualization as if to reality.

The Processes in Curriculum

Centering is the aim of a transcendental ideology. As such, it is a process one enters into. Thus, the question of the objectives of a transcendental curriculum must be seen in process terms also. But processes are not ends in themselves. The ends are infinitely varied and unknowable in any finite sense with reference to a given individual. Processes, rather, refer to the engagement of the individual in human activity, which facilitates the process of centering.

For the sake of clarity an analogy may be made at this point to Dewey's developmental ideology. That is, if centering is viewed as the long-range developmental goal of curriculum, then process and content may be seen in terms of this goal. Content is selected in terms of the readiness and interest level of the students, primarily by the person involved coming to know what their immediate concerns are that are related to cultural substance. The essential component remains the processes or activities or events that occur. There are a number of possible processes that would facilitate centering.

Pattern making. This critical process reflects itself in the need to transform reality symbolically, to create order in search of meaning, and it is fundamental for locating oneself in time and space and for providing cognitive awareness that may facilitate centering. The pattern making process must be distinguished clearly from the transmission of preformed patterns to the individual. Although cultural substance can never be formless by definition, the emphasis placed upon the nature of the individual encounter is critical. Thus, pattern making would emphasize the creative and personal ordering of cultural data as the individual engaged in activity.

Playing. The attitude and activity of play is a critical aspect of the pattern-making process. Play in this sense refers to playing with ideas, things, and other people. To engage in the encounter with cultural substance in a playful manner provides the individual with a self-regulating potentiality. Playfulness is at the service of the individual and frees persons to order and create without the necessity of constant attention and direction of the adult world. Thus, the process of "playing" would seem to be necessary to facilitate pattern making and to provide for self-regulation of activity.

Meditative Thinking. "Why" is the fundamental thought question for a transcendental ideology, in the sense of examining the fundamental meaning of things. Technical or calculative thinking, so central to our society, is built into the very pores of our social skin. To facilitate centering in the individual we must encourage meditative thinking. Rather than fostering the activity of thought in a functional, utilitarian way, a problem-solving process, we must foster what Martin Heidegger called a "releasement toward things" and an "openness to the mystery."[18] Thus, nothing can be accepted simply on its own terms in its social utility. Rather, we must encourage the young to say both yes and no to culture and probe the ground from which our culture arises, through meditative thinking.

Imagining. Another way of approaching pattern making, play, and meditative thinking comes through the activity of imagining—imagining as a process in contrast to verbalizing. Our verbal culture and language culture and language forms, as useful and necessary as they are, have also become the dominant form of thinking and expressing ourselves. The danger of this one-sided verbal emphasis is the constant externalizing of meaning, of coming to name the object and manipulate external reality. Imagining on the contrary provides an internal referent for the external world. The work of Rudolf Steiner[19] and the Waldorf Schools provides considerable insight into this process. Steiner emphasizes the technique of presenting knowledge to the child first through his own imagination and only later following up with empirical observation. In essence the individual first forms his own images of encounters as he listens or actively creates. Thus, imagination as the ability to picture in the mind what is not present to the senses is a perceptual power that involves the whole person, that puts him in contact with the ground of his being.

The aesthetic principle. It is clear that the guidance of much of the arrangement of physical facilities, interpersonal facilities, interpersonal relations, and individual expression must come from what Herbert Read[20] called the aesthetic principle. Read called the guidance of human education by the aesthetic principle the natural form of education. The preadolescent education of individuals, Read argued, should move from feeling to drama, sensation to visual and plastic design, intuition to dance and music, and thought to craft. Then, from the play of children emerging from their feelings, sensations, intuitions, and thinking, the individual could gradually grow toward cultural art forms guided by the aesthetic principle. Thus, the activities of dramatization, designing, dancing, playing music, and making or crafting are important in a transcendental ideology.

The body and our biology. Physical education, Alan Watts has said, is "the fundamental discipline of life."[21] Watts, however, did not mean the games and skills of the traditional curriculum. Rather, he meant coming to grips with our own biological being and all that it means. Thus, he was able to propose that learning to husband plants and animals for food, how to cook, how to make clothes and build houses, how to dance and breathe, how to do yoga for finding one's true center, and how to make love were examples of this discipline. Although we rarely admit to a mind-body separation on a philosophical level, it is clear by the way we educate the young that we do not consider the biological aspects of the person to be relevant to the real business of education. Thus, the emphasis upon cognitive-verbal learning not only separates us from our inner resources but it divorces us from our biological organism. To be at home in our bodies is critical for human centering, and it would seem to me that far more attention should be paid to this phenomenon. It is interesting that the field of biofeedback is growing today. Thus, the use of machines to provide a conscious awareness of bodily functions, such as heartbeats or brain waves, may help to develop an integrated knowledge of the phenomena of our existence. It is perfectly reasonable to propose that the school curriculum processes may come to provide us with avenues for knowing ourselves as biological entities. Again, I would not claim biological and body knowledge as an end in itself. What I would say is that, in the centering of the human being, the awareness of "who I am" and "what my biological and physical potential are" are necessary avenues for the long-range development of the centering process.

The education of perception. This is the final area that needs exploring here. I refer to perception in the sense of William James's many other worlds of consciousness that exist aside from our present one, rather than in the sense of a functional psychological mechanism. The most impressive and exciting recent work in this area comes from an anthropologist—Carlos Castaneda's[22] fascinating trilogy, in which he relates his experiences with the old Indian medicine man. I am not sure what the implications of this work are, but I am sure that the creation of altered states of consciousness is a human potential that is important to the process of centering.

The Teacher In The Process

The developmental ideology of Dewey, Piaget, and others, as described by Kohlberg and Mayer perceives the teacher to be a person who comes to know the students but who also makes judgements about the long-range implications of experiences on the development of the children. So far as it goes, then, it is not incompatible with a transcendental developmental ideology. A transcendental ideology would, however, define this process in a different manner.

The teacher from a transcendental point of view is also in process. That is, the developmental aim of centering is as valid and important to the person of the teacher as it is to the child. Thus, the teacher does not "stand back" in a judgmental stance in the same manner. Rather, the teacher is immersed in the process of centering from her own point of view. Thus, the relationships between students and teachers are mutually responsive to the aim of centering.

The key distinction between these two developmental ideologies is the fundamental difference between knowing and understanding. In a secular or psychological developmental ideology, knowing the child, knowing his developmental status, and knowing the long-range developmental goals are essentially explicit cognitive acts. They are dependent upon being once removed from the children in a judgmental stance. This implies a maturity that is static in its essence, an end point which only the teacher has access to and only the teacher has arrived at. Thus, the predominant rationality of the teacher is still a technical process of planning, manipulating, and calculating, even though the intentions and relationships are, for example, more humane, perhaps, than those found in cultural transmission ideology. A transcendental ideology would shift the predominant rationality toward the aesthetic, intuitive, and spontaneous in the mutual process of centering.

Children learning and teachers teaching are fundamentally dependent upon the tacit dimension. Explicit awareness or knowledge of each other and of teaching or learning tasks is embedded in a tacit realm that provides the ground for understanding, for making activity meaningful. Teachers cannot be said to understand children simply because they possess a considerable amount of explicit knowledge about them. Understanding is a deeper concept. It demands a sort of indwelling in the other, a touching of the sources of the other. Understanding others is not a "useful" procedure in the sense that knowing is, in that it does not provide the basis for planning, manipulating, and calculating. Understanding provides the grounds for relating, for being fully there in the presence and as a presence to the other. The explicit knowledge of child development or of specific children may facilitate our understanding of them if it is internalized and integrated into our inner self. It is, however, only one avenue toward understanding.

There is another path, much harder but more direct. This is the process of locating one's center in relation to the other: to "see" one's self and the other in relation to our centers of being; to touch and be touched by another in terms of something fundamental to our shared existence.

This act of relationship, called understanding, is only known after the fact. "*Now*, I understand!" It is an act of listening, but not to the explicit content that a person is expressing. Rather, it is "tuning in" to the "vibrations" of bodily rhythms, feeling tone, inward expressions of a person's attempts to integrate and to maintain his integrity as a whole person.

Explicit content may facilitate this process, but often it creates a cognitive dissonance, an interference with really listening to the center of the person. We can easily be led away from this center by the way in which the other's explicitness reflects upon our own needs for centering. This interference raises barriers in ourselves to understanding, and shuts down our own expression of our being. So much of the explicit expression of cognition is really no more than dignified "cocktail chatter." Whether it is the weather, religion, sex education, politics, another person's foibles and problems, or the latest gossip does not matter.

Dialogue is different. Explicit cognitive expressions are oriented in dialogue toward creating something from the inner resources of two or more people. It is entered into with the intent of listening, and listening beneath the surface. The hope is that out of the explicit dialogue the creative inner workings of the participants will be freed and combined. Short of dialogue, even the expression of ideas, of philosophical or religious truths, of psychological insights, is often in the service of the cognitive ego of the participants. Dialogue does not just occur in a face-to-face relation; it can take place for the person through reading a book, or even, heaven forbid, listening to a talk on curriculum theory. Inner verbal and visual activities are possible without direct interaction.

Problem solving as a vehicle for a progressive interactive method in this context, on the other hand, necessitates the introduction of social power structures in order to facilitate activity. Thus, when development is based upon problem-solving schema, the orientation of activity is externalized, and it necessitates the organization of human activity into a social power structure. It further implies that development is a process of mastering the outer world through solutions by problem-solving methods of intelligence. When centering is the main process in relationships, problems are not always solved. As centering evolves, some problems disappear, still others become redefined, and some are solved in a sense of bringing to bear the unity of self through thought, feeling, and action.

Psychoanalysis, one supposes, is a recognition of the phenomena of inner meaning in each person. Yet as valuable as the process may be, the difference in the ability of psychologists to help others lies mainly in their ability to listen and understand, not in terms of their cognitive developmental theories but in interpreting the explicit data of the other as symbolic or in getting individuals to solve their own problems. The successful psychoanalyst is probably one who listens and reveals his own centeredness, who helps the patient gather his own inner resources for centering by *being* and revealing, by listening and responding, by offering and receiving.

Implicit understanding is to poetry as explicit knowledge is to science. The explicitness of science is in contrast to the unity and expressiveness of poetry. Science "adds up"; poetry integrates. It is becoming less clear to scientists whether explicit knowledge even "adds up," not at least until we have made a poem of the other in our own being. When we make a poem of the other in ourselves, we do not trap either in categories and classes. When we understand each other, we create a shared poem of our existence. Understanding is the crystallization of our aesthetic knowing; explicit knowledge is its rational handmaiden. To know a child is to describe his characteristics; to understand him is to be able to write a poem that captures his essence.

The teacher in such a process is, therefore, engaged in the art of living. The task of both student and teacher is the development of their own centering through contact with culture and society, bringing as much of their whole selves as they can to bear upon the process. There is no specifiable set of techniques or of rules or of carefully defined teaching roles. It is primarily a willingness to "let go" and to immerse oneself in the process of living with others in a creative and spontaneous manner, having faith in ourselves, others, and the culture we exist in as a medium for developing our own centering.

In concluding, I would like to clear up one possible misconception about the processes of curriculum and teaching leading toward centering in the educational ideology of transcendence. These processes are not haphazard; nor do they operate upon the romantic notion of the natural unfolding of the child. I quote from Mary Caroline Richards:

> It is a terrible thing when a teacher gives the impression that he does not care what the child does. It is false and it is unfaithful. The child hopes that an adult will have more sense and more heart than that. The teacher therefore seeks to understand what the child hungers for in the life of his imagination, his mind, his senses, his motion, his will. This means that he (the teacher) does not take things at their face value, but sees elements in relation to a lifetime process of deep inner structures.[23]

Notes

1. Lawrence Kohlberg and Rochelle Mayer, "Development As the Aim of Education," *Harvard Educational Review* 42, No. 4 (November 1972), pp. 449–496.

2. Paulo Freire, *Pedagogy of the Oppressed* (New York: Herder and Herder, 1970), p. 186.

3. Peter Berger, *A Rumor of Angels* (Garden City, NY: Doubleday Anchor Books, 1969), p. 10.

4. Herbert Marcuse, *An Essay on Liberation* (Boston: Beacon Press, 1969), p. 91, and *One Dimensional Man: Studies in the Ideology of Advanced Industrial Societies* (Boston: Beacon Press, 1964).

5. C.G. Jung, *The Basic Writings of C.G. Jung*, V.S. De Lazlo, ed. (New York: Modern Library, 1959), p. 544.

6. William James, *Varieties of Religious Experience* (New York: New American Library, 1958), p. 396; John Wild, *The Radical Empiricism of William James* (Garden City, NY: Doubleday Anchor Books, 1970), p. 420.

7. James, *Varieties of Religious Experience*, p. 388.

8. *Ibid.*, p. 391.

9. Michael Polanyi, *The Tacit Dimension* (Garden City, NY: Doubleday Anchor Books, 1967), p. 99.

10. *Ibid.*, p. 20.

11. Arthur Koestler, *The Roots of Coincidence* (New York: Random House, 1972), p. 158.

12. Sir James Jeans, *The Mysterious Universe* (Cambridge, England: Cambridge University Press, 1937), p. 172.

13. Koestler, *Roots of Coincidence*, p. 140.

14. Olexa-Myron Bilanvik and E.C. George Sudarshan, "Particles Beyond the Light Barrier," *Physics Today* (May 1969), pp. 43–51.

15. Mary Caroline Richards, *Centering* (Middletown, CN: Wesleyan University Press, 1962).

16. Lawrence Kubie, "Protecting Preconscious Functions," in *Nurturing Individual Potential* (Washington, DC: A.S.C.D., 1963).

17. Colin Wilson, *New Pathways in Psychology* (New York: Taplinger Publishing Co., 1972), p. 289.

18. Martin Heidegger, *Discourse on Thinking* (New York: Harper and Row, 1966), p. 93.

19. Rudolf Steiner, *The Essentials of Education* (London: Rudolf Steiner Publishing Co., 1968).

20. Herbert Read, *Education Through Art* (London: Faber and Faber, 1956), p. 308.

21. Alan Watts, *In My Own Way* (New York: Pantheon Books, 1972).

22. E.g., Carlos Casteneda, *Journeys with Don Juan* (New York: Simon and Schuster, 1969).

23. Richards, *Centering*, pp. 101–102.

Chapter Five

Curriculum and Human Interests

Gunnar Myrdal posed the basic problem in relation to social science that I wish to deal with in this essay in relation to curriculum thinking. He focused on the methodological problem of how to maintain objectivity.

In the process he asked specifically how can the student of social problems (and I am convinced we may read "student of curriculum" here) liberate himself from three pervasive influences:

> (1) the powerful heritage of earlier writings in his field of inquiry, ordinarily containing normative and teleological notions inherited from past generations and founded upon the metaphysical moral philosophies of natural law and utilitarianism from which all our social and economic theories have branched off; (2) the influences of the entire cultural, social, economic, and political milieu of the society where he lives, works, and earns his living and status; and (3) the influence stemming from his own personality, as molded not only by traditional and environmental but also by his own individual history, constitution, and inclinations.[1]

In the field of curriculum we have been fussing about with the problem of values and perspectives for some time. Ubblelohde's dissertation is an example of the recognition of the importance of this problem.[2] He has attempted to analyze curriculum theorizing from an axiological viewpoint. It is clear from this analysis that curriculum thinkers have been unaware of the different levels and kinds of value perspectives that are involved in curriculum thinking.

Recognition of value concerns in curriculum can be illustrated in terms of the designs that have arisen when priorities are established among the basic referents of curriculum. Thus, subject matter curricula are sets of value judgements that prize knowledge (cultural heritage) over social uses or personal interests. Problems of living designs prize society first; and emerging needs proposals have individual welfare primarily in mind.

At another level the justification of curriculum decisions also reflects value commitments. Different value positions result in describing curriculum variables in different patterns (or even different variables). This can be illustrated easily with the four basic psychological positions one may take. It makes a considerable difference in curriculum decisions whether one is a behaviorist, a gestaltist, a psychoanalyst, or a third force psychologist (self-realization). These are value positions that affect curriculum thinking.

Ubblelohde, for example, concludes among other things that curriculum theory is essentially an attempt to construct a theory of values, whereas curriculum designs are patterns of value judgements. The task of justifying the curriculum design is not completed simply by making the judgement.

Goodlad and Richter[3] appear to recognize something of this sort when they examine the decision-making process in the Tyler rationale and suggest that values must be clearly identified before the specification of objectives rather than used as screens in the decision-making process.

Thus, there are two levels of value that I wish to focus on as illustrations at this time (recognizing, as Ubblelohde demonstrates, that there are still other relevant value levels); and these are problems of value at the theory and design levels. I shall refer to these two levels as: (1) structural perspectives; and (2) rational values.

At the level of structural perspectives it appears that we approach the world or mediate reality through fundamental perceptual structures. Thus, the implication that it is possible to deal with curriculum as a purely objective descriptive phenomenon is apparently a naive wish rather then a real possibility. Instead, we are from the outset asserting a stance or an orientation even at so fundamental a level as our perceptual orientations to curriculum phenomena.

In another way, this level of structural perspectives may be at a level of meta-ethics where we discuss the character of the value judgements at the rational level, and where we dispute the applicability of these judgements to curriculum. It is, however, already a stance that has value components.

Thus, for example, we may dispute the adequacy of a given curriculum design on the grounds that it does not meet the criteria of good design, or we may dispute the criteria that another uses to examine a specific design. In either case we have implicit orientations involved which ground our logical activities. Perhaps these groundings are in a kind of tacit knowledge, as Polanyi talks about it;[4] but it is a personal knowledge that is more than cognitive in its content.

When we move to the level of curriculum designs the value components are even more obvious. It is clear that adherents to such supposed curriculum designs as "disciplines," or "interdisciplinary studies," or "person-centered," are basing and deriving considerable direction from value positions they hold. Thus, values appear clearly here as the source of objectives and as determinants of significant elements to account for in the curriculum design. As previously mentioned, Goodlad and Richter recognize the problem and suggest procedures to improve the "Tyler" model.[5]

It is clear that curriculum theorists or designers have not clarified the problems of value. It is probably primarily this failure that gives curriculum thinking such a diverse and circular character. We are often, for example, talking at different value levels and thus miss the whole point of each other's thinking. But it has not clearly been realized that the most fundamental level—structural perspectives—is also grounded in a value matrix of some sort. Thus, people have either assumed that we all shared the same basic perspective, or that you simply could not communicate with certain other persons.

This fundamental realization that we are all not working out of the same basic structures (or metaphors, if you wish) and that it is not sufficient simply to reason together for everything to become clarified and agreeable leaves us with the fundamental problem of objectivity noted by Myrdal. I would like to present a possible conceptual solution for clarifying and communicating among ourselves and for stimulating curriculum activity. At this point I am primarily in search of understanding for myself but optimistic that some progress is possible within the conceptual orientation I shall propose.

Knowledge and Human Interests

During the past year I have discovered a book that might have been written specifically for me at this time; that is, it spoke to me as only a few books can in a lifetime. This is probably an example of what J. McV. Hunt calls "the problem of the match." Somehow the cultural content and my personal interests and reading were "matched." At any rate, the book, by Jürgen Habermas, is called *Knowledge and Human Interest*.[6] I should like to summarize briefly the concepts proposed by Habermas and discuss these in terms of curriculum. At this point, I feel that these ideas could provide a basis for greatly improving our understanding of the problems of curriculum.

Habermas sets forth the basic proposition that knowledge cannot be divorced from human interest. He attempts to deal at length with crucial persons and ideas that demonstrate how the scientific aura of the nineteenth and twentieth centuries have resulted in a substitution of concern for a theory of knowledge by the concern for a philosophy of science. Thus, we have come to think that knowledge is derived only by empirical analytical means and that other sources of knowledge are misleading. He reminds us of Nietzsche's remark that what distinguished the nineteenth century from previous ones was not the victory of science but the victory of the scientific method *over* science.

Knowledge, in a scientific sense, has become a product of an empirical-analytical methodology. The circumstance or grounding of methodology is ignored. Where did the methodology come from, and why did it arise? Is this an example of pure random, historical trial and error learning? Habermas thinks not and I am inclined to agree with him.

On the contrary, people have historically considered knowledge to have a broad base in what are now known as the arts and sciences. It is only the positivistic methodology of science that has misled us into denying the knowledge base of the arts. Habermas distinguishes between these two as the *monologic* and *hermeneutic* understanding of meaning.

By monologic he means the abstraction of facts from value and the creation of theory explaining facts in an empirical-analytical fashion. The process of verification is a linear one called, variously, for example, education, induction, or abduction. A formalized language (e.g., calculus) is used to facilitate objectivity.

Hermeneutic understanding of meaning arises in the context of different cultural life expressions such as ordinary language, human actions, and nonverbal expressions. All of these experiences carry symbolic meanings, which, however, need a dialogic interpretation rather than monologic verification. The methodology is circular rather than linear in that the interpretation of meaning in hermeneutic understanding depends on a reciprocal relation between "parts" and a diffusely preunderstood "whole" and the correlation of the preliminary concept by means of the parts. It is a method that discovers the empirical content of individuated conditions of life while investigating grammatical structures.

Habermas further argues that hermeneutic understanding has fallen prey to objectivistic tendencies, in that historians, for example, have labored under the illusion that the facts are separate from the values and ground of activity. The trouble with both modes is that they have divorced themselves from self-reflection; for objectivism deludes the knower by projecting an image of a self-subsisting world of facts structured in a law-like manner, and thus conceals the a priori constitutions of these facts. The overriding concern for methodology that follows an objectivist stance hides from our self-reflection the ground and sources of the "facts," as Habermas notes, "representations and descriptions are never independent of standards. And the choice of these standards is based on attitudes that require critical consideration by means of arguments, because they cannot be either logically deduced or empirically demonstrated."[7]

Thus, Habermas proposes that an emergence in the nineteenth century of a self-reflective science will begin to transcend the problems of objectivism and scientism. He sees psychoanalysis as an exemplar case in illustration of a process of knowing that transcends the problem of monological and hermeneutic meaning.

Fundamental to the whole argument here is the assertion that all knowledge is grounded in human interest. This interest may be fundamental self-preservation, but even self-preservation cannot be defined independently of the cultural conditions of work, language, and power. Thus self-preservation becomes preservation of one's fantasy of the "good life." Thus, the mortality of human interest enters as a meaning structure served by knowledge and nicely caught by Bertrand Russell's comment "without civic morality communities perish, without personal morality their survival has no value." In either case knowledge is at the service of our interests.

There are, then, if Habermas' analysis is valid, three fundamental cognitive human interests that are the ground for knowledge. They are (1) a technical cognitive interest in control underlying the empirical-analytic approach; (2) a practical cognitive interest in consensus underlying the hermeneutic-historical approach; and (3) a critical cognitive interest in emancipation or liberation underlying the self-reflective approach.

I think an understanding of these three basic interests can be usefully and insightfully applied to the analysis of problems related to the knowledge of curriculum and curriculum thinking. But before examining this proposition, I should like to return to the third interest, the critical cognitive interest and its self-reflective methodology since this is the more recent conceptual emergent.

The objectivist stance toward both monological and hermeneutical knowledge tends to separate the knower from the known and facts from values. Objectivists see theoretical cause-effect relationships or practical means-ends continuities. Neither of these serve a critical interest, since both accept the status quo as descriptively given and as separate from the knower. But the history of mankind is tied to the "good life," which is a fundamental interest related to the degree of emancipation that historically is objectively possible under given manipulable conditions. It is, in other words, an interest in *overcoming causes* and *redefining means-ends relationships* as social conventions in the service of persons.

The methodology of this approach is self-reflective. Thus, using psychoanalysis as an example, one begins with a metapsychological construct that, though not empirically verifiable, does provide a systematically generalizable schema that accounts for the history of infantile development with typical variations.

This allows the analyst to make interpretive suggestions for a story the patient cannot tell. However, these suggestions can be verified only if the patient adopts them and tells his own story with their aid. In this methodology the object of inquiry participates in the inquiry process via self-application of general ideas. Generally, this methodology (1) provides a general scheme for many histories or particulars with alternatives; (2) must be validated by self-reflection but cannot be refuted this way; and (3) has explanatory power in overcoming "causes" (rather than explicating them).

Curriculum and Human Interests

Although there is a great deal more that could and should be said about knowledge and human interests, moving into some possible meanings for curriculum seems more provident at this time.

I hope this discussion of knowledge and human interests will provide a setting for getting at the problem of value in curriculum thinking. The applicability of concerns about knowledge to curriculum concerns should be obvious, since knowledge about curriculum is not only part of our total knowledge, but also is composed of the very knowledge, knowers, and processes of knowing that we are concerned about. Thus, the application of ideas from a theory of knowledge is a fundamental activity of curriculum thinking.

My basic proposition about curriculum is that at all levels and specifically at what I called the structural perspectives and rational values level (curriculum theory and design), the basic phenomena that underlies all activity is the existence of human interest that precedes and channels the activity of curriculum thinking.

The second proposition, following from the same source, is that three basic cognitive interests—(1) control, (2) consensus, and (3) emancipation—may be seen as the basic sources of value differences in curriculum.

Providing the evidence necessary to test these propositions necessitates a lengthy and laborious process that has not yet been completed. At this time it seems only reasonable to touch possible areas for further exploration.

At the level of structural perspectives in curriculum where our theorists describe the elements and variables with which we are concerned and set the ground rules for designing, we are perhaps most implicitly influenced by human interests coming through the forms described by Myrdal (i.e., tradition, environment, and personality).

After careful examination of twenty-six leading theorists Ubblelohde concluded that a categorization of their work at different levels was possible.[8] His argument is reasonably compelling to me and I suggest that we may select as examples for the brief examination possible here from his categories. At what I call the structural perspectives level this would include Virgil Herrick, Dwayne Huebner, Joseph Schwab, Alice Miel, Ivan Illich, and some of my own work. (This group is, of course, only as representative as the original sample of twenty-six theorists).

It is, I believe, possible to identify major structural perspectives shaped by dominant cognitive interests in many of these theorists. I shall try to illustrate this briefly with reference to Schwab, Illich, and Herrick. It should be noted that I am taking the liberty of inferring a general thrust and position for all three men through examination of some of their specific works.

It seems to me that Herrick illustrates as well as any theorist at this level a cognitive interest in control. That is, the social theory base of his work and the empirical thrust of his research are reflected in his two basic theoretical tasks: (1) defining the relevant elements or variables involved in curriculum; and (2) creating a system of decision making for curriculum designing.

Perhaps the best single statement of his position can be found in his chapter in *Toward Improved Curriculum Theory*, where he deals at length with both tasks.[9] It is clear that he had an overriding concern for cognitive forms that would make for more effective decision making in the development of curriculum designs.

Schwab, on the contrary, performs the interesting role of designing by theorizing that theory is useless or not possible in curriculum. At this fundamental value level Schwab would appear to be motivated by more practical means-ends cognitive interests in arriving at common consensus about the nature of education practice. Schwab's monograph dealing with the practical in curriculum goes to some lengths to propose (among other things) the above position and to urge a practical consensus by examining in detail what actually goes on in the classroom.[10]

When we move to Illich, we are in another realm of interest.[11] Illich would appear to be saying that his major thrust in the critical cognitive interest is in the emancipatory realm. He agrees that curriculum designs can be constructed from theory, but abhors the process as *control* in the service of a larger system that is oppressive. Thus, Illich would dissolve curriculum theory because of its control potential and develop a curriculum in a much less institutionalized or formalized basis.

Whether other theorists who could be identified might be so easily associated with the three major interests proposed here is difficult to say. I suspect not; the curriculum field may be likened to all growing persons, eventually the categories or the shoes pinch. However, it probably matters less whether anyone is pure in interest than whether the theorists know what interests they represent.

Moving to the level of rational values, or the curriculum design level, rather than dealing with individuals, I shall suggest that traditional types of designs reflect basic cognitive human interests. The corollary, again, will be only loosely fitted to the categories, but suggestive of the value base from which these designs arise.

Following from the idea of three basic referents for curriculum we have witnessed the development of curriculum designs that have been roughly classified as subject or discipline centered. Each of these, it is suggested, flows from a structural perspective that reflects a primacy of one of the three basic conjunctive interests.

The control interest has been mainly associated with the subject matter or disciplines approach. (For example, see Bloom, Bruner, etc.[12]) This has been most recently elaborated into a definition of structures of the disciplines, and modes of inquiry that have been defined in terms of behavioral objectives and programmed for individualized instruction. This process is a logical outcome of a fundamental interest in control of learning as an outcome of any curricula.

The problems of living or social issues design (for example, see Stratemeyer, et al.[13]) primarily reflect a fundamental interest in consensus, or resolution of conflicts between mutual social expectations. Solutions of problems are not given ahead of time, but it is expected that objective dialogue and study of these problems will lead to consensus on action. These designs reflect a practical concern for knowledge rather than the more theoretical concern of the discipline.

The third type of design, called person or child centered, or emerging needs, can most closely be associated with the emancipatory interest. Then the rhetoric of developing individual potential or fostering self-realization is embedded in a cognitive interest in freeing people from limitations and creating new conditions and environments. This fundamental interest shapes the implied values (as is also the case of each of the others) of the selections of variables, psychologies, ethical theories, and what have you, that goes into developing curriculum designs.

Thus, a cursory look at basic perspectives and design values suggests that the analysis projected by Habermas will clarify the problems of objectivity and source of values, which pervade curriculum thinking. The initial attempt to relate individual theorists and specific types of designs is promising, at least suggestive of future activity.

Illustrations of Value Orientations

As an illustration of the potential meaning of the ideas that have been presented, I should like to move to an action context in curriculum development. Thus, it appears to me that the application of values around three kinds of human interests lead to varying designs and to varying praxis.

The concept of praxis is a valuable one, especially when used as Paulo Freire does to mean action with reflection, in distinction from either reflection without action (intellectualism) or action without reflection (activism). Thus, curriculum development is seen as praxis or action with reflection.

What I shall briefly propose is that three different prominent models for development can be seen as related to the cognitive human interests of *control, consensus*, and *emancipation*. It is these fundamental human interests I propose that explain most of the variations in approach rather than some other sorts of empirical or rational criteria.

The three curriculum development models (proposed as exemplars or as ideal types) are: (1) the linear-expert model, (2) the circular consensus, and (3) the dialogical model.

Linear-Expert Model

A basic interest in control leads to a common linear-expert dominated model. Thus, the procedures employed most advantageously by the national curriculum projects in science and mathematics over the past fifteen years or so fit this model.

In very general terms, the projects are initiated by experts (usually in discipline areas), who begin by preparing materials to be tried out, fed back to the experts, rewritten and piloted, and then revised for broad distribution.

The central features of this procedure are expert domination of the process and the attempt to maximize control by aiming all feedback procedures at gaining the greatest possible amount of student achievement and teacher satisfaction. Thus, the whole process is controlled and monitored with specific goals in mind, and it is the experts who make the initial and final decisions about the validity of the content and process.

This approach, I may add in passing, finds its logical fruition in the behavioral objectives movement.

Circular Consensus Model

A second model might be likened to what used to be called "grass roots" curriculum development. Essentially what this approach sought to do was engage the local staff of schools in the clarification and specification of aspects of the curriculum (experts are on call).

This approach requires considerable faith in the use of group process and a conviction that unless teachers are centrally involved in the process of curriculum development, texts, documents and materials will be misused or relatively meaningless.

There is some rhetoric of control in this process, but it appears for purposes here that consensus and communication are more important outcomes in this process. Thus, the teachers, staff, and community participate and knowing appears central.

At present the community school curriculum development activities seem to be the direct outcome of this basic interest.

Dialogical Model

The third approach might best be called the dialogical model in the sense that it is out of a dialogical process that the curriculum emerges.

We in the United States do not have a great deal of experience with this model because it actively involves the student in curriculum development. Paulo Freire, on the other hand, has demonstrated this sort of model in literacy programs for South American peasants.

In general, this approach would follow from the idea that leaders (staff and other adults) would identify student leaders and with their help try to find major ways of providing a "match" between the cultural resources the adults know about and the needs and interests of students.

General curriculum themes or topics would be prepared by leaders who would engage students in dialogue, and the worth and direction of this material would be validated and verified by each student in his own self-reflection. The closest available illustration of this process would, I suppose, be some of the core curricula, or interdisciplinary activities.

Conclusion

What I have offered here might be generalized to all education much as Paul Goodman talks about progressive education. Goodman says that progressive education is a political movement. I suspect that in many ways all curriculum design and development is political in nature; that is, it is an attempt to facilitate someone else's idea of the good life by creating social processes and structuring an environment for learning.

Thus, objectivity is not simply the province of the science or control element of education. This approach also has a political position. (See, for example, John S. Mann and Michael Apple for insightful analyses of this theme).

Curriculum designing is thus a form of "utopianism," a form of political and social philosophizing and theorizing. If we recognize this, it may help us sort out our own thinking and perhaps increase our ability to communicate with one another.

What has been said here is offered in the spirit of an emancipatory interest. If the general scheme has meaning for individuals, each must use it within the self-reflective area of his own experiences and validate and/or verify it on that basis.

The kind of analysis offered here will not do away with disagreements, of course. But if this analysis has validity we may at least hope that understanding, if not agreement, will be enhanced among curriculum thinkers. It might also help bring curriculum thinking and development under a more rational scrutiny; if so, the ideals of Virgil Herrick will have been further enhanced.

Notes

1. Gunnar Myrdal, *Objectivity in Social Research* (New York: Random House, 1969), p. 3–4.

2. Robert Ubblelohde, "An Axiological Analysis of Curriculum Theory" (Ph.D. diss., University of Wisconsin - Milwaukee, July 1972).

3. John Goodlad and Maurice Richter, "The Development of a Conceptual System for Dealing With Problems in Curriculum and Instruction" (USOE Contract No. SAE-8024, Project No. 454, 1966); see Ralph Tyler, *Principles of Curriculum and Instruction* (Chicago: University of Chicago Press, 1950).

4. Michael Polanyi, *Personal Knowledge* (Chicago: University of Chicago Press, 1958).

5. Goodlad and Richter, "Development of a Conceptual System."

6. Jürgen Habermas, *Knowledge and Human Interest*, Jeremy J. Shapiro, trans. (Boston: Beacon Press, 1971).

7. *Ibid.*, p. 312.

8. Ubblelohde, "Axiological Analysis of Curriculum Theory."

9. Virgil Herrick, "The Concept of Curriculum Design," in *Toward Improved Curriculum Theory* (Chicago: University of Chicago Press, 1950), p. 37–50.

10. Joseph Schwab, "The Practical: A Language for Curriculum," in *Curriculum and the Cultural Revolution* (Berkeley, CA: McCutchan, 1973).

11. See, for example, Ivan Illich, "The Breakdown of the Schools: a Problem or a Symptom?," *Interchange* 1, no. 4 (1971).

12. Benjamin Bloom, "Mastery Learning and Its Implications for Curriculum Development," in *Confronting Curriculum Reform*, Elliot Eisner, ed. (Boston: Little, Brown, 1971), p. 17–48; Jerome Bruner, *The Process of Evaluation* (Boston: Harvard University Press, 1960).

13. Florence Stratemeyer et al., *Developing a Curriculum for Modern Living* (New York: Teachers College Press, Columbia University, 1957).

Chapter Six

The Quality of Everyday Life in Schools

Observation: The teacher was sitting with a group of eight children in a circle of small chairs. Each child was holding a reading book. The children took turns reading aloud to the teacher. She corrected and encouraged them. More often than not, the children had to be told where they were supposed to be reading when it was their turn.

In another part of the room nine children were copying a handwriting lesson off the board. There was considerable commotion in this area; especially a great deal of movement and low-toned talking. Three children seemed absorbed in work.

The third group of ten had been given work sheets with structural analysis tasks. They were asked to make new words out of double vowels such as "oo"; and work on endings such as "er," "ing," and "s." Most had either finished quickly and were waiting for further directions, or they had not bothered to do it.

Comment: The actual observation above does not seem unusual in terms of the general quality of existence observed at many levels of schooling over the years. Fundamentally, the hour was characterized by routine, boredom, and busywork. I have often asked teachers why they waste their own and children's lives dealing with trivia and meaningless tasks. I have even accused them of being immoral for doing so! My attitude was summed up by a well meaning principal friend of mine who asked, "How can I change the perspective of my teachers?"

I was wrong, and so was he. We should have been asking, "Who *really* makes the decisions, and in whose interest are these boring, routine, and busywork decisions made?"

Everyday Life[1] and Meaning

We live in a modern society which is fundamentally characterized by technology and bureaucracy with an economically consumer-oriented ethic. But society is not simply structures acting upon passive individuals, it creates a concomitant consciousness in individuals which then acts back upon society. It is the kind of modern consciousness that is being developed in schools through everyday life experiences that I wish to explore here.

Consciousness in this context does not refer to the curricular learnings the school intends. The consciousness of everyday life is more tacit or pre-theoretical. It is as Berger says, "the web of meanings that allow the individual to navigate his way through the ordinary events and encounters of his life with others."[2]   In toto, they make up his social life-world.

The school is not a primary carrier of the modern consciousness, but along with the mass media serves as a major transmitter of consciousness derived from the primary sources. "Through school curricula, motion pictures, and television, advertising of all sorts. . . the population is continuously bombarded with ideas, imagery, and models of conduct that are intrinsically connected with technological production."[3]

Technological Production

There is a press for technological rationality in the function of the schools. This concept results in attempts to order the nature of teaching functions around the idea that there is a large body of educational knowledge which is potentially available to school staffs, but is organized around a hierarchy of experts. The teachers' activity is seen as a participation in a large organization and as part of the sequence (grade, unit, etc.) of production.

Implicit in this scheme are ideas, such as teacher competency, which suggest that teachers are potentially interchangeable, that productive activity may be learned and performed mechanistically, and that any "good" teaching act is reproducible by another teacher. And, finally, that all teaching is measurable in terms of the criteria of accountability in use.

The acceptance of this orientation demands that teachers view their work in compartments. Each discipline must be seen separately and each step in the teaching "plan" capable of being broken down and analyzed; then reassembled in a sequentially rational pattern or sequence.

Means and ends are separated also. Since the "knowledge and skills" passed on to students may go into the production of a doctor, a lawyer, a mechanic, or a housewife, the teacher is still capable of performing his or her function without knowing the long-range ends in mind.

Thus, teaching becomes implicitly abstract, that is, it is based upon a frame of reference that is not directly related to the ongoing uniqueness of everyday life in the classroom, or even to the long-range goals of "production." The "Tyler rationale" is one such abstract decision model: (a) specify objectives in behavioral terms; (b) select activities; (c) organize the activities; (d) evaluate outcomes.

Thus, work for teachers and students is seen as segregated from their private lives. This fractional consciousness not only puts a premium on seeing specific students (and their learning) in terms of problems to be solved, but creates the kind of innovation we have lately experienced as "tinkering." The frame of reference is abstract and not related directly to everyday living.

Social relationships tend to become anonymous and a split in individuals' identities develops. Individuals come to experience themselves in a dual manner: as a private and unique person and as a public functionary. Considerable internal psychological management then becomes necessary and the existence of discipline problems may be largely due to the constant press and struggle to maintain an appropriate dual identity (on the part of either or both teacher and student).

Thus, emotional management and control becomes extremely important with priority placed upon passive, controlled behavior, acceptant and even-keeled. Then students are incapable of managing their own emotions (that is, split their public and private lives), so the teacher must spend considerable time doing so.

Technological consciousness also leads to prizing optimum growth, or maximum efficiency and effectiveness, the greatest amount of learning in the shortest period of time. This in turn enters the consciousness of students and teachers and helps shape their self-concept in terms of their relative place in this scheme of things.

Bureaucratic Social Relations

Given a technological orientation, there is an imperative directive to follow out the above kinds of procedures and enter into the modern consciousness of technocracy. Bureaucracy on the other hand does not have the same imperative. Bureaucracy is not intrinsic to a particular goal. Thus, it is possible to witness the displacement of the school's goals for learning by the functioning of the organizational bureaucracy. School bureaucracies may easily become self-serving. The arbitrariness of much bureaucracy means that contrary to the technological orientation, "production" is not necessarily the major goal.

Thus, schools are political organizations as well as technical producers. The "school" may in fact be almost entirely a politically oriented organization. If this were the case the "school" may actually subvert the technical achievements of learning most efficiently and effectively. The cry for "teacher-free" materials and "deschooling" can be seen as the effects of bureaucracy upon schooling.

The fact of the matter is that schools do exist, they are bureaucracies, and they deflect or support, as the case may be, the general technological consciousness.   In the process they create further aspects of the modern consciousness which pervade everyday life.

The bureaucracy of the school deals essentially with the social relations (rather than the technical acts) of the organization. The two are, of course, not unrelated, but any person who has worked with preservice teachers (and many in-service people) will be quick to note that the two overriding concerns of these teachers are "How to teach" (methodology of technology) and "How to manage" (control and organize the social relations in the classroom). In a very real sense these two major concerns reflect the deeply embedded modern consciousness which teachers-to-be have picked up from our modern technological and bureaucratic society.

Bureaucracy creates its own form of knowledge and this knowledge relates to, for example, the definition of roles and status, appropriate agencies, procedures of referral, proper procedures per se, and avenues of redress. Thus, students and staff, in and out of classrooms, must "learn" the rules, procedures, norms, policies, statuses, of the school above and beyond the tasks of technical achievement.

Order becomes the overriding element of bureaucracy. But contrary to the analytical order of production, bureaucratic order is essentially "classificatory." Categorization of students by ability, grade level, unit level, etc., are obvious elements of this phenomenon. The results of ability grouping (in technical terms) are clear indications (that is, generally no significant differences) that the categorization serves primarily bureaucratic order needs and not technical achievement goals.

Bureaucracies are set up to serve clients, not produce "goods." As such the workers of the bureaucracy (school staff members) are always "active," whereas clients (students) are mostly "passive." Thus, in encountering school bureaucracy the student encounters a general sense of impotence that is not present in his or her later work experience.

Thus, in bureaucracies, in contrast to pure technical production situations, the bureaucrat (teacher) and the client (student) have different goals and problems rather than different perspectives on the same goals. This is a fairly critical distinction that has often been overlooked by educational psychology. The teacher's problem is not "how students learn and develop," as useful as this knowledge should be, but how to construct effective and orderly activities within which students learn and develop. The actual learning and developing are the students' "problems." If the student were not also a living agent in the process the bureaucratic structure could be eliminated and only the goal of the producer (teacher) would be relevant.

Because "desired" relationships are paramount, bureaucracy has a distinctively moral quality that is not apparent in technocracy. The moral quality, however, is an anonymous one, not a personal one. Thus, the axiom of equality among persons within their bureaucratic categories is an axiom of bureaucratic ethics. Further, means are not separable from ends in the bureaucracy of schooling. A student who gets the "right" answer with the "wrong" method, for example, is not appreciated for this achievement.

Consumer Consciousness

The third major characteristic of modern consciousness facilitated by schools is the concern and indeed demand for consumption. The knowledge and skills we produce are made available through bureaucratized social relations for the primary purpose of student consumption. What this entails is a massive publicity operation and a concerted legitimization of the "goods" of schooling. The student by and large does not see the personal need in everyday life for much of what the curriculum deals with. Thus, we psychologize the problem as one of motivation, which results in an analogous function of public legitimization of relatively unneeded "goods," similar to the advertising industry.

Consumption then becomes in schools the substitute for production in real life. What is consumed eventually is the student, not in flesh and blood, but in living time. Thus, it is not difficult to see the consumption of six hours a day for twelve years of a student's life is the act of consuming what are essentially imaginary "goods, that is, abstractions of life rather than productive realities.

This constant consumption has its corollary generalization in the consciousness of the modern person. The act of consumption becomes a good in and of itself, a criterion of worth and "living." What is lost is the consciousness of everyday life in its active, creative, and productive vitality.

Critique to What End?

Decisions about schooling, its form, program, curriculum, in structures and activity, are social policy decisions. They are in fact not appreciably different from legislative acts in their intent. In both cases we assume that the decision will improve the quality of life of the society in some appreciable manner and toward some valued end. Thus, legislative action which makes the Equal Rights Amendment into law is no different in kind (although level and degree obviously vary) than a school system policy decision to remove textbooks which display sexist attitudes or to provide equal funds for girls' athletic programs. Both are (legislative and school policy) social policy decision areas. Thus, school critique is critique of social policy decisions and it is imperative that the end or standard of a critique be made explicit.

The end which I propose as the standard of critique is the quality of everyday living in the schools. This is equivalent to saying that what one needs is essentially a cultural revolution and that economic and political arrangements are key variables or means toward those ends.

In schools the analogy to broader economic variables is related to such things as the curriculum, social access to learning, equitable allotments of materials, personnel, and resources. The "economy" of the school is mirrored in the learning tasks (work) and all its contributing factors. This often is the realm of the technical.

Political processes in the schools are analogous to party politics, law, and access to power in decision making. In schools it is reflected in the politics, management practices, patterns of interpersonal relationships, and social control mechanisms. The "politics" of the school is most often the realm of the bureaucratic.

Yet changing the "economy" or the "politics" of the school is only a public means toward the end of a change in the cultural conditions and private quality of life. If these are seen as ends in themselves they tend toward polarizing ideologies and change takes on a tendency toward "inversion." Thus, the swings back and forth in curriculum innovation over the past century appear to be due to mistaking the "economic" and "political" as innovative ends rather than analytical and practical means of reaching a higher quality of existence, through reuniting the public and private aspects of living.

This is true, I would argue, in Western society at large, where Socialist doctrine (originally grounded in a *social*-ism) aimed at making the quality of one's social existence as humanly fulfilling as possible but which has been short-circuited by Socialist acceptance of change in public economic policy and political control as the ends, rather than reintegration of the public and private realms through social change. Thus, we tend to see the same technological and bureaucratic domination of everyday life in, for example, both Russia and the United States. Somewhere along the line the means have become the ends. The Western democratic processes and capitalist economics and Western Communist party processes and socialist economics are in neither case sufficient as ends in themselves. They are only valid and meaningful as they contribute to the quality of cultural experience—of everyday living. Both "worlds" may be faulted heavily for destroying everyday living reality. That they are more similar in this respect than different is readily seen in the policy of "détente"—a reflection of the easy movement of technical and bureaucratic consciousness and meaning between the two worlds.

Loss of Personal Living in Schooling

The source of meaning of the schools in society and the source of meaning for persons engaged in schooling resides in the human activity that takes place in school. We have for too long paid attention to the rhetoric of goals, objectives, and product assessment as if these statements or measurements reflected the fundamental meaning.

That this is not so is now patently clear. Meaning resides within persons regardless of the societal traditions, social conditions, or verbalized goals. Traditions, conditions, and goals are merely boundaries and directives that enter into the shaping of activity, they do not represent the meaning of activity itself. If we are to understand the meaning of the schools we must search for the social meaning of the human activity that takes place there; and if we wish to examine the meaning implications of schooling we must look at the personal activity of people in the schools.

This is not necessarily the same thing as saying that "we learn by doing" or that "all learning is experientially based." The concern here is not for learning in its traditional sense, but for the development and/or explication of meaning structures in human consciousness which are inherent in the activity itself and not necessarily what is learned from that activity.

Let us look first at the activity in the schools in our society and then move toward reflection on the social and personal meanings of that activity.

Activity in schools, according to Philip Jackson,[4] may be characterized by the phenomena of (a) unequal power, (b) living in groups or crowds, and (c) evaluative or judgmental qualities in relation to activity and rewards.

What this in effect means is that all school activity is controlled by the staff, in the sense that even the power to let students exercise control is given to them by teachers or other staff. Further, it means that all activity has a social meaning. Every activity has implicit connective tissue among the people engaged in schooling. And, still further, all activity is constantly being evaluated and judged in process through the normative threads of at least three kinds: (a) the effect of activity on others; (b) the desired direction of activity in terms of those who control; (c) and "objective" utility of the patterns by which activity is shaped. Thus, the major concerns of teachers are easily understood as discipline (or control), methodology, and content: (a) how to control the social behavior of the students; (b) how to teach it; and (c) what to teach. Thus, schools pattern activity, direct its flow, and monitor the social relationships within the process.

At this level of analysis it makes little if any difference what the substantive nature of the activity might be, for example, arithmetic or music; it is the formative character of the activity that guides the development, the personal meaning, and the interpretation of its social meaning. Thus, if we are to understand what school "means," socially and personally, we must understand the formative quality of the activity that takes places there, not simply the substantive learning outcomes of this activity.[5]

It is in fact the phenomena of school activity that are the primary justification for having schools at all. If the substantive quantity of learning were the primary concern, we have within our technical power a variety of ways to transmit knowledge and develop skills. In fact, we could most likely with certain creative rationalization such as Illich's Learning Webs, cable TV, or community learning centers, do a better and more equitable job of the substantive learning than is now attempted in schools.

The activity in and of the school is not neutral. The activity embodies the quality of experience which infuses and symbolizes meaning rather than the quantity of learning; and as school people we have tended to accept our practice in a framework of technical neutrality. Thus, school people have mistakenly thought that in their practices, activities, and aims they are value free (or perhaps better—free of having to commit themselves to values). This misguided "centrist tendency" has actually resulted in an acceptance of broader social values which are destructive of the development of personal meaning and which are representative of a form of oppressive social meaning.

Thus, the activity characterized above is reflective of, and communicative of, social meanings inherent in the social power structure of the broader society. In this context the criticism of the "mindlessness" of the schools takes on a powerful meaning. It is a mindlessness which does not critically identify the public behaviorist values embodied in the activity of schooling. It is a mindlessness that continues to accept through its practical activity a process by which persons are alienated from one another and from their own potential as human beings. This in turn makes the dominant social meanings ones which foster the oppression or dehumanization of other people; and is seen as a natural way of existing because it has been created in the "natural" context of the activity of school life. The schism between our liberal rhetoric and our practices is easily seen to be related to the mindlessly oppressive character of school activity which accompanies the discussion of our higher values. Thus, we study justice in an activity context characterized by injustice. As, for example, our knowledge of the tradition of justice grows, our ability to act justly decreases through the implicit meaning structures of the learning activities. Thus, we leave schools knowing about justice, and "that" justice is a good thing, but knowing "how" to unjustly oppress people effectively.

On the personal side of the picture the corollary of social oppression (our acting out of the practice in relation to others) has other destructive effects. Inwardly the activity of the schools represses the uniqueness of our own meaning structures. Our personal meanings are consistently delegitimated through the activity of schooling, and this is not the same as losing an argument or having unresolved conflict of values in an open situation.

The exercise of unequal power, the use of praise and blame in group settings, and the general judgmental aura of the school activity clearly communicate that the personal meanings of the person are not legitimate for common sharing with others. Further, the expression of personal meaning under these circumstances involves high risk on the part of the student.

Personal meanings when expressed or felt thus become anxiety laden and often result in guilt or shame reaction when not accepted or praised. As a result individuals engage in a "forgetfulness" concerning their own meanings. Thus, they repress or submerge the unique meaning structure growing out of their own activity and take on the attitude and posture of the control agent.

When this happens the students have completed the personal-social connection by an accommodation to social alienation with the added dimension of becoming alienated not just from others or their work, but also alienated from their own personal potential through repressive "forgetfulness."

Personal response to this process is reasonably predictable and is characterized by student withdrawal and passivity, lack of initiative, and destructive personal coping behaviors such as "apple polishing" or "schoolmanship." These behaviors are personally destructive of individual meaning structure regardless of how well they adopt one to the oppression and alienation of the school activity that is implicitly reflective of the "neutral" stance of the school.

Anger and aggression are further predictable behaviors in such circumstances, although they appear not to be as prevalent as withdrawal and destructive coping simply because the unequal power situation provides much greater risk to the aggressive student.

In the long run it is certainly reasonable to predict that constant immersion in the dominantly characteristic school activity contributes to neurosis, psychosis, fanciful romantic nonsense, drug experience, and social violence. Having systematically submerged one's own meaning structure for years, the hope of self-realization (or making oneself more real) becomes less possible in the usual context of social activity.

The struggle for personal meaning goes on within persons, but if we have done our job well, students are effectively cut off from the personal sources of their own creativity and growth, and accommodated to an alienated view of the social world. Thus, the person who attempts to exercise choice and direction, lacking clear personal grounding or adequate social reality frameworks, creates further socially and personally destructive behavior. Thus, the hope of developing or facilitating the development of responsible personal meaning structures and activity becomes less and less likely.

Contradictions in Schooling

When the technological, bureaucratic, and consumer ethos enter the consciousness of staff and students the personal activity of everyday living, the fundamental quality of existence, becomes counterfeit and is replaced by a kind of "false consciousness." This "false consciousness" can be seen clearly when we look at certain contradictions which are revealed in traditional everyday school living activity. The contradictions are viewed in terms of what Habermas[6] has called the three aspects of practical activity: (a) work, (b) power, and (c) language. The contradictions are, of course, grounded in the acceptance of the quality of living as the cultural end of social policy. In other words, we must assume that the answer to the basic question, "In whose interest is the activity of the school?" presents contradictions when the form and quality of work, power, and language create conflicts between the everyday living interests of those experiencing the activity, and other explicit or implicit external agencies imposing school activity in the service of their own interests.

Contradictions in Work ("Economics")
1. **"Seriousness vs. irrelevance and triviality."** Work in the schools for teachers and students is supposed to be serious and "task oriented"—a serious business. Teachers are expected to be professional about their jobs, to know and

process the correct rhetoric. They are thus expected to take their job seriously, to serve the student and the system. Schooling is to be seen by students as the most serious and important event in their social lives.

Students are expected to take school seriously. Discipline problems and other disruptions which interfere with the seriousness of learning are cardinal sins. Further, students who lack "motivation" or school game playing skills are a constant irritant to the business at hand.

The contradiction lies in the fact that there is a general lack of conviction about standards and worthwhileness of tasks imposed in the schools. Many teachers wonder "why" they are teaching what they are to disinterested youngsters. Promotion is more than likely automatic no matter what youngsters achieve. Graduation is usually a test of endurance for nonacademically oriented students. However, the compulsion to act "seriously" is still felt by all involved.

What this does is debase the nature of labor or work in the schools. It clouds the development of values in the productive activity of the persons there, since all work must be taken seriously whether clearly justified or not. As a result, people become alienated from their work because the pleasure of worthwhile activity is reduced to satisfaction in the external rewards offered in the absence of justifiable standards. Everyday life loses its potential reality as persons in schools become divorced from a sense of worth in their activity.

2. **"Consumption of quantities of 'goods' vs. production of quality in work."** The industrial ideology of consumption of material goods is reflected in the structure of school activity inasmuch as schools emphasize the quantitative accumulation (or consumption) of skills and knowledge. It is correlated with the idea of expansion rather than development, growth rather than progress or balance.

Schools assume that the more one knows, the better one consumes and accumulates skills and knowledge, the better one becomes. Thus, as in society, a continuous accumulation becomes the end in itself.

Opposed to this is the idea that the quality of productive work enhances human development in schooling, and skills or knowledge are part of the contributing means for this development. This contradiction is as old as the Socratic and Rhetoric schools of thought—men of virtue or men of consummate skill (that is, knowledge + technique). It is also as new as the present concern for formative aspects of moral and intellectual development rather than the substantive outcomes of morals and intellect.

People in schools experience life as the facilitation and acquisition of a never-ending accumulation of substantive outcomes. Whether or not they contribute to the personal quality of human development is not a major concern.

Teachers and other staff even experience their own professional growth as the accumulation of courses and credentials, and not in terms of the increasing quality of their own professional work and personal development.

In effect then the activity of the classroom is coercive in the use of power since the emphasis upon accumulation of the past divorces people from their own sense of development in the present and they must be "motivated," "structured," and "controlled" in order to foster brute accumulation.

Work is divorced from the everyday meaning structures of the individual. Accumulation as a goal demands dependence upon external rewards, not the developmental relevance of present activity, which provides intrinsic reward.

Verbal acquisitions, as concepts, ideas, facts, or skills, are seen as the major "goods" to be accumulated. These acquisitions are not viewed basically as a means to enlightenment and development. As such they deal fundamentally with language about language rather than common language (words about the reality of immediate activity).

Once again, everyday living and the quality of development are devalued by the accumulative consumption ideology of the schools.

3. **"Compartmentalization of work vs. lived experience of wholeness and continuity in activity."** Compartmentalization of activity takes place in terms of time, behavior, and tasks in the schools. Thus, we are able in the interest of outside agencies to "divide and conquer" the young by adult compartmentalization of subject matter, by external sequencing and limitation of true involvements, and by dividing behavior (and shaping objectives) in cognitive, affective, and psychomotor realms. The rationale for these compartmentalizations is of course not available through the lived experiences of the young.

This in effect detaches the work of students in school from their own sense of wholeness and experiential continuity. The quality of their engagement and the sense of control over their experience are submerged in the imposition and compartmental manipulations of their work experience.

Inherent in this procedure is the technically rational planning and organization of work tasks and pupil activity which, in the interests of others, destroys the spontaneity, creativity, playfulness, and essential risk-taking potentials of everyday living experiences.

Contradictions in Power ("Politics")

1. **"Compulsion for order vs. the ideology of democracy."** Democratic processes, and especially the sharing of power through participation, are cornerstones of democracy. In schools, as in many other places of work, the Bill

of Rights is effectively "parked at the door."

Democracy becomes politicized through this process and is removed from the everyday living of the participants. It becomes an abstraction that is not lived, but talked about.

The perceived need for order which has become almost a compulsion preempts democratic processes. Thus, the compulsion to have things run smoothly, to be efficient, to be accountable for goals, and thus to control the social behavior of students contradicts the meaningful embodiment of real, everyday democratic living in classrooms.

As a result the quality of human relationships is infused with a hierarchical domination in everyday life. In the process democracy loses its everyday meaning as power is abstracted from living and exercised authoritatively. In the process work tasks and human relations are imposed for the sake of order.

Closely correlated with this contradiction is the ideology of "maturity" which both legitimates imposed order and seduces the student. Full participatory living and sharing of power are denied on the basis of the "maturity of the adult" (or immaturity of the student). This rationalization allows adults to impose their order on the student and at the same time allows the student certain "immature" trade-offs in behavior. Thus, students are not expected to be "responsible" for many kinds of behavior because they are immature.

In effect, classroom life becomes (again) a form of activity abstracted from everyday life. The consequences of behavior are sheltered from reality because students learn they are immature, and the imposition of activity is legitimated because adults are "mature."

2. **"Social reward of satisfaction vs. personal reward of pleasure."** The need for order and bureaucratic control, abstracting personal participation from its lived practice, necessitates a concomitant abstract reward system.

Whereas in the everyday life of experience reward comes through the personal pleasure gained from productive activity, it is now necessary to legitimate imposed activity by "teaching" a substitute and abstracted need for rewards that are socially satisfying rather than personally pleasurable.

Students, thus, work for grades, teachers approval, test results, parental approval, and to competitively best other students. These rewards are not "in the interest" of students in terms of the intrinsic value of activity in their everyday lives. They provide a pale copy of pleasure in the form of satisfaction (or socially abstracted pleasure).

Satisfaction is in the "pleasing" of others and the achievement of rewards which have future "meaning" rather than direct meaning in everyday life. Thus, slowly, students lose their own sense of value in inactivity and substitute social satisfaction which makes them dependent upon abstract rewards for their sense of worth.

By the age of nine or ten this reward system has been completely internalized, most creative behavior has been repressed, and the alienation of the "losers" (predominantly the lower classes) has become almost complete. It is clear that the substitution of social satisfaction for personal pleasure in the interest of persons and processes outside the living context of the school diminishes the quality of lived experience there.

Contradictions in Language ("Culture")

1. **"Disembodied intellect vs. organismic presence."** In everyday life communication in its cultural context is a complete organismic response involving facial gesture, bodily posture, emotional mood, tacit understanding, and personal organic needs. The activity of the school in contradiction focuses almost entirely upon formal structures of communication, primarily language. Thus, the curriculum goals are essentially divorced from the concrete biology of the student.

It is not simply that the school justifies its role in terms of the intellectual development of the student. This, again seen from the point of view of the quality of everyday life, is a form of compartmentalization of abstraction from practical living. The school, its rewards, and its tasks become focused upon a highly restricted (though highly socially useful) set of human capacities. In a fundamental sense the student as organism is disembodied in the process, since even primary bodily functions such as erotic pleasures, elimination, and ingestion are ordered and subordinated to verbal learning goals.

The body, when recognized at all, is related to a segmented physical education consisting in most cases of exercise gained through the enduring of a social games and skills oriented program.

This divorcement of the verbal from affect and psychomotor activity provides a highly useful control and sorting mechanisms for society, but in the process destroys the fabric of everyday living in the sense of full organismic participation in life. In the process it helps teach students to distrust their own values, emotions, and bodies as basic aspects of life and to this extent diminishes the full meaning of being alive.

2. **"Language as words about words vs. language as words about reality."** The verbal focus of the schools is further destructive of full living to the extent that the primary emphasis is not related to connecting language activity to concrete experience, to self-expression in the act of full participation in living; but to manipulating words whose referent is other words. The

development of the language experience approach to teaching reading is one such recognition of this fundamental contradiction. In this case learning to read is hopefully connected to concrete experience of the students' immediate lives.

But beyond certain early practices, the school curriculum quickly becomes a "definitional" experience. That is, previous words are utilized as the referent for constructing and understanding new words (or ideas). In a very real way this results in a means of masking or mystification of the understandings hoped for rather than revealing meaning to the student through verbal processes that serve their own practical possibilities.

There can be no quarrel with the need for words about words at some point in schooling. But the fact of the matter is that this approach is fundamental and pervasive throughout schooling. Further, as presently operational it is essentially self-defeating since it rejects the building of language in concrete reality and divorces meaning structures from active potentials of human beings.

Again, it is useful to ask "in whose interest" this process operates—for it is clear that it basically contradicts the goal of developing full, active meaning structures related to the practical everyday life of students, and thus is not an enhancement of their own development and the quality of their living.

Conclusion

In conclusion, further exploration of life in schools could uncover other contradictions, perhaps even more important than those examples provided here.

The fundamental point of this analysis is the highlighting of contradictions between things deemed important in the schools and the quality of living in the schools. And, if we accept the improvement of cultural conditions of everyday life as the fundamental goal of social change (that is, enhancement of the quality of existence), then the resolution of contradictions becomes a first order of business for schooling. The pattern of these contradictions is of course not unique to the schools. The same kinds of contradictions can be seen in our other technological, bureaucratic, consumer oriented institutions throughout our society.

The analysis of schooling from the viewpoint of the everyday life in the schools leads me to the conclusion that fundamental attempts to "re-form" the schools must focus upon the activity in the schools as a cultural milieu, with the technical and political concerns as major means for constructing environments that enrich the quality of living.

This proposed conclusion is both value oriented and practical. That is, it reflects a basic concern for cultural change rather than technical or political change, per se; and it reflects a practical conviction that what we are best able to change (should we wish to) is the activity of schooling, rather than change in the "outputs" brought about by technical acts.

If we wish to get at the root of the problem of schooling, that is, take a radical approach, it would seem to be clear that a cultural re-forming is the end goal and that this cultural reform must deal directly with human activity in its qualitative aspects.

Notes

1. Many helpful ideas for this essay were stimulated through the works of Henri Lefebvre, especially his *Everyday Life in the Modern World* (New York: Harper & Row, Publishers, 1971).

2. Peter Berger, Bridgette Berger, and Hansfried Kellner, *The Homeless Mind: Modernization and Consciousness* (New York: Random House, Inc., 1973), p. 12.

3. *Ibid.* p.40

4. Philip Jackson, *Life in Classrooms* (New York: Holt, Rinehart and Winston, Inc., 1968).

5. "Formative" and "substantive" are used here in an analogous sense to the way Jean Piaget uses them. Thus, the formative aspects refer to basic private developmental growth and not the arbitrary substantive content of a given society. In this sense the formative base of everyday living develops attitudes, feelings, dispositions, and cognitive orientations rather than the specific substantive content of the curriculum.

6. Jürgen Habermas, *Theory and Practice* (Boston: Beacon Press, 1973).

Chapter Seven

Living Democratically in Schools:
Cultural Pluralism

The movement toward multicultural education arises from the practical reality of the failure of assimilation of subcultures into the historically dominant culture of American life. We do, in fact, remain a pluralistic society. This reality has been ignited in recent times by our awareness of minority groups striving for social equity and justice via civil rights movements and other forms of liberating pressures.

Analysis of the schools and how they function, especially with more recent concerns about output variables, has raised serious questions that do not yet lead to comfortable answers for educators. How does one explain the differences in performance of youngsters representing varying minority, religious, social class, racial, and sex groupings?

The answers do not "fall out" easily although there is no dearth of hypotheses. We, most of us, had naively assumed that providing equal facilities with equal access to the dominant culture was primarily what was needed. We have little evidence, even where these have been successfully embodied in school programs, that the outcomes are reasonably equitable.

It is now eminently clear that schools and school goals are directly affected by the family background and the broader social structure and uses of schooling. As in most other aspects of life we are now aware of the social ecology, the interrelationship of all our social institutions, reflected in this case in schooling. This is simply to say, in old-fashioned terms, that education is not synonymous with schooling. What we really have gained lately is a much more sophisticated set of data to document this truism.

What this, in effect, means is that equal access and equal facilities in school programs can never hope to solve the problems of equal access to the "good" life for a large number of youngsters in our society. The good life is, of course, defined by the patterns of success that have evolved through the dominant culture in the context of our industrialized urban society. The critical variables from a dominant cultural viewpoint would seem to be the need for standardization of cultural experience in the family lives of children, and a complete acceptance of the status quo in our social structures, if subcultural groups are to enter fully into success patterns.

Problems and conflict immediately arise with these suggestions. There is little agreement that cultural values, norms, and behavior patterns learned in the home in the dominant culture represent the best attributes of human beings. What was once so easily dismissed as cultural deprivation now is seen more lucidly as cultural difference. Further, there is no assurance that the present social structures, characterized by technology, bureaucracy, and a consumer citizen's role, are the epitome of the good life. In fact, one would suppose that in a democratic society social structures would continue to evolve toward more and more humane conditions.

The options before us would appear to boil down to three:

1. Leave things alone.
2. Impose greater control over the lives of individuals.
3. Accept and facilitate differences in a non-punitive manner.

The first, I suggest, is untenable if for no other reason than that minority groups will not settle for this. Between the second and third the only viable way to proceed in the spirit of our democratic ideals would appear to be the option of developing human potential, increasing participation, and opting for pluralism. In this sense we must face up to the acceptance of multicultural schooling.

Multicultural Schooling

The advocates of multicultural schooling have proposed many courses of action. One such proposal is multiethnic studies (begun primarily by the black studies movement). Another thrust has come under the aegis of local control, a return to separatism and segregation in many cases. Still a third is based in developing greater understanding of children from various backgrounds so that they/we may learn how to "motivate" them to accept and achieve in the standard curriculum.

To my way of thinking, none of these definitions is satisfactory, although there may be circumstances in which they are positive and desirable. Each, in its own way, is directly acceptant of a dominant school culture. To me, the promise of multicultural education rests in the enlightenment of human potential by the actual living in multicultural situations in classrooms. Thus, it seems to me that education has as its basic meaning the process of helping each person transcend the parochialism of his/her own time and place, and the creation and fostering of human possibilities that may be entered into and eventually chosen as the most fulfilling personal values and life styles.

Thus, what multicultural education means to me is the recognition of each person in the context of his/her cultural background. In this sense the individual is not abstracted from a living context and placed upon the gridwork of standardized norms. Further, the recognition of the power of a cultural upbringing demands the acceptance of the real worth of the context from which a person comes as a self-confident stepping off place for personal development.

Culture

The critical need in multicultural education is a clarification of what we mean by culture, for we really will have very little opportunity to distinguish meaningful activity in schools if we are not clear about the term. This is not an easy task, since there is really not a clearly accepted agreement among social scientists.

On the broadest level culture tends to be related to or defined as the symbolic universe of a group of persons. In this sense it refers to the meanings people attach to relationships to self and others, to humankind's extensions, for example, tools, technology, etc., to institutions, ideas, and other groups of people, and to each human's relations to cosmic circumstances.

This leaves all areas of the school curriculum within the definition of culture. However, it seems to me that the cultural heritage as the course of study is perhaps the least important from a cultural analysis point of view in terms of the multicultural education movement.

Rather, I suggest that, for example, Edward T. Hall's concern is of more import and value for viewing school activity from a multicultural perspective. From Hall's viewpoint, the so-called cultural heritage, that is, the body of cultural knowledge and skills, may be the very danger that must be transcended. As Hall states:

> I would suggest another alternative, namely that once man began evolving his extensions, particularly language, tools, institutions, he got caught in a web of what I term extension transference and was both alienated from himself and incapable of controlling the monsters he had created. In this sense, he was advanced at the expense of that part of himself that he has extended, and as a consequence has ended up by regressing his nature in its many forms. Man's goal from here on out should be to rediscover that self.[1]

What seems to me to be infinitely more important than the course of study of schooling is the quality of everyday life in schools. Excluding the practical reason that there appears to me no way we can construct totally different courses of study for each subcultural group to be operational simultaneously, the real impact and promise of cultural diversity appears in, as Berger says "the web of meanings that allow the individual to navigate his way through the ordinary events and encounters of his life with others."[2]

The assumption here is that the traditional dominant cultural course of study, its programming and sequencing, are completely arbitrary. This shared technological-consumer knowledge and skill can be learned at any time and in a variety of places given the willingness of an educative society to provide the access. What is infinitely more important is the self-concept we hold of ourselves and the potential for our human possibilities by the encounter of cultural differences in our everyday lives. In mundane terms, an analogy may be made to the learning of a foreign language. If we wish to learn it well and experience the culture and its impact on us for our development as human beings, it is far better to go live in a foreign country than to sit in a booth with earphones at any high school. What focusing on the everyday life of youngsters in our schools in a multicultural setting does is to provide the same kind of living laboratory. Quite frankly, I think it is the only really meaningful embodiment of multicultural education in schools. The precedent for looking at schools in this manner is already with us in the concern for the hidden curriculum,[3] or the unstudied curriculum,[4] or life in the classrooms,[5] or the everyday quality of classroom living.[6]

Dimensions of Living Culture in Schools

Given these premises, assumptions, and opinions it would make sense to examine more critically the dimensions of cultural activity and the multicultural implications of such activity.

What this in effect means is that multicultural education must be conceptualized and organized in terms of the daily lives of students. Further, it will be of little value simply to place students from diverse cultures together and hope that by some process of osmosis learnings will be picked up. Nor does it mean that we should didactically teach multiple cultures as the ideational beliefs of diverse groups. Each of these options, it seems to me, is bracketed by a standard culture which encapsulates and overpowers the multicultural intentions.

One avenue that is worth trying comes from an exploration of the idea of culture. Culture has often tended to mean differences so that multicultural education becomes education for many different groups of youngsters. It is as least worth asking whether the key to such educational efforts may lie in a more careful analysis of the knowledge we possess about the dimensions of culture.

Here, again, it is important to note that the cultural "media is the message," not the linguistic content of messages. Thus, as Hall has argued, it is the hidden dimensions of culture that make the greater impact. These are primarily nonverbal and are the structural glue which organizes our activity and directly impact upon self-concepts and visions of our possibilities. It is in these aspects of culture, rather than the products of culture, such as art, religion, philosophy, and language, that I would look for lead to creating viable multicultural education programs.

Hall identified ten interrelated and dynamic non-verbal systems of culture. They are, again, structural ways of organizing human activity that are normally hidden from us. These ten systems are: (a) interaction, (b) materials, (c) associations, (d) defense, (e) work, (f) play, (g) bisexuality, (h) learning, (i) space, and (j) time.

What these subsystems represent in school terms are ways of organizing or structuring the human activity regardless of the subject matter content of the program; and as such in our traditional and standardized educational system are reflections of the dominant culture, variously called "Anglo" or "white middle class" or "Western European urban," etc. It is this "structure" which most clearly relates to the sense of the quality of living in schools and most directly to the emotional/attitudinal/motivational/self-concept nexus of the schools.

Reflecting Upon Cultural Subsystems
in Schooling

When we think about the implications of this school culture it reveals a number of familiar awarenesses, some not so familiar, and all in a somewhat different perspective which may prove more useful than earlier ones.

In schooling terms these cultural subsystems are interrelated (as in any cultural setting). Thus *work*, for example, is distinguished from *play* and given priority over play in the serious business of the school. The serious business refers to using *time* in a serial nature (one thing at a time, that is, work activity), in a specific *space*, and with movement in space carefully prescribed. Materials are also work-appropriate and to be used in prescribed ways for work tasks. Interaction and associations, that is, the process of approved communication and the groupings of people, are also work specific, prescribed, and supposedly facilitative. Sexuality is carefully repressed on the one hand, but utilized in its bisexual implication for many management facilitative tasks such as lining up (boys and girls). Learning is the outcome of working, but also it is embedded in time, place, interaction, association, material, bisexuality, and play. One learns in school, under appropriate prescribed procedures, by doing work (not playing) in facilitative interactions and associations, with identified relevant materials in specific spaces under carefully controlled time sequences.

The standard procedures, structures, and organizational patterns are well known from our own observation and experience. It is proposed here that the cultural subsystems and the standard nonverbal patterns are dominant culture specific. In this sense they provide a tacit cultural dimension which is more or less at odds or alien to the tacit organization of nonverbal culture for a great many (probably the majority) of youngsters in the American schools.

This realization, of the tacit subcultural dimension, helps explain one of the major problems with special programs for culturally "deprived" or "different" youngsters. The emphasis has seldom been placed upon examining the nonverbal or tacit cultural patterns that are built into the work (school) situation. It is really very little wonder that culturally different youngsters, that is, from the dominant culture, cannot overcome their own nonverbal cultural conditioning and compete equally in a different nonverbal cultural pattern. The possibility of doing so would, of course, vary with different subcultural groups (as it does).

In this light cultural pluralism or multiethnic education (as discussed here) becomes one of the main schooling possibilities for providing equal access to the overt and symbolic substance of the total culture.

Culturally Pluralistic Programs

We are immediately faced with a plethora of problems when considering what culturally pluralistic programs would look like. It is necessary, in other words, to identify the basic structure(s) of schooling that would facilitate pluralism. It should be clear that pluralism has little meaning outside the context of comparison and that any attempt to escape structures is an illusory one. Freedom, whether it be personal or cultural, is always within boundaries.

Here I would agree with Gibson Winter[7] that acceptance of *pluralism* necessitates commitment to the goals of human *liberation*, and the social processes of equal *participation*. In less lofty terms (and more educationally comfortable ones), this means that programs designed to facilitate human development in culturally pluralistic contexts must be committed to the development of individual potential through the cultural nexus of the specific individuals and by utilizing democratic processes which allow for full participation of the persons in schools in making decisions which determine the quality of their experiences. In even more mundane terms, there is no substitute for acceptance of each person for what he/she is and could become; and, for legitimizing this acceptance through the process of full participation in the determining of activity.

One of the most promising directions for realizing the above ideals would appear to be making the latent cultural subsystems mentioned earlier (time, space, etc.) manifest to the persons involved (bringing them to verbal awareness) and then making the subcultural systems negotiable by deliberation and reflection on the part of all concerned. This would indeed be a "tall order" for most schools. Yet, it seems hypocritical to foster concerns for cultural pluralism without going to what is premised here to be the heart of the matter.

The implications of this approach suggest that a concern for "coming to know" each other and for entering into negotiation through planning and deliberation are basic cornerstones. Beyond this the making and remaking of the patterns of structure for school activity would be a continual process.

The learning environment (or curriculum) takes on special meaning here. That is, cultural pluralism will demand a much broader and more flexible kind of encounter for the people involved. The program will by necessity need to be based in each classroom with adults, but evolve out of these settings into the community at large, interdisciplinary study themes, and special interest centers.

Probably the most critical problem will reside in what is usually called the definition of objectives. It should be clear that if learning expectations are defined purely in terms of traditional school goals, then pluralism will continually collapse into a rigid, dominant cultural orientation, since the standard expectations of the school already are embodied in this culture. What will be needed are goals which transcend these limitations and provide a more universal orientation to the school.

In place of the usual cognitive, affective, and skill objectives, goal statements will need to deal with some qualities such as "life values"—values in the sense that they represent the integration of cognitive, affective, and action components of culture into meaning and behaviors which are meaningful in the total life (not just school) of the learner. In other words, learning will need to be redefined to focus upon value as coming to know through cognitive awareness, emotionally positive affect, and commitment to action as behavioral wholes and not separate aspects of behavior.

In summary then, one projected program format for cultural pluralism concerns redefining goals in broad holistic terms; providing an environment which allows for activity in the community, in interdisciplinary study, with special interest and need centers; and with full participation in the school community, all evolving out of the close personal relationships with knowledgeable, helping adults.

Final Note

There is no need to concern ourselves about multiethnic education in the context of cultural pluralism if we are not committed to a democratic society. If we are committed to democracy then there is no alternative but to respect the individual in his/her cultural difference and provide for each person's development through his/her own life history and unique characteristics.

Programs based upon cultural pluralism are affirmative action programs, not simply programs which affirm the rights of individuals in the context of structures which predispose the competitive success of certain subcultural groups. Further, the dignity of the person, as Gabriel Marcel points out,[8] is not best represented by either the concept of *liberty* or *equality*, but rather by commitment to *fraternity*. Liberty, per se, leads to domination by subcultural "privileged" groups. Equality is meaningless beyond abstractions in a society composed of differing subcultural groups. It is concern for each as a brother-sister that provides the cornerstone of real democracy for a program built upon cultural pluralism.

Notes

1. Edward T. Hall, *Beyond Culture* (Garden City, NY: Doubleday & Company, Inc., 1976), p. 4. See also, by the same author, *The Silent Language* (Garden City, NY: Doubleday & Company, Inc., 1959); *The Hidden Dimension* (Garden City, NY: Doubleday & Company, Inc., 1966).

2. Peter Berger, Bridgette Berger, and Hansfried Kellner, *The Homeless Mind: Modernization and Consciousness* (New York: Random House, Inc., 1973), p. 12.

3. Michael Apple, "The Hidden Curriculum and the Nature of Conflict," *Interchange* 2, 1971, p. 4.

4. Norman Overly, ed., *The Unstudied Curriculum. Its Impacts on Children* (Washington DC: Association for Supervision and Curriculum Development, 1970), p. 127.

5. Philip Jackson, *Life in Classrooms* (New York: Holt, Rinehart & Winston, 1968).

6. See Chapter Six in this collection.

7. Gibson Winter, *Being Free* (New York: Macmillan, 1970).

8. Gabriel Marcel, *The Existential Background of Human Dignity* (Cambridge, MA: Harvard University Press, 1963).

Chapter Eight

Value Bases and Issues for Curriculum

Curriculum as a field of inquiry, and curriculum theory in particular, have been said to be moribund. Moribund means "in a dying state" or, "on the verge of extinction or termination." Persons of no less stature than Joseph Schwab[1] and Dwayne Huebner[2] have pronounced this diagnosis; and it is my opinion that they should be taken seriously, that is, their assertions should be examined carefully.

What follows here is the result of a reexamination on my part (stimulated by the assertion of moribundness) of my basic formulations, assumptions, and concerns in relation to curriculum. In the process of this reexamination the fundamental problem of the value bases for curriculum and the value bases I hold in my curriculum work became important concerns for me. Thus, what follows will be a reflection upon the problems, questions, assumptions that emerged when asking myself whether "curriculum is moribund" and the problems of, and assertions of, a value basis for curriculum that evolved in the process of rejecting the assertion of the moribundity of curriculum.

The first question that presented itself was—"Why be concerned about curriculum?" There are, after all, a variety of other specialties in the field of education, most of them more popular and prestigious. And, of course, the world is open to many other callings.

Each of us would find a different answer to this question. My answer surprised me in some ways.

Curriculum, it seems to me, is the study of "what should constitute a world for learning and how to go about making this world." As such it implies, in *microcosm*, the very questions that seem to me to be of foremost concern to all of humanity. Such questions as "what is the good society, what is the good life, and what is a good person," are implicit in the curriculum question. Further, the moral question of how to relate to others or how best to live together is clearly a critical part of curriculum.

Thus, "why be concerned about curriculum" can, for me, be expanded to "why be concerned about life." For me, the school setting is a potentially manageable microcosm of a rather unmanageable macrocosmic society. Schools lack none of the elements found in the larger context, and they do provide, for me, concrete entry points for thought and action growing out of my own experiences. Thus, for example, I have experience with politics *in* schools that gives me a concrete referent for generalizing beyond that context.

If, on the other hand, I felt that curriculum talk and work were only specific socially available roles limited in their meaning to concrete processes and situations in schools, it would hold little interest for me. It is the human intentions embodied in curriculum making, and the micro-macro relationships that bring curriculum work alive, and create processes and situations that become more than technical problems. If curriculum's only real meaning lies in schooling, then it is fundamentally a technical problem.

Thus, from my perspective, if curriculum is moribund, then society as we know it is also moribund. This view of the decadence, disorganization, alienation, degeneration, estrangement, anomie, loss of community, etc., in modern society is a well known thread of intellectual history, especially apparent in the work of sociologists such as Weber, Simmel, Durkheim, and Tonnies (as well as de Tocqueville, Burckhart, and Nietzsche). In fact, the tradition of classical sociology to the present day is one which casts a pessimistic pall upon human endeavors.

If, for example, we are to take completely to heart Max Weber's concern about the rationalization and bureaucratization of society in curricular terms and turn to examining the tangle of rules, policies, self-serving bureaucratic goals, rationalized testing, behavioral objectives, etc., in schools, one might come to agree about the moribundness of the field. It is, however, misleading, I think, and both fruitless and destructive to focus this critique of society upon curriculum without clearly pointing out the broader intentions and meanings.

This pessimistic view comes through our intellectual tradition in the form of hermeneutic methodology. It is committed to the quest of human understanding, and it assumes a sort of "objectivity" which I believe masks basic value questions. It is a form of curriculum theorizing that is not terribly helpful.

The presently competitive antidotes to this classical academic pessimistic "objectivity" rest in two diverse but interwoven value patterns: (a) The Marxist and/or Socialist position and (b) religion. I shall return to these "answers" a bit further on.

Theory and Praxis

A second concern that arose out of my reflections was a theory/praxis problem. Curriculum talk consists of talk about both theory and praxis. It is important to keep in mind, however, that there is a necessary and desirable difference between talk and action. Talk about theory is talk about ideational boundaries with which we are concerned in our thinking about "making a world";

whereas talk about praxis is planning talk. (Again, neither *is* praxis.) Thus, there are three critical activities inherent in curriculum: (a) talk about curriculum, (b) talk about praxis (planning talk), and (c) praxis (including talk-in-praxis).

One of the most destructive aspects of the general techno-rational and anti-intellectual ethos of American life is the idea that social action or praxis is a preemptive activity. Thus, we hear such things as "It's only talk," "Put your money where your mouth is," etc.—as if the action would have any meaning without the communication that surrounds it. As Paul Ricouer remarks, talk has to be different from praxis in terms of the way talk functions in human existence.[3]

Jürgen Habermas makes a similar distinction between work and communication.[4] When we consider Habermas' third element—power—some interesting insights emerge.

Rather than simply ask whether our actions or praxis reflect our talk in some linear hierarchical pattern, we can more fruitfully ask what the relationships between talk and action are? Thus, for example, in what ways does our present praxis distort our talk or communication? In what ways are the so-called failures of talk being translated into action—really not failures of talk, but outcomes of power realities? We have moved a long way when we can separate clearly the difference between "that talk is impractical" and "that talk is not politically viable." In the first case there is a suggestion of the violation of reality, whereas in the latter we recognize the feasibility of the talk to be in existing, arbitrary human arrangements. Existing praxis, held in activity by power arrangements, is thus quite capable of distorting the meaning and value of curricular talk.

This can readily be seen in explicit and implicit criteria applied to the evaluation of curricular talk by practitioners and/or non-curriculum oriented educators (the predominant group being psychologists). In both cases there is often the claim to be unable to understand or see the value of curriculum talk due, I believe, primarily to the distortion of thought processes brought about by work and power. As for the moribundness of curriculum, I would suggest that this conclusion results from the distortion in judgement brought about by the existing macro social praxis and power arrangements—not by the lack of potentiality, or possibility, or vitality in curriculum talk.

Thus, having justified my concerns for curriculum and having dignified the role of curriculum theory, I would like to quickly raise three sub-questions which occurred along the way.

For example, what is the prelogical or tacit ground for curriculum talk? It seems to me that we are faced with the very question posed and discussed by phenomenologists. What brackets surround curriculum talk?

There tend to be two (at least) sets of brackets that are implicit in varieties of curriculum talk. On the one hand are those, who (as I do) tend to bracket curriculum talk by the human condition—who most probably would agree or at least accept the possibility that curriculum praxis is a reasonable microcosm of the macroscopic world, and thus curriculum talk is bounded only by its concrete referents within the human condition.

An obvious disagreement is apparent, however. The tacit as prelogical boundary for curriculum talk for many other persons would appear to be a given cultural and social definition, located in time and space in the now of social functions. Thus, this tacit bracket channels curricular talk into technical or "objective" modes, which restrict legitimate talk to planning talk, to talk about praxis. This, I believe, is what Schwab hoped to do with his emphasis on scientific examination of praxis.

This assumptive base or ground is a fundamental problem in curriculum communication. If curriculum talk is moribund, is it dying because of its tacit or prelogical bracket of meaning? Is the source of validation, the ground of validation, no longer viable? Or, has the dominant socio-cultural bracket (the technical) established its truth? Is it now moribund to inquire into the human condition?

Another concern of mine asks if curriculum theory is only talk about talk, or is it also talk about work and power? Thus, are we dealing only with talk about cultural communication (such as subject matter), or do we speak about social settings and human activity also when we talk curriculum talk? Many curriculum persons would have us talk mainly about cultural communications if we are to revitalize curriculum.

I disagree, for, it seems to me that a considerable amount of legitimate curriculum theory has been talk about power and work in the schools. In fact, I find it incredibly naive to assume that curriculum talk can be limited to examining the cultural manifestation of education in exclusion from the nature of educational experience (work), and social power.

This was (or is) in fact the point of departure between the Existential and Marxist, the human consciousness and political action wings of the so-called reconceptualist curriculum theorists. This dispute, or concern, has provided an existing basis for intellectual growth and challenge among curriculum theorists.

Another way of expressing this concern is with the question " Is curriculum talk essentially descriptive or is it talk about change?" Again, we have to grant talk a legitimate role in human endeavors in order to consider this question, for it is not the same as asking whether in proto-Marxist terms, curriculum theory is intended to understand schooling or to change it.

Much of the curriculum theory of the reconceptualist kind has not dealt with exhorting or recommending prescriptions for change. This may be a reaction to technical talk, which fundamentally deals with "getting things done." Nevertheless, the question remains as to whether a Marxian, or a phenomenological, or an Existential analysis of the human school condition is enough. Certainly it throws light upon our problems, and many new insights are created which could have meaning for us. But, have we completed the task of curriculum talk without dealing directly with prescriptions for schooling?

It is especially interesting to see Marxist analysis in this pattern. This form of analysis is usually a sweeping structural critique which then fails to state its values and prescribe its remedy. As I understand it Marx was clear that the role of the intellect was to change the world not simply to analyze it.

The existential position may be equally ludicrous, since it is very difficult to understand how freedom, choice, and authentic being get translated into some sort of general objective analysis of the human condition without being in "bad faith." Or, how can we be convinced by an abstract, general, objective statement which, as a media vehicle, contradicts the substance of its position?

Another concern I have is not unrelated but can be asked in a different way. "What kinds of cultural tools are most appropriate for curriculum talk?" We have available a rather wide range of communicative tools: varying from aesthetic criticism to technological reasoning. This includes behavioral science talk, political theory orientations, phenomenological analyses, as well as a variety of philosophical approaches.

These issues or concerns have not been raised to be answered here, but to point toward a fundamental lack in curriculum theory which creates these problems. It is a failure of theorists to explicitly state the value base of their work. There is no way theorists can avoid assuming choices of value and implying them in their work. The basic choice of communication style or cultural tool, the problems, or issues dealt with—all these concerns perceive *threats to cherished values of the theorists*, and cannot be clearly formulated without acknowledgement of those values. Fundamentally, curriculum talkers (and workers) must face up to whether they are aware of the uses and values of their work and whether their values are subject to their own control.

It is clear (or seems clear to me) that many curriculum talkers and workers with a fundamentally technological orientation are not aware of their value base (thinking it to be objective and value free), nor are they aware that their values are not subject to their own control, nor do they thus show any desire to control them. It is this value-witlessness that is frightening in the technological approach, not the approach itself, since technological rationality is obviously a potential for either human good or evil.

Any person concerned with curriculum must realize that he/she is engaged in a political activity. Curriculum talk and work are, in microcosm, a legislative function. We are concerned about practical affairs, but with the goal of creating the *good* life, the *good* society, and *good* persons—this direction is implicit in the very institutional fabric of schools and curriculum. Even if we wish to deschool society and eliminate any formal curriculum agenda (in which case no need for school curriculum talk and work would exist), we still must commit ourselves to whatever values we believe create good societies, lives, and persons. And, if we curriculum talkers are to understand what *we* ourselves are saying, and communicate to others, these values must be explicit.

The Aims of Education

As an area of illustration of the value foundations of curriculum talk, let us look for a moment at perhaps the most fundamental educational value commitment, that is, *the basic aim of education*. In much curriculum talk these basic aims are implicit only.

Much of our curriculum talk is replete with concern about objectives but says very little directly about aims of education. There is, however, no way to escape a commitment to some long range goal or aim of education in any form of curriculum discourse.

Occasionally, curriculum talk will note all the possible aims, suggest that they all are valid, and then move into a discussion of objectives which does not reflect any clear rational connection between these values and these operating objectives. Curriculum theorists (and workers) have thus shown a great uneasiness about aims or basic directions.

Let us look for a moment at some major aims of education. (Remember an aim should be reflected in the construction of a curriculum environment which would maximize the attainment of that aim.) Parenthetically, I would like to suggest that talk about objectives at the curriculum level is misplaced. Objectives talk is instructional talk. At the curriculum level (the level of environment construction) the appropriate talk is about aims (directions). Three aims that appear clearly evident to me are: (a) socialization, (b) development, and (c) liberation.

Socialization, as an aim, relates to the training potential of schooling. It is the acceptance of the status-quo by definition and the replication of the present social class and role structure, ethos, and attitudinal sets by the most efficient and effective methods possible.

There are very few curriculum persons who will own up to this aim, even if it is by far the most prevalent. It is to the credit of Bloom[5] and his "mastery" disciples, and Bereiter,[6] that they do admit to this fundamental aim. At least one knows the values that underlie the process. Most persons working out of this value system, however, will not admit to this aim, but insist that these procedures are neutral and "in the service" of all aims. This aim is really a statement of a larger metaphor in curriculum terms. It is part of the Social Mechanistic analysis—human beings should fit into the social machine as interchangeable "parts."

Much of curriculum rhetoric has, however, been more "permissive" in tone. That is, the explicit or implicit goal or aim of education has been proposed as human development—most specifically, the development of the individual. One sees this today in the most recent fad called Moral Education. Kohlberg et al.[7] are, of course, developmentalists.

The developmental aim is an important statement of the American experience. It reflects an organismic or biological metaphor. This metaphor found its grounding in 19th century intellectual growth (e.g., evolutionary theory) combined with American agrarian and individualistic values, among other things.

The whole developmental approach, however, in formal educational terms (i.e., school curricular construction) does not always clearly specify the values or interests that are being served. Thus, development involves the concept of an elite group (e.g., mature vs. immature or educated vs. ignorant) that knows that direction "development" must take and how to guide this process. These directions and processes are not always clear to developers and *never* known to the developee (since they are immature or ignorant by definition).

An interesting analogy to this education process may be witnessed in a broader context in relation to the "underdeveloped" or Third World, especially in the case of South America. Development, in this context, is a process of becoming like the advanced capitalistic countries (mainly the United States). Development, in other words, has a direct relationship to the status of the elite or advanced group, whether researchers, teachers, or economists. Maturity, in other words (for education), is defined by the "mature" members of the society as being "like us."

A third general aim, often embedded in a developmental position, is more adequately called liberation. This is a much riskier aim and is, thus, often put in developmental terms. But, essentially, it is an aim of freeing persons from the parochialness of their specific times and places and opening up the possibilities for persons to create themselves and their society. Because one might be called a communist or something equally derogatory and threatening (Utopian, etc.), many curriculum talkers who apparently accept this value, camouflage it in a rhetoric of developmentalism. I suggest that many of them are not willing to face up to the action implications of their values.

The point here is that it would be a great service if curriculum talkers and workers would clearly specify their aims and begin to reflect this consistency in their work. It would greatly facilitate understanding in the communication process and it would provide a clear basis for dialogue and improvement of the state of the field.

Domain Values

Curriculum, however, not only has directional value problems, it has definitional value disjunction. A second major area of value concerns is those values that are best called domain values. According to Gotshalk, "a domain is any well established area of human value activity that has an established and distinctive telic pattern."[8] Curriculum certainly qualifies as a domain (and sub-domain of education). The activity of constructing a curriculum is a purposive set of actions—a telic pattern. The question remains as to what domain values reside within the activity of curriculum making. The relevance of the question is obvious, for if there is no agreement among curriculum talkers and workers concerning domain values, there can be little communication or dialogue about curriculum.

I suppose another way of asking is: "What are the subpoints (variables as values) that curriculum talkers and workers feel have to be dealt with?" Tyler says he is satisfied after 25 years, for example, with his four basic questions about objectives, selection, organization, and evaluation.[9] Assuredly, he also thinks *rational decisions* are the critical unit values of the curriculum domain. I personally disagree, as do some other persons; nevertheless, it would be of great value if we *could* identify our domain values (i.e., units of conception and significant variables).

In the past (within the decision making unit value) other variables have been suggested also. Decisions about (a) significance, (b) balance, (c) scope, (d) sequence, (e) integration, and (f) continuity have also been thought to be important.

But more important, with the belated discovery of the latent or hidden curriculum, the decision making unit (i.e., rational planning) becomes somewhat suspect as the critical domain value. As a unit of action or activity, some aspect of the praxis of curriculum is suggested as a more critical unit than "rational decision."

This problem again parallels broader intellectual dialogues about praxis and consciousness and signals a point of potential dialogue and disputation in curriculum talk and work (what would be more fundamental in curriculum?) that belies the moribundness of the field, and signals its intellectual vitality and its challenge in the relatedness to broader intellectual movements.

There is one sense in which we might as well close up shop in curriculum (or at least any of us other than walking and talking technicians). This is if one fully believes that all values are relative and that all dominance of value is a result of the strong and elite (whomever they may be) having the political and social power in their hands to impose values. If one believes this, then any social manifestation of the good life, good society, or good person is most likely a reflection of simple power—someone's dream for the masses. Making history the villain doesn't change the picture. If this is a true representation of educational reality, then those of us who strive for "other" values are surely misplaced in education. We should be seeking power, and probably by any means we can get it, or, of course, we could sink into the sleeping arms of technical activity and forget the significance of values. But curriculum talk and work as an area of integrity *is moribund* under these conditions. In its most general form, the pronouncement of value relativity is that "God is dead."

I challenge this conclusion. In fact "God" is very much alive. By God, I do not necessarily point toward anyone's personal idea or any person-being. I am referring to the source or ground of the religious impulse and spirit that pervades human history and activity. In this sense, it is a course that informs humanity about itself and the potential and possibility for creating. Thus, I would suggest humanity is not created in God's image, but is busily in the process of creating itself in the image of "God."

In any case, we are faced here with the acceptance of very fundamental values which are preserved in our definitions of good (society, life, persons); this leaves us with questions about where these values come from and what are they?

Clearly, curriculum talk and work imply "goodness" by someone's definition. What is, or should be, curriculum talkers' and workers' idea of goodness? What fundamental values inform our own activity, arise out of that activity?

It is here that I shall express what values I feel ought to undergird curriculum talk and work; I *propose* to illustrate the point, although hopefully *to convince someone also*. Here I am afraid I am rather parochial, rather American in my makeup for I believe that a kind of religious socialism should be that central core. These are in other words two fundamental value questions that inform and form the human condition. They are (a) what is the meaning of human life?, and (b) how shall we live together?

To me these two vague value loadings belong inextricably together. I think any fairly adequate reading of history suggests that the major source that gives socialism its dynamic impulse and desire for bringing about progressive human betterment *is* that core of basic spiritual value found in the human religious tradition. At the very least, it is where such values and concerns as justice, equality, fraternity, and liberty seem to arise and make their appearance.

This approach irritates almost everyone. Few religious people like socialism and even fewer socialists like religious people. Not only that, but allow yourself to be identified as either "religious" or "socialist" outside either of those small minorities is likewise to risk immediate censure.

This is unfortunate, but true. Yet it doesn't change the fact that, for me, all of those persons who are revolted by either of the combination or both, are in fact blindly or unwittingly riding piggyback on these very values as the basic impetus toward betterment in Western civilization—and, it is clearly so fundamental that I believe it *ought* to be seen as underlying our curricular talk and work.

We may wish to go on sounding like pragmatists and certainly hoping that people see us as nonideologists, to continue the illusion that we are socially or affluently beyond the need of ideology; but our need for fuzzing up or covering the source of our sentiments and directions does not change the reality of where these directions came from. At a curriculum theory level, of course, to admit this would be nonacademic, not reputable, or not objective enough. Somehow, at the university level, one must pretend that one creates knowledge out of nothing, with no help from the social or biographical past, the present or hoped for future. Every bit of curriculum talk and directed work is shot full of this basic value (some basic) assumption about *goodness*. The problem is we cover it up or sugarcoat it, or are really unaware of our debts. In any of these cases, we fuzz over and disconnect the value base from the topic of our rhetoric and action. Reading much curriculum theory is like pretending the writers have no *presence* in their work—why not make that presence the central, the integrating agent of the work rather than ghosts in the machine?

This is really not the place to argue both the politics of socialism, or religion. But I should like to conclude with a few remarks about this grounding which those of you who disagree, would like to agree, or are curious, can pursue at your own leisure.

In a sense, this makes me very old fashioned and conservative for I find two basic ideas which are very old to be the cornerstone of religious socialism. These ideas or concepts are those of the *person* and *social democracy*.

I have great difficulty beginning or ending our concern for good societies, lives, or persons without the concept of *person* as my grounding point. Further, the only meaningful social process that manages to violate personness least is what historically has become known as *social democracy*. Social democracy is, as Michael Harrington so adroitly describes, the underlying socialism that has been allowed to appear in America due to Americans' unique development.[10]

What I am proposing is a challenge to curriculum talkers and workers to explicitly profess their basic grounding values of goodness that underlie the work they do. How do they answer the questions of the meaning of human existence, and what form of living together? What do they substitute for such concerns as *persons* and *social democracy*? And if they agree with these, why is the connection between their values and their activity (whether talk or work) so vague?

Conclusion

In conclusion, the major premise of my work is a simple but important one. It is: *that all curriculum talk and work is value based. Further, examination of much of our curricular talk and work often reveals a failure to clearly identify and relate the values to the work in process.* I have suggested some critical questions and some basic areas where values need to be clearly stated, and I have hypothesized that most of the "progressive" values that transcend our dominant technical witlessness, are those which are basically derived from our religious and social democratic history. This being the case we would be well advised to pronounce *these* values and work directly through them.

Notes

1. Joseph Schwab, *The Practical: A Language for Curriculum* (Washington, D.C.: Center for the Study of Education, National Education Association, 1970).

2. Dwayne Huebner, "The Moribund Curriculum Field: Its Wake and Our Work." Invited address, Division B, American Educational Research Association, San Francisco, April 1976.

3. Paul Ricouer, "Work and the World," *Existential Phenomenology and Political Theory*, Hwa Yol Jung, ed. (Chicago: Henry Regnery Co., 1972), pp. 36–64.

4. Jürgen Habermas, *Theory and Practice* (Boston: Beacon Press, 1973).

5. Benjamin S. Bloom, "Mastery Learning and its Implication for Curriculum Development," *Confronting Curriculum Reform*, Elliot Eisner, ed. (Boston: Little, Brown and Co., 1971).

6. Carl Bereiter, *Must We Educate?* (Englewood Cliffs, NJ: Prentice-Hall, Inc., 1973).

7. Lawrence Kohlberg and Rochelle Mayer, "Development as the Aim of Education," *Harvard Educational Review* (November 1972).

8. D.W. Gotshalk, *Patterns of Good and Evil* (Urbana, IL: University of Illinois Press, 1963).

9. Ralph Tyler, "Two New Emphases in Curriculum Development," *Educational Leadership* (October, 1976), pp. 61–71.

10. Michael Harrington, *Socialism* (New York: Bantam Books, Inc., 1970).

Chapter Nine

Curriculum as a Political Process

The basic referent for curriculum is not the student, nor society, nor the cultural heritage. It is instead the political process of schooling.

By this I mean that the political process is that web of interpersonal relationships, norms, roles and structures that operate in the process of schooling.

I do not refer to the "politics" of education, nor the "political" processes brought to bear upon the educational establishment. Although relevant to any total picture of education, it is my conviction that all relevant variables in curriculum are monitored, colored, or shaped by the political processes of schooling.

It is, thus, the schools' bureaucratic definition that gives curriculum its generative shape.

With this in mind we may trace three major ideal types of instructional milieus which are potentially possible. These will be called: (1) the autocratic, (2) the democratic, and (3) the anarchic.

Given these choices we are apt to promote the *democratic*, of course, as the ideal of our cultural value system. Leaving this reaction in abeyance for a moment, it is abundantly clear that the predominant mode of bureaucratic schooling is *autocratic*.

Almost none of those civil liberties or freedoms associated with "democracy" as we are used to thinking of it in America are enjoyed by students in school.

Some doubt can be raised about compulsory education itself, but given this as a necessary boundary within which we operate a system of schooling, a cursory examination reveals that student have almost no civil liberties, few rights, and little freedom.

Students do exercise choice. Choice, however, varies from total withdrawal from the "system" through "going along with it enough to get by" to acquiescence and acceptance. In essence this means "playing the game" or rejecting it. There are no viable alternatives of cooperative definition of the game (democracy), or of personal choice of the game (anarchy).

Let me make it clear that choice here refers to choice which embodies the rights, liberties, and freedoms of determining social conditions within which one lives and interacts with others—the institutional nexus of existence—and not choice to fight the system or alternatives within acceptance of the system.

The evidence for my assertion that schools are almost entirely autocratic in structure is almost self-evident to anyone who has taken any time to visit, study, and/or talk in depth with teachers and administrators. Social conditions are seen almost entirely as means of facilitating the goals of the teacher, subject syllabus, or school and are thus in the province of the hierarchy (adult staff) to determine.

A few examples are all that should be necessary. Students have little to say (if anything) about why, what, when, where and with whom they will engage in school tasks. The same amount of institutional control would arouse all sorts of indignant reaction and direct action on the part of most adults in our society.

Thus, students do not choose whom they will associate with in school, where they will go at any given time, why they are doing what they are, what they are doing or when they will do it. This seems about as complete a picture of autocracy as one could imagine.

Autocracy is justified by two major lines of argument: the need for order and the need for disciplined encounter with subject areas. Both are impressive arguments since the listing of each as justification implies the lack of either under any other sort of institutional arrangement. Thus, to be against autocracy appears to be opting for disorder and irrelevancy and insignificant learning.

We have much in the immediate era to thank the child-centered enthusiasts for providing the ammunition for autocratic justification. As well meaning as this approach is (or was), its mystical reliance on the ability to know the *needs* of children and channel the *emergence* of meaningful tasks simply doesn't hold water.

The roots of autocratic schooling go far deeper than this, however, since it is reasonable to believe that Comenius, Rousseau, Pestalozzi, Dewey, Kilpatrick, etc., all represent, in some form or aspect of their thought, reactions against autocratic schooling.

Dual themes can be found throughout these thinkers—the emphasis upon the nature of the child and the unfolding of individual talent, and the concept of the shaping of the child by his group living in schools.

Perhaps due to the 20th century emergence of the "science" of child development and the growing awareness of psychoanalytical thought, school theorists became overly centered on the child rather than the social conditions of schooling. Whatever the case may be, the absurdity of a planless school with unfolding flowers in each seat is really no answer to order and disciplined enquiry. This is so primarily because the rhetoric of a child centered approach removes any general operational (or practical if you must) discussion from the level of general discourse. Instead we must substitute for procedure an equally mystical (to that of the unfolding child) reliance on the creative teacher.

It is, of course, completely unfair not to recognize the substance of the child centered approach or its good intentions. It is, however, disastrous to fail to recognize that this approach is almost uncommunicable without expert and specialized study, and impractical in terms of concrete common operational action referents.

Having accepted the fact earlier that we shall compel children to attend school, we can also accept the fact that the substance of learning will be involved with something which resembles the disciplines of our fields of knowledge. This is to say, the study of the systematic accumulation of our cultural heritage or symbolic systems must appear in some form in schooling.

Given our captive audience and a broad target area, it seems eminently plausible that the only practical way to plan for schooling is to proceed by a consideration of the political actions or arrangements of living together in school settings.

By this way of thinking the individual is always seen in terms of the group setting and the necessity of living together. Further, the beginning point for determining how the curricular substance will be encountered is clarified by the prior decision of the kind of political processes that one prizes and prefers.

Rather than behavioral objectives as a beginning point, which are concrete but free floating in terms of group living, we should rather begin with the actual concrete behavioral relationships among people living together in schools that we desire. These kinds of behaviors are concrete, specifiable, communicable, and eminently practical in that they are based on the ongoing reality of day-to-day living from which learning hopefully accrues.

Thus, we return to the three ideal types of arrangements—autocratic, democratic, and anarchic. The autocratic, as was discussed, is the predominant pattern in schools.

At this point I shall alienate all those readers who are still with me by rejecting democracy as a viable alternative. I do so on the simple grounds that it is not a practical possibility. Children and adults simply are not "equal" and cannot maintain a cooperative arrangement which does not become subtle autocratic manipulation or almost total abdication of adult responsibility. Further, democracy as an acceptable form may often result in the subjugation of minorities of children to majority interests, a substitution of childish autocracy for adult control. This being the case, it would be preferable to have adult control.

I would rather argue that *bounded anarchy* is the only viable approach to political circumstances in schooling. Bounded anarchy is not a contradiction since no action can take place outside boundaries. There are always limits to what one can do, even if they are only physical in nature.

Bounded anarchy in schools would simply mean that the limits are set by adults prior to childrens' appearance, and that these limits do not operate as interpersonal dictates, but rather as natural environmental boundaries within which children exercise free choice and develop self discipline.

Chapter Ten

Curriculum, Consciousness and Social Change

"Three things cannot be retrieved
The arrow once sped from the bow
The word spoken in haste,
The missed opportunity."
                              —Islamic Proverb

It is becoming very fashionable to take a dim view about the field of curriculum and curriculum development. We are, I suspect, overly harsh on ourselves, perhaps because we have had high and unwarranted expectations. We are, I believe as the proverb suggests, missing opportunities.

It is important to note that although we have always had our own special set of complexities and problems, we also share a broader social and intellectual context that can be said to be experiencing considerable disillusionment, anxiety, and confusion.

Our alternatives seem fairly clear. We have the option of giving up the whole enterprise (negating it, if you wish); simply living through whatever resolution occurs; or continuing to try to provide better conceptualization and practice that can lead to the improvement of curriculum environments for human beings. I, personally, have not yet lost my passion for continuing the quest for improvement.

Those of us who continue on this path are faced immediately with a very difficult question. "Is there anything we can do at the level of schooling that does not necessitate prior or concomitant broad social change before it can happen in any meaningful way?" Or, perhaps stated in another way, we can modify George Count's "Dare the Schools Change the Social Order" to "Can the Schools Change the Social Order?" If we decide we can make a difference, then we must justify the implicit "should" that rests in the very asking of it. Personally, I believe that we both can and should attempt to "change" society.

The "should" question will not be dealt with at any length here, in order that I may focus my attention on how I believe we can make a difference.

Yet, I must, at least, say that although schooling is a major social vehicle for socializing the young and conserving and transmitting our culture, there is no special reason why we ourselves must not act upon the basis of the very best values we are trying to communicate to the young.

Thus, there is little reason that I can see to propose to the young that the freeing of the human spirit, mind, and body from arbitrary social and psychological constraints—that is, the liberation of human potential in a framework of democratic rights, responsibilities, and practices, leading toward a better realization of justice, equality, liberty, and fraternity—should not be reflected in our own work with schools. Thus, I think we should work toward change in the direction of human liberation.

Turning to the question of what we can do in curriculum and curriculum development in the schools, we must be clear about our expectations. At the most abstract level, it is analogous to food—do we have a synthetic, instant potato, set of expectations—or an organic set? I shall opt for the organic approach here.[1]

What I shall attempt to do in the balance of this chapter is to provide an analysis of the setting for the derivation of reasonable expectations, and then proceed to suggest ways we might meet these expectations.

What do we expect?

Having declared my intention to enter into the work of curriculum for the sake of human liberation, rather than shaping and controlling behavior, or understanding, per se, as end points, we need to have our expectations (as distinguished from objectives) rather clearly in mind.

What we can expect to achieve is grounded in our conceptions of the nature of human nature and the nature of change in society and culture. I shall explicate rather briefly, basically from the works of two rather disparate scholars, the position and thus setting from which my expectations come.

Historically, at least over the last 2,500 years in Western culture, we have witnessed a basic confrontation between brands of idealism and realism. Pushed to their polar extremes, this has amounted to positions which may be stated as consciousness versus materialism. At one extreme, it may be argued that reality rests in our consciousness and the material objects of the world are appearances. The extreme materialist position would posit that reality is what it appears to be (what we sense), and that mental phenomena are epiphenomena of our actions in the world. This debate is a continuing one and the diversity in viewpoints about this problem are almost beyond cataloging.

I will utilize the work of Michael Polanyi[2] as a basis for illustrating the concept of human nature that I believe makes most sense in relation to this fundamental problem of consciousness and materialism, now translated into the old mind-body argument for purposes here.

Polanyi posits that all knowledge is personal knowledge. By this he does not mean that all knowledge is relative and idiosyncratic to individuals, but that all knowledge involves a person knowing (a knower). Further, knowing involves a focus for our coming to know and a tacit subsidiary ground or context is needed to form the elements of personal knowing.

Coming from a Gestalt psychology perceptual understanding, Polanyi combines this with an organismic biological orientation that posits a hierarchy of organization in organic systems whereby the higher level systems are not the sum of their parts (though dependent upon them) but provide an organizing function for lower levels.

I shall not argue the case here, but refer you to Polanyi's work for your own decision; rather, I would like to present what Polanyi feels are implications of his framework in terms of the mind-body problem, or consciousness.

Polanyi states that the relation of mind and body has the same logical structure as that which exists in focal awareness and subsidiary awareness (i.e., figure-grounded relationships). As he says, acts of consciousness are conscious *of* something but also *from* something. Fundamentally, we attend *from* the body (subsidiary clues) to something through our mind (focal entity). The mind sets the boundary condition of focal awareness and, thus, is an entity which organizes the subsidiary clues for focal use.

There is, he notes, no concept of consciousness in physics or chemistry. Thus, for example, a psychologist who observes the mechanism of the brain observing a cat, can never observe what is in our consciousness but only the mechanism of our observation of the cat. Thus, he says, something else must exist (i.e., consciousness), since we all have it.

What Polanyi concludes from his analysis is that the mind or consciousness exists as a separate entity, but dependent upon the body to which it serves as a higher principle in the organization of the organism's functions. He concludes by saying: "Though rooted in the body, the mind is, therefore, free in its actions from bodily determination—exactly as our common sense knows it to be free."[3]

The second set of clues for our setting in projecting expectations are taken from the work of Antonio Gramsci. Gramsci was an Italian Marxist theoretician whose major work ranges over the period of 1916–1937. His work was and is (to my knowledge) rather unique in Marxist theory. It has special relevance to my position here because it contributes from a Marxist orientation on social and cultural change the kind of perspective that helps us focus on reasonable expectations for curriculum and curriculum development.

Gramsci's major themes, according to Carl Boggs,[4] were as follows:

1. He focused upon the active, political, and voluntarist side of theory rather than the fatalistic reliance upon objective focus and scientific laws of capitalist development.
2. He focused less on historical analysis and empirical description and more upon issues of strategy and political methods necessary to destroy bourgeois society.
3. Revolution or change necessitated passionate emotional commitment, not just rational-cognitive activity, integrated through the concept of praxis.
4. Most important of our purposes here—Gramsci gave a high priority to the role of ideological struggle in the revolutionary process. He insisted that socialist revolution be conceived as an *organic* phenomenon, not an event; and, that transforming consciousness was an inseparable part of structural change (i.e., economic and social conditions of work and production).
5. Thus, revolutionary change must embrace all aspects of society and culture, not simply the economic.
6. Further, he rejected the elitist and authoritarian tendencies in the Communist movement and strove to develop a "mass" party rooted in everyday social reality.
7. And, finally, he strove to build a theory that would be visibly relevant to the broad masses of people.

What is selectively critical for my purposes here is Gramsci's concept of *ideological hegemony*. Where many Marxists emphasized the dependence of politics, ideology, and culture on the economic substructure, as a reflection of the material base, Gramsci clearly felt this was not broad enough to encompass the needed analysis for change.

By positing the idea of ideological hegemony, Gramsci meant to elucidate, as Boggs says:

> . . . the permeation throughout civil society—including a whole range of structures and activities like trade unions, schools, the church, and the family—of an entire system of values, attitudes, beliefs, morality, etc., that is in one way or another supportive of the established order and the class interests that dominate it. To the extent that this prevailing consciousness is internalized by the broad masses, it becomes part of "common sense". . . . For hegemony to assert itself successfully in any society, therefore, it must operate in a dualistic

manner: as a general conception of life for the masses, and as a scholastic program or set of principles which is advanced by a sector of the intellectuals.[5]

What Gramsci posits and develops through the context of his Marxist theory is the critical role of consciousness and the necessary changes in values, attitudes, morality, and beliefs that are necessary as a pre-condition in order that revolutionary change be possible.

One further point of Gramsci's theorizing should be noted for our purposes—his conception of the role of intellectuals in the process. Assuming that curriculum thinkers are intellectuals, his points may have relevance for us.

Gramsci rejected the establishment of an elite group of theoreticians and proposed what he called an "organic intellectual" immersed in the everyday activity of the different groups of workers. New ideas would be integrated into the very fabric of the life styles, language, and traditions in those environments. As Idries Shah, the leader of the Sufis says, "Please do not start to teach the blind until you have practiced living with closed eyes."

Turning now to the problem of expectations for our own hopes for positive change in schools, the positions described by Polanyi and Gramsci, from widely separate experiences and intentions, have provided a setting which is representative of many other scholars.

The importance I wish to attach to these views may be summarized quickly. First, the existence of a separate entity called human consciousness is apparent; and next, change in human social consciousness is necessary and a precondition of later political change. And, it is precisely in the realm of changing consciousness that I believe our expectations should reside.

Thus, in Jürgen Habermas's[6] terms, there are two moments in the dialectic—work and communication. If we utilize the concept of a dialectical relationship over longer periods of time between consciousness and structural change, it is at the "moment" of consciousness in this dialectic whereby we may expect to have any meaningful input in the change process.

Our activities, efforts, and expectations should, in other words, be focused upon the ideas, values, attitudes, and morality of persons in school in the context of their concrete lived experiences; and our efforts should be toward changing consciousness in these settings toward more liberating and fulfilling outcomes.

Furthermore, there is no one brand of liberation. There is no predictable absolute outcome that we should expect from our efforts. On the contrary, a diversity and apparent inconsistency of comparative efforts is to be expected. Any concrete or spontaneous concern on the part of educators for repressive or oppressive structures, practices, and ideas should be treated as valid and a point of entry for changing consciousness.

William Irwin Thompson[7] makes a similar point when asking why our good intentions so often lead to evil outcomes. One answer to this, he feels, is simply that if the good is seen shining in the immediacy of the act itself, it should be adopted. All appeals to long-range goals, fixed outcomes, expediency and efficiency are the foci that wreck our ideals. In terms of our activity then, the good of it for liberating human beings resides in the validity of the immediate activity in concrete contexts.

Our expectations then should be focused upon the consciousness of educators, stimulated through the analysis of existing practical conditions and the introduction of new frameworks for looking at school life and by providing leadership through which new experiences with these perspectives can be internalized in a wide variety of seemingly disparate (on the surface) activities. Let us examine some of these areas and activities that can be done.

Some of the Possibilities

The proposals and/or prescriptions I am about to present must obviously remain in the realm of possibilities. I believe we must be much more opportunistic and flexible, more adaptable to practical situations, if we are to hope to foster the realization of our expectations. To attempt to be definite at this point would obviously be inconsistent with the view presented here. Nevertheless, I think there are some areas of activity and some potential alternatives within these areas that may legitimately be suggested.

The areas that I see at this time which are more relevant to the task of changing consciousness toward a more liberating existence are the areas of (1) ideas and perspectives; (2) personal growth; (3) substance or subject matter; (4) preference rules; and (5) constitutive rules. In addressing myself to these areas, I shall refer primarily to the roles of teachers and other workers in the curriculum field.

Ideas and Perspectives

Perhaps the most important and overriding concern is in the realm of ideas and perspectives we bring to bear on our activity. At least it has seemed to me. Through my experience I have become convinced that a major prerequisite for liberating changes necessitates a rather dramatic change in the consciousness of persons in how they "see" the meaning in the activity they engage in with students and colleagues. It is not enough simply to change the structures or provide new techniques without new lenses of perception and conception. What I propose is the attempt to shift the perspective of educators from the dominant quantitative achievement task orientation toward nebulous future goals to a perspective which focuses directly upon the quality of the lived everyday life in our working situations.

The quality of lived experience resides in the relationships that exist in our lives. Thus, the way we relate to other people, the way we organize and administer power, the relationships of our work to our self-esteem, how we feel about what we are doing, and what meaning our lives have in concrete contexts are all ways of thinking about the quality of our experience.

As a teacher at the University, after many frustrating years, I have realized that if one wishes to influence others' ideas and perspectives, one must literally embody these ideas and perspectives.

By this, I do not mean "teaching the way you recommend others to teach." This old bromide is both too simplistic and futile. Our styles are our own, rooted in biography and personality. What we must reveal is our passion, our values and our justification. To focus simply on our behavior is near to selling our souls to the devil at the price of our own vital energy.

What we must ask ourselves then is to really profess; to reveal and justify from our own viewpoints what we believe and value. There need be no loss in the setting forth of others' views divergent from our own in this process; but what must be risked is the loss of the posture of neutral scholarship suffused with the aridity of living an uncommitted life.

There are inherent dangers in this process. The temptation to slide from legitimate justification to propaganda and indoctrination is not always easy to resist. Yet the very process of challenge and the creation of dissonance in the mind of the student embodied in the living presence of another and infused in a living relationship is often the source of the beginning of liberation. Most university teachers of my acquaintance would rather be neutral and let their readings give divergent views. I would reverse this posture if I hoped to influence students toward their own liberation and new liberating perspectives.

We are coming perilously close at this point to the concept of transcendence. We are asking persons to transcend the limitations and restrictions of their social conditioning and common sense and to venture beyond by seeing and choosing new possibilities. Thus, the human spirit becomes engaged in the direction of this transcendent activity through the guidance of the meaningfully valued goodness toward which these possibilities may lead.

Philip Phenix[8] has spoken insightfully about curriculum transcendence. He posits that we by our very nature are drawn toward transcending our present state via our consciousness of temporality. Thus, the impetus for choosing and becoming in us is not something that need be externally imposed, but is rather a process of helping others see possibilities and helping them free themselves for going beyond this present state of embedded existence.

Paulo Soleri captures this eloquently in another context which should be seen as an analogy for our purposes, when he says:

> I do not bow to the death wish we exhibit cynically as a sign of existential responsibility, nor do I sympathize with the pietist sporting flowing robes, beards and sandals of the simple and the meek. I find the hard-headed technocrat utterly pulp-minded; and the politician too busy to know and be serious. I find him smothering the soul while flushing history into the past as if it were an undigestible but somehow homogeneable slut.
>
> I see most of the equivocation, the inability to act, as the gap between the nuts and bolts fanatic and the spiritualist . . . the bridge between the matter and spirit is *matter becoming spirit*. This flow from the indefinite-infinite into the utterly subtle is the moving arch pouring physical matter into the godliness of conscious and metaphysical energy. This is the context, the place where we must begin anew.
>
> If the reference point is spirit, then whenever spirit is not incremented, pollution is present in its most comprehensive form: entropy. Entropy and pollution are one and the same.[9]

What we must ask of students is equally important. It should be clear by now that our goals, broadly conceived, should be: (1) develop new liberating perspectives; (2) clarify values; (3) stimulate and develop educational thinking; and (4) communicate significant knowledge and ideas in the area we are dealing with. The statement of, or intent to achieve, highly specific goals in curriculum courses is neither necessary nor desirable, for this process is both fruitless and antithetical to freeing students for achieving our significant goals.

In the late 1920s, W.W. Charters, through analysis of the teaching role, produced approximately 1,000 teacher competencies. No one is quite sure what happened to these necessities of good teaching, but some say their ghosts have come back to haunt us today. At any rate, in my understanding about the phenomena of ghosts, they are more to be pitied than taken seriously and their only power resides in the fear they produce in the observer.

What is at stake here is close to the distinction Rene Spitz[10] makes between education and learning. He sees these processes as radically different, both structurally and developmentally. Spitz illustrates this from his work with infants and toilet training. In the 1930s the Children's Bureau recommended toilet training begin at two months of age. Babies actually learned when placed on the toilet to do their duty. By the end of the first year, the training broke down. At this time, says Spitz, it came in conflict with their developing personality and it proved exceedingly difficult to right the breakdown. Toilet training based on education calls for a later age, but also an effective relationship which facilitates identification with a significant others' wishes and standards. Humanization can only occur via education, which comes through affect-charged relationships which help develop self-governance, autonomy, and independence.

In passing, I shall share one general approach that I believe is a real possibility for achieving the broad liberating goals mentioned earlier. It is a holistic approach in that all the aforementioned goals are embedded in the same general approach.

Students and school personnel in curriculum courses or in the field can be asked to develop and share their own creative models of educational contexts that are relevant to their own work. In the process they are asked to specify the basic intention of the model, i.e., *control, understanding*, or *liberation*.   Value assumptions concerning the cosmos and human nature are also identified. The model itself, once constructed, must have boundaries, variables, and specify the relationships among the variables within the model. And, finally, each may be asked to state what new insights for them or what practical implications for them the model may have. These models are then shared and critiqued by a group of peers.

This form of curriculum activity engages the person not only in an exercise of thinking, but of revealing and clarifying values, of searching for new perspectives, and engaging in moral, political, and aesthetic discourse—so much needed in education, as Huebner[11] has pointed out.

Let us turn now to what might loosely be called the "content" of the liberating thrust.

There are at least four fundamental emphases that we must constantly hope and attempt to recognize, analyze, and encourage deeper understanding of their meaning at the levels of values, attitudes, morals, and ideological thought processes. These emphases are: (1) technological rationality; (2) bureaucracy; (3) human rights; and (4) economic substructures. All of these are, of course, to be focused upon in terms of their meaning for the quality of lived experience in our lives.

Technological rationality refers to the dominant mind-set of our culture. It is in Marcuse's[12] terms a one-dimensional orientation toward tasks and problems characterized by a complete commitment to an instrumental thinking which separates means from ends. Thus, in the process this empirical and socially behavioristic aura emphasizes the efficiency and effectiveness of measurable achievement and divorces human activity from the source of valued meanings or qualities. Thus, an irrational rationality predominates. In social terms, this is both an ideological set and political act of destroying the validity of possible change as concerns are narrowed to the efficiency of the domination of the status quo.

School personnel must be constantly alerted to this cultural mind-set. They must be helped to see where it enters our lives through such practices as behavioral objectives, behavioral modification, management by objectives, systems analysis, teacher competency approaches, and accountability movements. They must be constantly encouraged to shift from the "How?" to the "What?" and the "Why?"

In terms of bureaucracy we are witnessing a form of institutional organization that facilitates the rationalization and specialization necessary to carry technological rationality into social structures, work tasks, and communication networks. Thus, examination and analysis of the intentions and effects of bureaucratic practices are critical elements toward developing liberating values and procedures.

There also exists in bureaucratic structures the phenomenon of displaced goals that must be revealed and examined. Much of the policy and form of bureaucracy tends to become self-serving and related to the institutions as a place of work, rather than its professional goals or purposes. This too must be noted.

A third emphasis is a concern for human rights. If we are to affect the quality of our lives in schools, we must ask if the "Bill of Rights" should be parked at the door when we enter the school, as it tends to be in most other work situations.

We have, I believe, relegated our concern for our rights to our homes as private citizens and our political system participation. This is a critical aspect of domination, since the impact on our perceptions, attitudes, values, and morals in living in institutional work settings is a perverse factor in our mind-set or perspective.

Thus, every reasonable opportunity must be taken to raise the issue of human rights in the context of our conduct and the impact of that conduct upon the quality of living in the environments we create.

The final major substantive emphasis to be mentioned here has to do with the economic system (and especially the substructure) that we are a part of. There can be little doubt that many of the policies, practices, and procedures we utilize in schools are built upon a "factory" model or analogy. Further, the basic thrust of justification for schooling seems to be shifting more toward preparation for occupations. Also, there is the fact that education is a major "industry" itself, at least in the sense that the expenditure of monies is directly related to the private world of commerce through such acts as the purchase of books and materials.

The examination of these (and other) economic factors upon our daily lives in schools is a critical need, and we should take every opportunity to examine and raise questions about our activity in relation to these economic forces in our society if we wish to build a clearer perspective on the potential for liberating experiences.

The four perspective emphases just alluded to are not seen as topics for study, but should be utilized as liberating lenses when dealing with our curricular substance in the course of work we do as curriculum persons.

Personal Growth

The second broad area of concern beyond building new perspectives is the area of personal growth. Personal growth is not divorced from perspectives, of course, but I refer here primarily to the idea that there is little chance that persons will be concerned about liberating human potential in others unless they themselves are also involved in their own personal structures in a liberating quest and set of experiences.

The work of Gramsci (and many others) clearly suggests that liberating social change by necessity involves the breaking up of conditioned and pre-set attitudes, values, and meanings attached to present social phenomena in a manner that allows the person to sense the potential within themselves for change and growth, from powerlessness to power, and from alienation toward relationship and commitment.

I do not believe that there is any fundamental contradiction in the long run between those theorists who advocate a personal change position and those who advocate a social change orientation in terms of changing consciousness toward a liberating praxis. This assumes that the social approach does not involve a highly individualistic orientation without meaning for communal living. Neither approach need be exaggerated to the point of exclusion of the other.

There is, thus, a need for us as curriculum teachers and workers to be in the process of continuous liberating growth ourselves, and to facilitate personal growth in those we work with through our own caring for them as total persons.

We should also select working processes which enhance a person's self-esteem, as well as selecting experiences which will facilitate the development of awareness of growth potential.

One relevant example comes from my year's experience as a member of the staff at the Curriculum Laboratory of Goldsmith College, University of London. Teachers and Heads (as teams from various schools) were brought on campus for twelve week workshop sessions with one day a week back in their schools. They were attending in order to work on developing curricula for an innovative program loosely labeled "Interdisciplinary Inquiry."

I was immediately and forcefully struck, and puzzled, by the provision of about a third of the workshop time in the engagement of the participants in a wide variety of activity in the areas of arts and crafts. This came to be one of the most significant aspects of their curriculum work, for not only did they learn art and craft substance for building into interdisciplinary studies, but far more important, it provided a rich personal experience of their own potential for seeing themselves as creative and growing persons.

Group sessions on the curriculum were organized to facilitate the kinds of issues, values, and decisions that were inherent to the task of curriculum development and design. The teams worked to develop their own plans in a full participatory manner in relation to their unique practical situations. In the broad context of attempting to innovate under the loose rubric of "Interdisciplinary Inquiry" toward a more liberating curriculum, the result was specific team plans which were widely varied.

The following year, I was asked to return to England to do a follow-up study of the then some two hundred persons who had experienced the Goldsmith program. One technique used was an open-ended interview with a random selection of some forty participants (ranging over five years). The most common response to their experience was its meaning to them personally, the impact upon the way they saw themselves, as persons and professionals. Their judgements about the value of the actual curriculum plans produced and subsequent implementation were much more varied.

A final note on personal growth refers to the use of such experiences as group therapy, encounter groups, and similar activities. Frankly, I am not competent to evaluate these possibilities with a fair appraisal. I should think, from what I know, that there is a great potential here for personal growth if these practices can be sensibly related to the tasks of curriculum teaching and working. A caution, gleaned from the comments of Keen's remarks in Floyd Matson's "Behaviorism versus Humanism," is in order. He suggests that some varieties of the humanistic encounter group activities may be as dehumanizing as behavioristic techniques when they result in stripping all human dignity away from the person in the process.

Substance or Subject Matter

When we approach the task of the actual content substance of the curriculum, and wish to provide liberating possibilities through this avenue, we must keep some fundamental epistemological assumptions clearly in mind. Among these epistemological assumptions are:

1. Knowledge is uncertain, not absolute.
2. Knowledge is personal.
3. Knowledge is for use, not simply storage.

And, perhaps of a slightly different order:

4. Knowledge of social arrangements is knowledge of human creatures that reflect more than anything else historical accidents within the broad organizing trends of such areas as growing technology, sciences, industry, and religion.
5. Knowledge is not disparate or segmented in a broad human sense of lived meaning, but rather unitary and only by specific highly rationalized human interests and tasks has it seemed so.

Given these epistemological assumptions (which I believe can be justified satisfactorily), we may look at the total curriculum plan for substance or at any given aspect, areas, or subject within, keeping in mind that the quality of lived experiences resides in relationships. In this case the relationships are basically: (1) person to subject matter; (2) subject matter to subject matter; (3) society to subject matter; and (4) person to society.

Kliebard,[13] at the Genesco Conference, restates what he sees historically to be the basic questions of curriculum as "What knowledge is of most worth?"; "How is this differentiated for learning?"; "How do we teach it?"; and "How is it integrated?" He says the central question is the basic question of objectives.

I have little difficulty accepting the four questions as basic to curriculum but I believe he is in error from a liberating point of view in the priority he attaches to the questions of objectives. As a matter of fact, they can easily be transposed into the Tyler rationale, with the one notable exclusion being the evaluation question.

Care must be taken here to also note that this represents a "back to basics" in the curriculum field. It reflects a general trend that I see to refocus the definition of curriculum back to the subject matter to be taught. One might suppose that this is related to the frustrations suffered over the past years in dealing with the complexities of experience and/or activity models of curriculum.

Accepting these four questions as central to curriculum for purposes here, I would posit that from a liberating value base, the critical question must be the question of integration (or in terms used earlier—relationships). The question of goals, procedures and differentiation, it would seem to me are to be answered in the dynamics of relationships. It is this network of relationships that Maxine Greene[14] has spoken about so eloquently.

Given these comments we may turn to a possible set of suggested design guidelines that focus upon the four relationships, (i.e., subject to subject; person to subject; society to subject; and person to society). These guidelines are not new. They not only would lead toward developing new consciousness for social change, but have also been known over the years to many persons as good, sound educational premises. What follows is an illustrative reminder.

1. Curriculum substance must be directly related to needs, interests, past experiences and capabilities of persons.

2. Substance should be so organized as to allow for maximum possible variation among persons.

3. Substance should be organized so that it reveals to the greatest possible extent its instrumental and interpretative relevance to the social world.

4. Substance should be organized so that its meaning for the everyday living of the persons is apparent.

5. Substance should be organized so that the cognitive and affective relationships within and between usually disparate areas are apparent.

6. Substance should be organized so that all areas of the curriculum contribute directly to the creation of meaning structures which deal with the human condition.

7. And finally, substance should be organized so that the overall concern is the development of broad meaning structures, human values, attitudes, and moral understandings.

This by no means exhausts the possible guidelines. Designs which tend to be consistent with these liberating guidelines go under such titles at present: Core Curriculum, Interdisciplinary Inquiry, Open Education, Broad Fields, Emerging Needs, Affective Education, and Problems of Living.

Essentially what is needed is a continued effort to help workers in curriculum to see the meaning of these types of designs for freeing human potential and, thus, raising consciousness, but in a way that provides a creative development in relation to their everyday lives in schools. We are, as I am sure many of us can testify, in desperate need of new and better design possibilities which will facilitate this movement.

Preference Rules and Constitutive Rules

The last two elements to be discussed are the preference and constitutive rules. I shall deal with them together.

Michael Apple[15] has discussed the implication of these rules in relation to the hidden curriculum. Fundamentally, it amounts to recognition that there are rules which we may vary by preference, such as the rules for the use of the toilet facilities; and rules that constitute basic boundaries that cannot be varied if the system or cultural milieu is to retain its integrity and function. One such constitutive rule in most settings is the rule against cheating.

I would posit that in the cause of liberation that three things are necessary. First, that the distinction between these kinds of rules be brought into everyone's awareness. Second, constitutive rules must be made cognitively accessible to all through analysis and discussion. Finally, that to the degree possible, attempts be made to move constitutive rules into the realm of preference rules.

Apple's illustration of a chess game is useful here among other reasons because it also is utilized by Polanyi in establishing the identity of consciousness. Thus, chess is played with boundary conditions such as definition of the use of the spaces, the acceptable directions and procedures for moving different pieces on the board, etc. On the other side, the strategy, sequence of moves, etc., are the preference of the players. In Polanyi's terms one focuses consciously upon the strategy (preference rules) from the subsidiary cues (ground). It would appear then that the boundaries or constitutive rules, once internalized, become a tacit dimension, or, if you wish, a hidden curriculum.

The importance of the hidden curriculum in relation to freeing human potential cannot be overestimated. It is squarely at this juncture that many of the most pernicious practices and procedures reside. The "return to basics" referred to earlier is essentially a turning away from this critical aspect of schooling. It is probably a product or corollary of the general retrenchment to conserve stability that we are witnessing throughout our society at this time.

Curriculum teachers and workers must continuously raise the reflective consciousness questions, "What are the constitutive and preference rules?," and "Why do you have them?," and "What (if any) is their connection to the broader society and culture?" This can be done on an abstract level or through techniques, such as observation, video-tapes, self descriptions of our own practices and procedures, and tapes and typed transcripts of learning episodes.

One very good avenue for helping us to locate constitutive rules lies in our passions. It appears sensible to me that basic rules are those boundaries which are most apt to arouse our emotional judgements. Following the position espoused by Solomon, passions are not imposed upon us but are fundamental judgements, such as love, anger, anxiety, hate, envy, with which we have interpreted our situation and which provide a key through our reflection of our definition of the situation.

When we are pleased or disturbed by the actions of individuals or the way things are going, it would seem quite possible that we are touching basic boundaries or rules and making judgements in terms of these rules that reflect our perspectives, values, attitudes, and morals. Thus school people can come to grips with identifying the constitutive rules in their activity via careful reflection on those very situations and actions which do arouse our passions.

This kind of reflective activity also has the merit of completing the human response to liberation by a momentary and sometimes tentative but real dissolution of the subject-object distinction so prevalent and humanly damaging in Western Civilization.

There are two other critical areas which are of special importance. These concerns are the testing and evaluation plans and procedures, and the differentiation of hidden structures that are rationalized by goals and efficiency in procedure. The structures are hidden in the sense that their full intent in relation to what constitutes their existence is not revealed in their function. Thus, to many school people and students they seem "natural" rather than arbitrary value commitments.

One dimension of this problem is the clear realization that many of the grouping, labeling, and tracking procedures utilized in curriculum and instruction provide an unequal access to the common knowledge in our culture. This has the effect of replicating the social structure in terms of a meritocracy, and convincing the winners and losers that they deserve the status they achieve. There exists a considerable lack of distributive justice in our schools or society—either materially or in terms of knowledge and consciousness.

In another sense, many of the constitutive rules, such as "Work is more important than play," "The teacher is the final authority," "Be on time," and "Don't skip school," are most probably functions of social conditioning for the work force, rather than necessary for stimulating and developing human creative potential or capabilities.

The evaluation dimension is at least as troublesome for persons concerned about human liberation. It perhaps is the epitome of domination for all persons in schools. What it essentially amounts to in practical terms is a system that can be characterized as a tyranny of knowledge and basic skills. It is interesting to note in passing that in the Business School at the University of North Carolina at Greensboro, the term "evaluation" is defined as control, perhaps a more honest approach than we take.

I am reasonably sure in my own mind that the major reason that technical rationales and the use of behavioristic approaches are dominant in curriculum is that they are logically (though not necessarily empirically) the most advantageous approaches to control. Further, the concerns for specifying and managing by objectives are not essentially related to the question of "what knowledge is of most worth," or "what relationships enhance the quality of living," but, become important only in the control nexus of evaluation. Though evaluation is often made to seem a necessary adjunct to reaching goals, I am afraid that statements of objectives are much more apt to be necessary adjuncts to the system of evaluative control.

There is really no point in detailing the problems with accountability, behavioral objectives, behavioral modification, management by objectives, systems analysis, teacher competencies, and other control and evaluation-oriented procedures. Let it just be said that they are the tools of domination for the tyranny of cognitive knowledge and skills in our schools.

Neither shall I, at this point, suggest strategies or procedures for changing evaluation procedures, for I am not sure that positive alternatives within the control orientation are even possible. What I shall say is that if evaluation were truly an adjunct to the goals of human liberation, its value would reside in the provision of data from the consequences of our actions which could serve as a basis in our consciousness for our further reflection and praxis.

Conclusion

In closing, I would like to reiterate the points I have presented. I believe that things are not hopeless and curriculum thinking is not moribund. It is essentially a matter of our expectations, and our expectations should be focused upon the development of cultural consciousness. Further, I assume that the major meaning of education relates to the liberation of human potential and not the control of human behavior, which to me is training. Consciousness is an essential entity of human beings, through existence in a material base. Any quest for liberating persons from arbitrary domination by others calls for a basic change in attitudes, values, morals, and perspectives, as well as change in social and economic structures. We in our roles as curriculum teachers and workers can only expect to have influence in the realm of consciousness. This is both a necessary and significant contribution.

Changing consciousness toward liberating activity can be effected by focusing upon school persons' ideas and perspectives, personal growth, subject matter, and upon the preference and constitutive rules, with the intent of bringing to bear our analysis upon the quality of the living relationships that exist in our school lives.

The avenues and aspects will be manifold, but essentially any change in consciousness or practice that moves one step closer to freeing ourselves from arbitrary domination by social structures or other persons (past or present) may be counted as a legitimate step toward liberation.

What we must do, if we are concerned about these matters, is to become somewhat more humble, but continue to work for what we believe to be right.

We must, as Erich Fromm[16] says, keep up our hope; which he defines as the willingness to keep working for what we believe in with the full realization that we may never see it come to fruition in our lifetime.

Notes

1. In doing so, I shall immediately be accused of liberal reformism rather than radical revolution. The weight isn't too heavy to carry, but I think there is a subtle difference in the position that will be developed here and traditional ideas of reform. In any case, what I propose seems to me the only sensible way to proceed.

2. Michael Polanyi, *Personal Knowledge* (Chicago: University of Chicago Press, 1958); and Michael Polanyi, *The Tacit Dimension* (Garden City, NY: Doubleday, 1967).

3. Polanyi, *Personal Knowledge*, p. 51.

4. Carl Boggs, *Gramsci's Marxism* (London: Pluto Press, 1976).

5. *Ibid*, p. 39.

6. Jürgen Habermas, *Knowledge and Human Interest* (Boston: Beacon Press, 1971).

7. William Irwin Thompson, *Evil and World Order* (New York: Harper and Row, 1976).

8. Phillip Phenix, "Transcendence and the Curriculum," *Teachers College Record* (Dec., 1971), pp. 271–283.

9. Paulo Soleri, *Matter Becoming Spirit* (Garden City, NY: Anchor Press/Doubleday, 1973), pp. 2 and 4.

10. Rene Spitz, *Fundamental Education Play and Development*, Maria Piers, ed. (New York: W.W. Norton, 1977).

11. Dwayne Huebner, "Curricular Language and Classroom Meanings," in *Language and Meaning*, James B. Macdonald, ed. (Washington, DC: A.S.C.D., 1966), pp. 8–26.

12. Herbert Marcuse, *One-Dimensional Man: Studies in the Ideology of Advanced Industrial Societies* (Boston: Beacon Press, 1964).

13. Herbert Kliebard, "Curriculum Theory: Give Me a 'For Instance,'" *Curriculum Inquiry*, vol. 6, no. 4 (1977), pp. 257–268.

14. Maxine Greene, "Curriculum and Consciousness," *Teacher College Record*, 73, no. 2 (Dec. 1971), pp. 253–269.

15. Michael Apple, "The Hidden Curriculum and the Nature of Conflict," *Interchange*, 2, no. 4 (1971), pp. 27–40.

16. Erich Fromm, *The Revolution of Hope* (New York: Harper and Row, 1968).

Chapter Eleven

Theory, Practice and the Hermeneutic Circle

"What does a fish know about the water in which he swims all his life?"
　　　　　　　　　　　—Albert Einstein

Einstein spent his whole life preoccupied with the interrelationships that give our world its structure and that link "us" with the "world about us." He sought to understand.

Now Einstein may have wished to have controlled these structures and relationships, and/or may have wished that knowledge of these structures and relationships would provide an emancipatory experience for humanity. What is clear, however, is that his basic intention, and one he shared with many others, was a desire to search for truth and to come to a better understanding of reality.

I have introduced this theme because we, in curriculum, have experienced a heavy input of control and/or emancipation oriented ideas in the past thirty years. The search for understanding—the *hermeneutic* quest—appears to have been relegated to a third neutral, non-action category of cultural consensus. This, I suggest, is a grave error on our part, for I believe the search for understanding is the basis in which scientific-technical and critical theory efforts are grounded.

Understanding, among other things, is not a totally rational process. It is not a goal which may be reached by a mathematical-logical process of reasoning. Understanding is not an outcome of problem solving, or a product which emerges rationally from preexisting structures.

It is most likely an overemphasis upon rationalism, dependent upon dualisms such as mind and body, subject and object, thinking and doing that has created the present situation in our intellectual lives and most assuredly therefore in curriculum theory.

"The essence of what we call rational thought is leaving out things—gut sensations, feelings, impulses to act," says Phillip Slater.[1] It leaves out the thinker, his or her unique horizon or place in the universe, with its associated urges, feelings and impulses. The main purpose of rational thought is to explain things so that we may predict and control them. Explain means to ex-plain or "flatten out."

The emotions that govern the need to be rational or "objective" (analyze, distinguish, and categorize) are anxiety, fear and tension. A thought, Slater remarks, is just a deed running scared, and "rational" or "objective" thought is the most frightened form of thinking. Rationality, Slater continues, is painting by the numbers. No matter how much information rationalists accumulate, or how many concepts they identify, they won't learn about those aspects of reality that frightened them into being cautious in the first place.

It is this rationalism that pervades curriculum theory in the clothes of science, or critical theory, or technique. This was brought home forcefully to me, for example, by William Doll's recent statement on "A Structural View of Curriculum."[2] What occurred to me then was the recognition that Doll's proposal to transcend the behaviorist-humanist squabble was another totally rational proposal. Doll's use of Piaget's structuralism is highly rationalistic, both in content and process. What could be more so than having the capstone of intellectual development rest in formal logic. Among other things, this discovery warrants the kind of feminist critique that Carol Gilligan gave Lawrence Kohlberg when she suggested that compassion was the highest female virtue, not justice as Kohlberg posits.[3]   Margaret Donaldson has laid some partial groundwork for that sort of analysis of Piaget.[4]

The point here is to emphasize that almost all of our curriculum theory efforts are attempts to explain (flatten out), which are usually intended to lead to prediction and control. Thus, implicit in this form of rational theory is the dualism of theory and practice and the assumption that the "proof of the pudding" is in practice. The paradox of rationalist theory is in effect that it leads to an anti-intellectual priority in doing. Rationalism, in other words, becomes the handmaiden of "good works."

The ancient Greeks distinguished between theory and practice as two ways of living: the contemplative and the political. I think that this understanding holds for what I wish to present. The rationalist in curriculum theory is living a political way of life, explaining in order to affect the living context of education in a direct controlling way—a political action. I personally suggest that it is time to reaffirm the legitimacy of contemplative curriculum theory. In Heidegger's terms, let us accept meditative thinking on an equal footing with calculative thinking.

Both the control and the emancipation curriculum theories have an optimistic buoyancy that suggests we can create and/or control ourselves, our relationships and the world. Archibald Wheeler, a theoretical physicist, reminds us that the physical world is not amenable to this when he says "what is hard is to give up thinking of nature as a machine that goes on independent of the observer. What we conceive of as reality is a few iron posts of observation with paper maché construction between them that is but the elaborate work of our imagination."[5]

Lyall Watson, a biologist, puts this another way:

In other words what we regard as ordinary physical matter is simply an idea that occupies a world frame common to all minds.   The universe is literally a collective thought, and we have a very powerful say in the reality manifest in our particular sector.

In our sanest moments we are all critical realists.   We know that there exists a reality "out there," and we know that as human beings that reality is known to us by the limits and creativeness of the human imagination. What we "know" is as much or more who we humans are: as it is what is there!

The age of the naive realist, the positivist with the delusions of one to one correspondence, is no longer at the forefront of our physical science.   Our knowledge and understanding has moved us beyond this, though the residue of this exists strongly in the common sense of our culture of positivism.   Thus, we live with naive realism in our lives and especially in our scientific-technical world, but also in the form of such emancipatory doctrines as scientific Marxism. As William Barrett suggests so persuasively, both capitalism and communism as they exists today are offsprings of the scientific-technical era.[6]

D.H. Wilkinson, another physicist, suggests that there are three kinds of limits to the knowledge of our natural world.   Essentially they are limitations placed upon our perceptual and conceptual ability by the nature of technology, reality, and the biology of the human species.   Wilkinson's major point is that scientists are limited in their knowledge and that at the point where knowledge no longer suffices, the scientist, like all other humans, creates explanation and meaning from an aesthetic feeling base.[7]

As Wilkinson says, "It is a truism with a capital T, that in man's description of the natural world, truth can never be accorded more that a 't' from the lower case. This is because you can with certainty prove a hypothesis to be wrong, but you can never prove a hypothesis to be uniquely wise." He goes on later to ask: "How do we choose between alternative scientific hypotheses when we have used up all our scientific criteria?"[8]

The remaining criterion of what is right rests in our feelings. It is precisely what we do when we are faced with a "regular" choice between two paintings, or poems, or any two courses of action. We sift and exhaust the evidence and then choose because we feel.

What this says is that human behavior and activity, though modified by experiences, issues from a basic capacity which is the same for whatever endeavor—art or science—in which humans engage in their personal and cultural experience.

The fundamental human quest is the search for meaning and the basic human capacity for this is experienced in the hermeneutic process of interpretation of the text (whether artifact, natural world or human action). This is the search (or research) for greater understanding that motivates and satisfies us.

The real, both Slater[9] and MacMurray[10] remind us, means important. What is real is what is important to us. Abstract thought is grounded in value, since a thought (or system of thought) can only be of value to someone—a matter of feeling, motive and desire. "We can't separate thinking from wanting, we can only think desirously."

Curriculum theorizing is potentially the creation of reality. Our rationalistic theory leads to what Slater has termed the "tinkertoy" style of reality, a sequential compartmentalized and categorized set of pieces which we put together through a language of nouns.[11]

Curriculum theory as a search for understanding, a meditative thinking, is an attempt to deal with unity rather than bits and parts additively. It is a theory which is experienced as a participatory phenomena, where the person engages in dialogue with the theory, bringing each person's biography and values to the interpretation. The intention is not to explain (flatten out) for control purposes, but to reinterpret in order to provide greater grounding for understanding.

Setting for Theory-Practice

What has been said up to now is a platform or frame within which I shall place my concern for theory and practice. Essentially, I shall propose that the problematics of theory-practice must be viewed in a larger framework, in a process which Paul Ricouer and Hans-Georg Gadamer call the hermeneutic circle.[12] Thus theory and practice are not only integrated through action and reflection, but are a larger interpretive endeavor which includes intention and direction toward the recovery of meaning and the development of understanding.

Practice, Barrett reminds us, is an abstract concept.[13] The idea of practice as separate from the world of everyday life is a specific development in human thought. Thus, the separation of theory from practice is only possible when each is abstracted from the concreteness of reality.

Theory as systematic and formal reflection is an abstraction from the ordinary thinking present in all human activity. Practice is abstracted from the constant action which accompanies ordinary reflection. Both theory and practice are embedded in social and cultural forms. All the human sciences start off by referring back to a lived experience, at least an implicit one, and they provide a certain understanding of this. Social science data provide us with a basis for our imaginations in terms of our experience of the life world.

Ricouer, for example, discusses hermeneutics in terms of whether the hermeneutic quest is focused upon the restoration of meaning or the reduction of illusion. He talks at some length about the theorizing of Freud, Marx, and Nietzsche in terms of their commitment to facilitating greater understanding through the reduction of illusion. Thus they enter the theory-practice problematic with the intention of reducing illusion, distortion and mystification. For these theorists, engaging in a theory-praxis relationship reveals the illusions that exist and provides us with a basis for new knowledge and understanding of reality.

Ricouer, however, raises questions about this form of hermeneutics and opts for the restoration of meaning as the more desirable intention of hermeneutics. He feels that what is at stake is what he calls the mytho-poetic core of imagination. He says that a demystifying hermeneutics sets up a "rude discipline of necessity." Following Spinoza, he characterizes rude necessity as: "first one finds oneself a slave, understands one's slavery, and rediscovers oneself within defined necessity." Ricouer feels this intention lacks "the grace of imagination, the upsurge of the possible."

Gadamer discusses a similar concern as expressed by Ricouer in terms of the distinction between "not understanding" and "misunderstanding." Attributing the shift from not understanding to misunderstanding to Schleirmacher, one suspects that Freud, Marx and Nietzsche (for example) are oriented toward clearing misunderstandings. Gadamer too, as Ricouer, feels that this is a mistake. It is not so much that we misunderstand but that we do not understand. For him the intention of hermeneutics is to reinterpret the situation, and the boundaries or horizons of the interpreter are a critical part of this process of understanding. In essence, what Gadamer and Ricouer are calling for is an ontological interpretation in hermeneutics rather than an epistemological or methodological stance.

Following from this it appears that the problem of theory-praxis must be seen in light of the interpretation of meaning as an attempt to reinterpret a context with the hope of reducing illusion, yes; but more fundamentally to come to understand what is not now understood.

It would appear that both the scientific-technical and critical theorists look specifically toward practice as the foundation variable. "By your good works shall ye be known." Theory, in this sense, becomes strictly an instrumental schema at the service of human activity. This attitude toward knowledge was articulated by Francis Bacon in *Novum Organum.* "Of all signs there is none more certain or noble than that taken from fruits. For fruits and works are as it were sponsors and sureties for the truth of philosophies. . ." This attitude is anti-theoretical and persists today in the idea that science or knowledge ought to be "practical," that is applicable to technological programs. . . and all men "ought to organize themselves as a sacred duty to improve and transform the conditions of life. . ."

This attitude turns out to be a limited concept of theory. Later science was to affirm the power of theory, and for our purposes it is proposed that both theory and practice are contributory to revealing greater understanding, to be a part of the hermeneutic circle.

Both enter in as a necessary moment in the hermeneutic circle, the quest for understanding and meaning, and as such the dialectic of theory-practice must itself be viewed in terms of what it reveals that creates new meaning for us through our interpretation. The test of "good" theory in practice is thus, not centrally that it works (i.e., that we can control practice), but that in the engagement of theory and practice we are emancipated from previous misunderstandings and are then freed to reinterpret situations and reach greater understandings.

Both science and critical theory are engaged in the theory-practice problem. In science, for example, you may treat theory as a set of hypotheses which are tested in the practice of empirical studies. Thus the concrete world of practice either responds as predicted or it doesn't. If it does respond as predicted this response is added to the larger corpus of related responses in the form of new knowledge. In science this process supposedly goes in a neutral value framework.

Critical theory recognizes the role of human interest in knowledge formation and creation. Science, critical theory claims, has an interest in control and critical theory has an interest in emancipation. Thus, critical theory calls its interest in practice, a problem of theory and praxis. What this means is theory which is self-reflective and with an interest in practices which release persons from domination, or speaking positively, with an interest in emancipation.

Critical theory then proceeds on the basis of a methodological paradigm much as psychoanalysis, as Habermas describes it,[14] or as a method of action such as Paulo Friere illustrates.[15] In either case there are common elements such as a general analytical theory (e.g., variations of Marxism) which are presented as a potential way of viewing the practical reality of a person or group of persons. This framework is related and integrated in relation to the way the person or group of persons sees their own reality, and then tested in their real life circumstances in terms of their emancipation (e.g., release from neurosis or improvement of realistic consciousness or practical freedom from the past domination by others).

Provided what has been said is a reasonable and valid portrayal of science and critical theory, two significant understandings emerge.

First, both science and critical theory are methodologies (epistemological approaches) which utilize a theory-practice (or praxis) relationship to create knowledge.

Further, each methodology utilizes the theory-practice relationship to increase their understanding of what *is*, as well as utilizing their knowledge to create technical functions or emancipatory praxis.

This leads to a recognition that both science and critical theory are participants in a hermeneutical process. Both methodologies lead to increased understanding of reality through the interpretation and reinterpretation of the reality with which they are concerned through the dynamics of the theory-practice/praxis relationship.

Whatever rests in this category which is truly separate from control or emancipation must rest in the area of poetics. I would thus propose that there is a third methodology, that of the mytho-poetic imagination, particularly related to the use of insight, visualization and imagination, which is essentially separate from science and praxis. Its practical method is surely similar to Polanyi's indwelling,[16] and, most probably what Steiner credits Heidegger's life work to be—that is, a process of "radical astonishment."[17] The mytho-poetic deals with "why there is being rather than nothing," at the awe, wonder, and anxiety of this puzzle.

I think perhaps this concern is most beautifully caught in Sören Kierkegaard's novel *Reflections*.

> One sticks one finger into the soil to tell by the smell what land one is on: I stick my finger into existence—it smells of nothing. Where am I? Who am I? How did I come to be here? What is this thing called world? How did I come into the world? Why was I not consulted?. . . and if I am compelled to take part in it, where is the Director? I would like to see him![18]

To me this clearly expresses the poetic practical interest in *meaning*. It is perhaps best called the methodology of "so what?" Its search is for meaning and a sense of unity and well being.

The methods of poetics also engage in the theory-practice relationship, only in a more personalized and uniquely biographical manner.   Here, broadly speaking, insights, images, and imaginative (or speculative) symbolizations are created as possible meaning structures. These meaning structures are however created as much or more by the concrete and practical experience of the participant in relation to the symbols, as they are in the coherence of the symbolic structure itself.   The process of self reflection in this case is the reflection upon the self, not reflection on the theory in a critical theory mode.

Science (in contrast to scientists) cannot deal with ultimate meaning, and critical theory in its concern for praxis leaves open the question of infinity and eternity.   For this and a host of more mundane aesthetic aspects of reality we need poetic participation in meaning.

But what of hermeneutics, per se? It is my opinion that the hermeneutic circle of understanding lies within each of the epistemologies and also transcends each method in the form of an ontological platform.

Each method, thus, uses a theory-practice interaction to create greater understanding and practical activity.   To the extent that we come to know and understand more through the theory-practice relationship, we are participating in a hermeneutic process.

The three methods (science, critical theory and poetics) are contributory methodologies to a larger hermeneutic circle of continual search for greater understanding, and for a more satisfying interpretation of what *is*.

The importance of this distinction lies in a differentiation between the ontological and epistemological understandings of hermeneutics and is illustrated by what I believe to be a misunderstanding by Habermas about the basis of hermeneutics.[19] This opinion is shared by Gadamer and there exists today a series of dialogues between the men.[20] I shall not review this literature here, but simply comment that Habermas' position issues from concern mainly for the social sciences and follows the work of Dilthey in both spirit and content. Gadamer's position of the larger view of hermeneutics comes out of broader religio-social concern.

Also, Habermas does not deal adequately with the aesthetic (a failing of many critical theorists[21]), and concludes that the humanities' hermeneutic methodology has become "objective" in its patterning after the scientific method. The hermeneutic, by his view remains merely method, and it is my contention, following Gadamer and Ricouer, that the hermeneutic circle is ontological in nature; and that at the level of method the appropriate category to accompany science and praxis is art, or the mytho-poetic.

Science, critical theory and poetics provide us with boundaries, or "landscapes" as Maxine Greene expressed it.[22] But Colin Wilson reminds us that although we need a frame to see the world, sooner or later this frame is seen as an absurdity. The frame is really a lie, for everything in it implies the existence of new vistas beyond. Yet we cannot grasp the world without a frame. This is the nature of mind.

And What About Curriculum Theory and Practice?

Curriculum theory, it is suggested here, is a form of hermeneutic theory. Thus curriculum theory is an ever renewing attempt to interpret curricular reality and to develop greater understanding. Curricular practice results from a hermeneutic process which both lies within the three methods (epistemologies) and transcends them.

Curriculum theory, as a movement in the hermeneutic circle, does not draw its reason for existence from practice. Schwab made this point clearly when he dramatically separated theory from practice through his discussion of the radical difference between theory and practice that may be witnessed in the methods of each, the source of their problems, their distinctly different subject matters, and outcomes of a different kind. Schwab did not, however, place the theory-practice relationship in a larger hermeneutic process.[23]

Theory, however, as Van Manen says, has meaning of its' own.[24] Theory is an act of imagining and it is *through* theory that we may hope to reach what theory points to. Not *in* the theory, for theory focused upon as a thing in itself becomes opaque, merely a "thing" in itself, which ends any vision it might possess. And, we don't reach our reality because of theory, for it is not a link in a logical chain, nor a conclusion in itself, or part of a syllogism. It is *through theory* that we see, think, know.

The act of theorizing is an act of faith, a religious act. It is the expression of belief, and as William James clearly expounds in *The Will To Believe*, belief necessitates an act of the moral will based on faith.[25] *Curriculum theorizing is a prayerful act*. It is an expression of the humanistic vision in life.

As such it should not be whipsawed into "accountability" by a set of "mind forged manacles," whether Aristotelian syllogism, Roman formulary, factualized hypothesis in scientific terms, or critical visions of someone's utopia. Curriculum theory is what speaks to us *through it* and what we do is informed by theory; but neither the specific words of theory nor the specific pedagogical acts of educators are the reality of education. What defines each is the spirit and vision that shines through the surface manifestations.

These methods provide us with technical and utilitarian control through technique, with emancipatory praxis through critical reflection, and with aesthetic, moral and metaphysical meaning through poetics.

What has been missing, and what has caused antagonism in curriculum theory, is a failure to realize that all three methodologies participate in the larger hermeneutic circle.

The necessity to reject the method of science and its positivism is essentially a political activity on the part of curriculum theorists by which the legitimacy of critical theory and poetics can be established in the field. The conflict between poetics and critical theory, perhaps best represented by the dialogue between the writings of William Pinar[26] and Michael Apple,[27] turns out to be sibling rivalry rather than a fundamental schism.

The three methods, in other words, provide instrumental practice (technique), emancipatory political praxis, and a personal awareness, insight, and vision for self reflection. Each is a valid basis for increasing our understanding, for helping us to interpret the reality of curricular circumstances.

The work of Dwayne Huebner, especially that dealing with language in the classroom, prepares us for this view.[28]   When we examine the technical, scientific, political, moral, and aesthetic language structures and potentials for talking about curriculum, we are clearly leading toward the three methods of knowledge that are called the scientific-technical, emancipatory (political), and the mytho-poetic (moral, aesthetic, metaphysical). As Huebner pointed out, all ways of talking are legitimate in some way, or for some purpose, or at some time. What wasn't explicated in his work was the ground of talking, which it is proposed here (in terms of methods) is the frame or horizon of the hermeneutic circle of understanding.

Returning to the presumption that curriculum theory is a form of hermeneutic theory with three contributing methodologies, it becomes explicable why non-scientific curriculum theory is a mystery to most educators. It is a mystery because it deals with *the* mystery.

Curriculum theory is not essentially instrumental. If we must counter with opposites, curriculum theory is basically expressive. We possess instructional methods which fall within the activity of curricular theorizing, but these instrumental methods provide a theory-practice dialectic which leads to the expression and interpretation of meaning, and to the development of greater understanding.

The focus of curriculum is not a context where a curriculum is in operation. The focus of curriculum is a microcosm of the universe. Blake's grain of sand;

to which we bring ourselves, our consciousness, and our cultural reality. We are in effect expressing this in a total context.

As curriculum theorists we should be reminded of what Barrett quotes Alfred North Whitehead as saying to Bertrand Russell. "There are two kinds of people in the world, the muddle-headed and the simple-minded. You Bertee, are simple-minded, and I am muddle-headed."[29]

The mathematical logic of Bertrand Russell no longer holds out the solution to reality. It was simple-minded as are most of the instrumental methods of curriculum. We are, as curriculum theorists, more aptly doomed to the expression of our muddle-headedness, since this appears to be the only long-range hope for the creation of meaning in our lives or our profession.

Van Manen carries this thought in another direction in his writing on pedagogical theorizing. Language is the vehicle of expression, but the words let the life world shine through them. It is an alternative to the silence that speech points toward. Pedagogical practice is the constant recovery of the pedagogical relationship through redemption, recall, regaining or recapturing the meaning of pedagogical activity.[30]

About theory, Van Manen says:

> Theorizing for the sake of theorizing, like an art for art's sake, is not a superfluous self serving exercise. . . . Theorizing contributes to one's resourcefulness. . . not in a simple means-ends as applied, technical, pragmatic sense, nor in an attitudinal or subjectivist psychological sense. Theorizing contributes to one's resourcefulness by directing the orienting questions toward the source itself; the source which gives life or spirit to (inspire) our pedagogic life. To theorize is to struggle to achieve one's limits, to find one's origins, one's grounding in that which makes our pedagogic life possible.[31]

The hermeneutical process is universal and basic for all inter-human experience, both of history and the present movement, precisely because of the fact that meaning can be experienced, even where it is not actually intended.

Notes

1. Phillip Slater, *The Wayward Gate* (Boston: Beacon Press, 1977), p. 19.

2. William Doll, "A Structural View of Curriculum," *Theory into Practice*, Fall 1979.

3. Carol Gilligan, "In a Different Voice: Woman's Conception of the Self and Morality," *Harvard Educational Review*, November 1977.

4. Margaret Donaldson, *Children's Minds* (New York: W.W. Norton and Co., 1978).

5. Archibald Wheeler, "Proving the Universe," *Newsweek*, March 12, 1979.

6. William Barrett, *The Illusion of Technique* (New York: Anchor Books, Doubleday, 1979).

7. D.H. Wilkinson, "The Universe as Artifact," in *Scientific Models of Man*, Henry Harris, ed. (Oxford: Clarendon Press, 1979).

8. *Ibid.*

9. Slater, *The Wayward Gate.*

10. John MacMurray, *The Self As Agent* (London: Faber and Faber, Limited, 1957).

11. Slater, *The Wayward Gate.*

12. See Paul Ricouer, *The Philosophy of Paul Ricouer*, Charles Reagon and David Stewart, eds. (Boston: Beacon Press, 1978); and Hans-Georg Gadamer, *Philosophical Hermeneutics* (Berkeley, CA: University of California Press, 1976).

13. Barrett, *The Illusion of Technique.*

14. Jürgen Habermas, *Knowledge and Human Interest* (Boston: Beacon Press, 1971).

15. Paulo Friere, *Pedagogy of the Oppressed* (New York: Herder & Herder, 1970).

16. Michael Polanyi, *The Tacit Dimension* (New York: Anchor Paperback, 1972).

17. George Steiner, *Martin Heidegger* (New York: Viking Press, 1979).

18. Sören Kierkegaard, *Reflections*, as quoted in Colin Wilson, *The Intelligent Universe* (New York: G.P. Putnam & Sons, 1975), p. 24.

19. Habermas, *Knowledge and Human Interest*.

20. See, for example, David Couzins Hoy, *The Critical Circle* (Berkeley, CA: University of California Press, 1978).

21. A notable exception is the recent work of Marcuse [Herbert Marcuse, *The Aesthetic Dimension* (Boston: Beacon Press, 1978).] who challenges the classical Marxist ideological conception of art, and discusses the truth that art expresses as necessity and experience, which is an essential component of revolution even though it does not fall in the domain of radical praxis.

22. Maxine Greene, *Landscapes for Learning* (New York: Teachers College Press, 1978).

23. Joseph Schwab, *The Practical: A Language for Curriculum* (Washington, DC: National Education Association, 1970).

24. Max Van Manen, "Pedagogical Theorizing." Paper presented at the Annual A.E.R.A. Conference - Boston, MA, April 1980.

25. William James, *The Will to Believe: Selected Papers on Philosophy* (New York: J. M. Deny and Sons, 1917).

26. See, for example, William Pinar, "Currere: Toward Reconceptualization" in *Curriculum Theorizing*, William Pinar, ed. (Berkeley, CA: McCutchan Publishing Co., 1975).

27. See, for example, Michael Apple, "Ideology, Reproduction and Educational Reform," *Comparative Education Review*, XXII, October, 1978.

28. Dwayne Huebner, "Curricular Language and Classroom Meanings," in *Language and Meaning*, James Macdonald and Robert Leeper, eds. (Washington, DC: ASCD, 1966).

29. Barrett, *The Illusion of Technique*.

30. Van Manen, "Pedagogical Theorizing."

31. *Ibid.*, pp. 12 –13.

Selected Bibliography

1958   "Practice Grows from Theory and Research," *Childhood Education*, 4(6), pp. 256–258.

1959   *The Professional Task of the Teacher* (unpublished manuscript).

1960   "A New Departure in Teacher Education," *Journal of Teacher Education*, 11(4), pp. 572–575 (with R. C. Doll).

"The Theme of the Conference," in *Research Frontiers in the Study of Children's Learning*, J.B. Macdonald, ed. (Milwaukee, WI: University of Wisconsin-Milwaukee), pp. 5–6.

"Curriculum Development" (paper presented at Anderson, NC).

1961   "Who is Ready for Teacher Education?," *Journal of Educational Sociology*, 35(3), pp. 123–127.

"Diagnosing Sources of Learning Difficuluties," *The National Elementary Principal*, 41(2), pp. 27–31 (with J. D. Raths).

Research Frontiers in the Study of Children's Learning (Milwaukee, WI: University of Wisconsin-Milwaukee) (monograph).

Cues to Effective Teaching and Teacher Education (New York: New York University School of Education) (monograph).

1962   *School Entrance Age and Achievement at the Third Grade Level* (Report of the Kindergarten Committee of the Lakeshore Curriculum Study Council) (unpublished report with J. D. Raths).

"Problems in Education and Research" (paper presented at Second Annual Meeting of Wisconsin Educational Research Association).

1963   "Human Development and the Emergence of Human Potentialities," *Pedagogia*, 11(1), pp. 113–28.

"The Nature of Instruction: Needed Theory and Research," *Educational Leadership*, 21(1), pp. 5–7.

"Curriculum Research: Problems, Techniques, and Prospects," *Review of Educational Research*, 33(3), pp. 322–329 (with J. D. Raths).

The Role of the Campus School at the University of Wisconsin-Milwaukee (unpublished manuscript with D. M. Matheson).

"Guidelines to Innovation" (paper presented at Fourth Annual Curriculum Research Seminar, Center for School Experimentation, College of Education, Ohio State University, Columbus, OH).

"Major Areas of Innovation Today" (paper presented at Fourth Annual Curriculum Research Seminar, Center for School Experimentation, Collegeof Education, Ohio State University, Columbus, OH).

1964   "Educational Research and Development as an Agent in Social Change: Research in Review," *Educational Leadership*, 22(1), pp. 57–63.

"Should We Group by Creative Abilities?," *The Elementary School Journal*, 65(3), pp. 137–142 (with J. D. Raths).

"An Image of Man: The Learner Himself" in *Individualizing Instruction,* R. C. Doll, ed. (Washington, DC: Association for Supervision and Curriculum Development), pp. 29–49.

Independent Study (unpublished manuscript)

"Curriculum Theory: Problems and a Prospectus" (paper presented at meeting of Professors of Curriculum, Miami Beach, FL).

"Educational Research" (paper presented at meeting of the Maryland Association for Supervision and Curriculum Development, Columbus, MD).

"Theories of Teaching" (paper presented at meeting of the State Teachers for the Deaf, Green Bay, WI).

1965   "Beginning Reading Research: A Reflection of Social Reality? Research in Review," *Educational Leadership*, 22(6), pp. 441–447.

"Myths About Instruction," *Educational Leadership*, 22(7), 571–576, pp. 609–617.

"Knowledge About Supervision: Rationalization or Rationale? Research in Review," *Educational Leadership*, 23(2), pp. 161–163.

"Moral Dilemmas in Schooling. Research in Review," *Educational Leadership*, 23(1), pp. 29–32 (with H. M. Clements).

Strategies of Curriculum Development: Selected Writings of Virgil E. Herrick (Columbus, OH: Charles E. Merrill), (with D. W. Anderson and F. B. May).

"Educational Models for Instruction" in *Theory of Instruction*, J. B. Macdonald and R. Leeper, eds. (Washington, DC: Association for Supervision and Curriculum Development).

"Educational Models for Instruction—Introduction" in *Theories of Instruction*, J. B. Macdonald and R. Leeper, eds. (Washington, DC: Association of Supervision and Curriculum Development), pp. 1–8.

"Independent Learning: The Theme of the Conference," in *The Theory and Nature of Independent Learning*, G. T. Gleason, ed. (Scranton: International Textbook), pp. 1–13.

A Research Oriented Elementary Education Stdent Teaching Program (Milwaukee, WI: University of Wisconsin-Milwaukee School of Education) (monograph with G. W. Denemark, B. J. Wolfson, B. J. Stillman & E. Zaret).

Theories of Instruction (Washington DC: Association for Supervision and Curriculum Development) (monograph with R. Leeper as editors).

"Inquiry in Teaching" (unpublished manuscript).

1965–66   "Helping Teachers Change" (paper presented at Eleventh Annual Meeting of the Association for Supervision and Curriculum Development, Washington, DC).

1966   "Thoughts About Research in Schools," *Educational Leadership*, 23(7), pp. 601–604.

"Praxiological Experience and Vocational Education," *Delta Pi Epsilon Journal*, 9(1), pp. 14–20.

"Gamesmanship in the Classroom," *National Association of Secondary School Principals Bulletin*, 50(314), pp. 51–68.

"Moral Concerns in Assessing Pupil Growth," *The National Elementary School Principal*, 45(6), pp. 29–33 (with H. M. Clements).

"Individual Versus Group Instruction in Reading," *The Reading Teacher*, 19(8), pp. 643–646, 652 (with T. L. Harris and J. S. Mann).

"The How of Core," in *Core Curriculum: The Why and the What*, R. Calloway, ed. (Milwaukee, WI: University of Wisconsin-Milwaukee School of Education), pp. 5–20.

"The Why of Core: A Rationale for Teacher-Learning" in *Core Curriculum: The Why and the What*, R. Callaway, ed. (Milwaukee, WI: University of Wisconsin-Milwaukee School of Education) pp. 5–20.

"Language, Meaning, and Motivation: An Introduction," in *Language and Meaning*, J. B. Macdonald and R. Leeper, eds. (Washington,

DC: Association of Supervision and Curriculum Development), pp. 1–7.

"The Person in the Curriculum," in *Precedents and Promise in the Curriculum Field*, H. F. Robinson, ed. (New York: Teacher's College Press), pp. 38–52.

An Experimental Study of the Group Versus the One-To-One Instructional Relationship in the First Grade Basal Reading Programs (Madison, WI: University of Wisconsin, Laboratory for Research in Basic Skills, School of Education) (monograph).

"Consideration About Content and Cognition" (paper presented as the Second Annual National Secondary Principals Symposium, Athens, GA).

"Curriculum Theory and Development in Vocational Education" (paper presented at Symposium in Vocational Education and Curriculum, American Educational Research Association, Chicago, IL).

"Research Design for Assessing Teacher Education Programs in Special Education" (paper presented at Fourty-fourth Annual CEC Convention, Special Education: Strategies for Educational Progress, Toronto, Ontario, Canada).

"Process and Change in Education" (paper presented at the Ohio State Department of Education Meeting, Columbus, OH).

"Perspectives on Technological Rationality in Education" (paper presented at the Association for Supervision and Curriculum Development Research Institute, Western Section, Minneapolis, MN).

1967   "The Dimension of Curriculum Planning," *Samplings*, 1(1), pp. 34–48.

"An Example of Disciplined Curriculum Thinking," *Theory Into Practice*, 6(4), pp. 166–171.

"Preservice and In-Service Education of Teachers," *Review of Educational Research*, 37(3), pp. 233–247 (with G. W. Denemark).

"Structures in Curriculum," in *Process for Curriculum Change* (Madison, WI: Wisconsin Department of Public Instruction), pp. 28–46.

A Study of Openness in Classroom Interactions (Milwaukee, WI: Marquette University) (monograph with E. Zaret).

Developing Human Potential (St. Paul, MN: Personal Services).

"The High School in Human Terms: Curriculum Design" (paper presented at the ASCD Western Invitational Conference, Portland, OR).

"The Necessity for Change in Schooling and Teaching" (unpublished manuscript).

"Developing Student Potential Through the Reading Program" (paper presented at Twentieth Annual Reading Conference, Cleveland, OH).

1968   *Education for Relevence: The Schools and Social Change* (Boston: Houghton Mifflin), (with C. E. Beck, N. R. Bernier, T. W. Walton & J. C. Willers as editors).

"School System Roles," in *Education for Relevance: The School and Social Change*, J. B. Macdonald, C. E. Beck, N. R. Bernier, T. W. Walton and J. C. Willers, eds. (Boston: Houghton Mifflin), pp. 177–205.

"The School Curriculum," in *Education for Relevence: The School and Social Change*, J. B. Macdonald, C. E. Beck, N. R. Bernier, T. W. Walton and J. C. Willers, eds. (Boston: Houghton Mifflin), pp. 207–229.

"The Schools Council and Curriculum Development" (paper presented at ILEA Conference at Garrett College).

1969   "A Proper Curriculum for Young Children," *Phi Delta Kappan*, 50(7), pp. 406–409.

"The High Scool in Human Terms: Curriculum Design," in *Humanizing the Secondary School*, N. K. Hamilton and J. G. Saylor, eds. (Washington, DC: ASCD), pp. 35–54.

"The School Environment as Learner Reality" (paper presented at the ASCD conference: The Nature of the Learner's Reality, San Fransisco, CA).

1969-70 "The School Environment as Learner Reality," *Curriculum Theory Network* 2(4), pp. 45–54.

1970   "On Tinkering in In-Service Teacher Education," *Instructional Development*, 1(4), pp. 3 & 6 (with M. Haberman).

"A Case Against Behavioral Objectives," *The Elementary School Journal*, 71(3), pp. 119–128 (with B. J. Wolfson).

"The Open School: Curriculum Concepts," in *Open Education—The Legacy of the Progressive Movement*, B. Spodek, ed. (Washington, DC: National Association for Education of Young Children), pp. 23–38.

"Strategies of Instruction in Adult Education," in *Adult Learning and Instruction*, S. M. Grabowski, ed. (Syracuse: ERIC Clearinghouse on Adult Education), pp. 46–59.

1971   "Curriculum Theory," *Journal of Educational Research*, 64(5), pp. 196–200.

"A Vision of a Humane School," in *Removing Barriers to Humaneness in High School*, J. G. Saylor and J. L. Smith, eds. (Washington, DC: Association for Supervision and Curriculum Development), pp. 2–20.

"Student Teaching: Benefit or Burden?" *Journal of Teacher Education*, 22(1), pp. 51–58 (with E. Zaret).

"Curriculum Development in Relation to Social and Intellectual Systems," in *The Curriculum: Retrospect and Prospect. National Society for the Study of Education Yearbook*, R. M. McClure, ed. 70(1) (Chicago: University of Chicago Press), pp. 95–112.

"Responsible Curriculum Development," in *Confronting Curriculum Reform*, E. W. Eisner, ed. (Boston: Little, Brown), p. 122.

"The School as a Double Agent," in *Freedom, Bureaucracy and Schooling*, V.F. Haubrich, ed. (Washington, DC: Association for Supervision and Curriculum Development), pp. 235–246.

Social Perspectives on Reading: Social Influinces and Reading Achievement (Newark, DE: International Reading Association), (monograph).

"A Position Paper on Curriculum Practices in Vocational Education" (unpublished manuscript).

1972 "Introduction," in *A New Look at Progressive Education*, J. R. Squire, ed. (Washington, DC: Association for Supervision and Curriculum Development), pp. 1–14.

"Teacher Competency," in *Competencies and Beyond: Toward a Human Approach to Education* (New York: Twenty-First Annual Teacher Education Conference Proceedings of the City University of New York), pp. 32–37.

1973 "The White Knight? (a reply to Henry Levin)," *Journal of the American Education Association*, 1(3), p. 2.

"Reading in an Electronic Media Age," in *Social Perspectives on Reading: Social Influences and Reading Achievement*, J. B. Macdonald, ed. (Newark, DE: International Reading Association), pp. 23–29.

"Education 2001: Destiny or Destination?" in *Dare the Social Order Build a New System of Schools*, R. M. O'Kane, ed. (Greensboro, NC: University of North Carolina), pp. 25–31.

"Critical Value Questions and the Analysis of Objectives and Curricula," in *Second Handbook for Research on Teaching*, R. M. Travers, ed. (Chicago: Rand McNally), pp. 405–412 (with D. F. Clark).

Reschooling Society: A Conceptual Model (Washington, DC: Association for Supervision and Curriculum Development) (monograph with B. J. Wolfson and E. Zaret).

"Organizing Centers as Alternatives to Behavioral Objectives" (unpublished manuscript).

"Potential Relationships of Human Interests, Language, and Orientations to Curriculum Thinking" (paper presented at American Educational Research Association Meeting, New Orleans, LA).

"A Radical Conception of the Role of Values in Curriculum: Praxis" (paper presented at Association for Supervision and Curriculum Development Meeting, Minneapolis, MN, with D. F. Clark).

1974   "An Evaluation of Evaluation," *Urban Review*, 1(7), pp. 3–15.

"Cultural Pluralism as ASCD's Major Thrust," *Educational Leadership*, 32(3), pp. 167–169.

"A Transcendental Developmental Ideology of Education," in *Heightened Consciousness, Cultural Revolution, and Curriculum Theory*, W. Pinar, ed. (Berkeley: McCutchan), pp. 85–116.

"The Domain of Curriculum" (paper presented at Annual Meeting of the American Educational Association, Chicago, IL).

1975   "The Person in the Curriculum," *Urban Review*, 8(3), pp. 191–201.

"Some Moral Problems in Classroom Evaluation/Testing," *Urban Review*, 8(1), pp. 18–27.

"The Quality of Everyday Life in Schools," in *Schools in Search of Meaning*, J. Macdonald and E. Zaret, eds. (Washington, DC: Association for Supervision and Curriculum Developmenr), pp. 78–94.

Schools in Search of Meaning (Washington, DC: Association of Supervision and Curriculum Development), (with E. Zaret).

"Biographical Statement," in *Curriculum Theorizing: The Reconceptualists*, W. Pinar, ed. (Berkeley: McCutchan), pp. 3–4.

"Curriculum and Human Interests," in *Curriculum Theorizing: The Reconceptualists*, W. Pinar, ed. (Berkeley: McCutchan), pp. 283–294.

"Curriculum Theory," in *Curriculum Therorizing: The Reconceptualists*, W. Pinar, ed. (Berkeley: McCutchan), pp. 5–13.

"Perspective on Open Education: A Speculative Essay," in *Studies in Open Education*, B. Spodek & H. J. Walberg, eds. (New York: Agnathon Press), pp. 45–58.

"Teacher Education: Politics and the Human Spirit in the United States," in *Ideas: Trends in Tertiary Education*, 30, L. A. Smith, ed. (London: Universoty of London, Goldsmith College), pp. 192–196.

"Reaction to Professor Eisner's Paper: *The Perspective Eye: Toward the Reformation of Educational Evaluation*" (paper presented at meeting of the American Educational Research Association, Washington, DC).

"Curriculum Theory as Intentional Activity" (paper presented at Curriculum Theory Conference, Charlottesville, VA).

"Women's Liberation and Human Liberation" (paper presented at The John Dewey Society Meeting, New Orleans, LA, with S. C. Macdonald).

1976   "Looking Toward the Future in Curriculum" (paper presented at Charlottesville Curriculum Conference, Charlottesville, VA).

1977   "Living Democratically in Schools: Cultural Pluralism," in *Multicultural Education: Commitments, Issues, and Applications*, C. A. Grant, ed. (Washington, DC: Association for Supervision and Curriculum Development), pp. 6–13.

"Scene and Context: American Education Today," in *Staff Development: Staff Liberation*, C. Beegle & R. Edelfelt, eds. (Washington, DC: Association for Supervision and Curriculum Development), pp. 7–14.

"Toward a Platform for Humanistic Education," in *Humanistic Education: Visions and Reality*, R. H. Weller, ed. (Berkeley: McCutchan), pp. 345–355.

"Value Bases and Issues for Curriculum," in *Curriculum Theory*, A. Molnar & J. Zahorik, eds. (Washington, DC: Association for Supervision and Curriculum Development), pp. 10–21.

1978   "Curriculum, Consciousness, and Social Change," *Foundational Research*, 5(2), pp. 27–45.

"Research: Methodology, Politics and Values" (paper presented at Southwest Education Research Association Meeting, Austin, TX).

"A Critical Perspective of Minimum Competency Testing" (paper presented at University of North Carolina School of Education Faculty Research Seminar, Charlotte, NC).

1979   "Managers and the Technical Mind Set: Minimum Competency Testing. A Case in Point," in *University Council for Education Administration Journal*.

"Evaluation of Teaching: Purpose, Context and Problems," in *Planning for the Evaluation of Teaching*, W. R. Duckett, ed. (A CEDR Monograph), pp. 13–26.

"Planning for the Evaluation of Teaching," in *Planning for the Evaluation of Teaching*, W. R. Duckett, ed. (A CEDR Monograph), pp. 2–12.

1980   "Is the Tyler Rationale a Suitable Basis for Current Curriculum Development?," *ASCD Update*, 22(8), p. 5.

"A Look at the Kohlberg Curriculum Framework for Moral Education," in *Kohlberg and Moral Education*, B. M. Mapel, ed. (Birmingham: Religious Education Press), Chapter 13.

1981   "Curriculum, Consciousness, and Social Change," *Journal of Curriculum Theorizing*, 3(1), pp. 143–153.

"Theory, Practice and the Hermeneutic Circle," *Journal of Curriculum Theorizing*, 3(2), pp. 130-139.

"Gender, Values, and Curriculum," *Journal of Curriculum Theorizing*, 3(2), pp. 299–304 (with S. C. Macdonald).

"Curriculum Design for a Gifted/Talented Program," in *Strategies for Educational Change: Recognizing the Gifts and Talents of All Children*, W. L. Marks & R. O. Nystrand, eds. (New York: Macmillan), pp. 79–85.

"Curriculum Theory: Knowledge or Understanding?" (paper presented at Second Conference on Curriculum Theory in Physical Education, Athens, GA).

"What Does It Mean to Be Practical?" (paper presented at Annual Association for Supervision and Curriculum Development Conference, St. Louis, MO).

"Thoughts on Continuing Good Work in Curriculum in the Eighties" (paper presented at Journal of Curriculum Theorizing

Conference: The Curriculum Field in the Eighties (A panel discussion), Airlie, VA).

1982   "How Literal is Curriculum Theory?," *Theory Into Practice*, 21(1), pp. 55–61.

"Social Studies and Personal Social Liberation" (paper presented at North Carolina Social Studies Educator's Group, Winston-Salem, NC).

1983   "Curriculum and Planning: Visions and Metaphors," in *New Trends in Education*, Z. Lamm, ed. (Tel Aviv: Yachdav), (with D. E. Purpel).

1986   "The Domain of Curriculum," *Journal of Curriculum ans Supervision* 1(3), pp. 205–214.

1987   "Curriculum and Planning: Visions and Metaphors," *Journal of Curriculum and Supervision*, 2(2), pp. 178–192 (with D. E. Purpel).

1988   "Curriculum, Consciousness, and Social Change," in *Contepemporary Curriculum Discources*, W. Pinar, ed. (Scotsdale, AZ: Gonsuch Scarisbrick), pp. 156–174.

Undated Material

"Comments on Future Committee Report" (unpublished manuscript).

"Curriculum and Instruction: Research and Evaluation" (unpublished manuscript).

"Curriculum as a Political Process" (unpublished manuscript).

"Curriculum Leadership for the Future" (unpublished manuscript).

"A Curriculum Proposal" (unpublished manuscript).

"Curriculum Referents, Process Decisions, and Design" (unpublished manuscript).

"Developing Curriculum Design Theory" (unpublished manuscript).

"The Education Game" (unpublished manuscript).

"An Essay on Curriculum: *Who is Killing Cock Robin*" (unpublished manuscript).

"Evaluation and Human Dignity in the Classroom" (unpublished manuscript).

"Ideology, Hegemony, and the Individualizing of Instruction: The Incorporation of 'Progressive Education'" (unpublished manuscript).

"Integration in the Curriculum" (unpublished manuscript).

"Is IDE a Good Alternative?" (unpublished manuscript).

"Meaning in and of School as a Process of the Development of Responsible Personal Activity" (unpublished manuscript).

"A Model of Teaching: The Facilitation of Sampling Behaviour" (unpublished manuscript).

"Moral Concerns in Elementary Education" (paper presented at Los Angeles, CA).

"Moral Problems in Classroom Evaluation and Testing" (unpublished manuscript).

"Myths About Schooling" (unpublished manuscript).

"The Nature of Evidence" (unpublished manuscript).

"A Note on the Emergence of Personal Intention of Theorists" (unpublished manuscript).

"Notes on the Aesthetic Process of Inquiry" (unpublished manuscript).

"Notes on the Study of Oppression" (unpublished manuscript).

"The Paradox: The Individual and Society" (unpublished manuscript).

"Plausible Logic in Educational Research" (unpublished manuscript).

"Problematics of Assessing Teacher Effectiveness" (unpublished manuscript).

"The Process of Teacher Study" (unpublished manuscript).

"The Referent for Theory Talk" (unpublished manuscript).

"Researching Curriculum Output: The Use of a General Systems Theory to Identify Appropriate Curriculum Outputs and Research Hypotheses" (unpublished manuscript).

"Response to Dr. Longstreet's Paper" (paper presented at Professors of Curriculum Annual Meeting).

"Sex Differences in Reading Ability and Achievement with Emphasis on the Elementary School" (unpublished manuscript).

"Skill and Abilities That Make For Effective Living" (unpublished manuscript).

"Social Change in the Schools" (unpublished manuscript).

"Strategies for Teaching for the Development of Cognitive Abilities" (paper presented as the National Association of Secondary School Principals Symposium).

"The Student and the Structure of the Discipline" (unpublished manuscript).

"A Study of the Impact of the Goldsmith Curriculum Laboratory In-Service Program" (unpublished manuscript).

"A Theoretical Viewpoint Underlying Curriulum: An Analysis of Robert Lindner's Viewpoint as Expressed in *Prescription for Rebellion* and *Must We Conform*" (unpublished manuscript).

"Value Questions in Educational Research" (unpublished manuscript).

"Where I Stand" (unpublished manuscript).

"Who Will and How to Assess the Compentency of Those Preparing Competency Based Education Programs" (unpublished manuscript).